Justin Quirk is an award-winning writer, editor and broadcaster from London. He first wrote for the *Guardian*'s music pages when he was nineteen and began contributing to *Kerrang!* shortly afterwards as a reviewer. Since then he has written for everyone from *Arena* and *Esquire* to *The Times*, *Sunday Times* and the *Independent* about art, music and culture, regularly appears on the BBC World Service and Soho Radio, and DJs at places such as Spiritland and Merchant's Tavern in London. As a teenage metaller he spent an inordinate amount of time hanging around Kensington Market (because his friend Chris had met Slash outside there), covered his schoolbooks in posters ripped out of metal magazines, saw Guns n' Roses twice, got stranded at a curfew-busting Skid Row show, made his older sister (a goth) take him to Donington Monsters of Rock, failed to get into an AC/DC video as an extra, played Metallica's 'One' for his music GCSE exam, saw everyone from Thunder to Mötley Crüe, and got regularly chased through suburban shopping precincts by skinheads. This is his first book.

Nothin' But a Good Time

Nothin' But a Good Time

The Spectacular Rise and Fall of Glam Metal

Justin Quirk

unbound

This edition first published in 2020

Unbound

TC Group, Level 1, Devonshire House, One Mayfair Place,
London, W1J 8AJ

www.unbound.com

ISBN (eBook): 978-1-78965-136-2

ISBN (Paperback): 978-1-78965-135-5

Cover design by Mecob

Printed and bound in Great Britain by Clays Ltd, Elcograf S.p.A.

*For my grandmothers, Ellen Healy and Mary
Frances Quirk, who should have had the
chance to write their own books.*

Super Patrons

Erol Alkan
Matthew Anderson-Ford
Neil Barrie
Adam Baylis-West
Chris Bell
Gav Brett
Colin Campbell
Andrew Carlson
Juan Christian
Garrett Coakley
Tony Coca
Laura Coman
Jon Cöscio
Paul Croughton
Jemma Cullen
Jennifer Daking
Karen Davidson
Mat Davies
Mark Davis
James Ervin
Eamonn Forde
Helen Francis
Alejandro Garcia Torres
Matthew Green
Judith Griffith
Giles Guest
Matt Hall

Alexander Hamilton
Matthew Hamilton
Andrew Hankinson
Rob Harborne
Pascal L Heureux
Scott Heydt
Emma Higgins
Matthew Hill
Andrew Hird
Will Hogan
Marcus Holzer
Matthew James
Anna Kibbey
George J Kokonas
Fraser Lewry
Marco Lo Giudice
Danny Lowe
Vivien Martin
Chris Meeke
Chris Mooney
Michael Moran
Gary Morgan
David Moynihan
Andrew Mueller
Paul Noble
Gregory Olver
Tim Pollard

Sam Redfern
Matthew Rickard
Claudia 'Dia' Rose
Annette Russell
Laurent Saffar
Mike Schwabauer
Lucy Scott
Ollie Scull
Dan Stacey
Emma Jane Stone

Michael Sutherland
Kathy Sweeney
Firouz and
Matt Thompson
Andy Vaccari
Genevieve von Lob
Camilla Way
Josh Woodfin
Iain Wright

Contents

Dear Anthony – thank you for all the long years of help, friendship and inspiration. And for all the Scorpions anecdotes which I've mis-remembered and then passed off as my own. \m/

Randy 'The Ram' Robinson: Goddamn they don't make 'em like they used to.

Cassidy: Fuckin' Eighties, man, best shit ever!

Randy 'The Ram' Robinson: Bet'chr ass, man, Guns n' Roses fuckin' ruled.

Cassidy: Crüe!

Randy 'The Ram' Robinson: Yeah!

Cassidy: Def Lep!

Randy 'The Ram' Robinson: Then that Cobain pussy had to come around and ruin it all.

Cassidy: Like there's something wrong with wanting to have a good time.

Randy 'The Ram' Robinson: I'll tell you something, I hate the fuckin' Nineties.

Cassidy: Nineties fuckin' sucked.

Randy 'The Ram' Robinson: Nineties fuckin' sucked.

The Wrestler, 2008

Prologue

January 27, 1992. The annual American Music Awards are held at the Shrine Auditorium in LA. This mock-Moorish theatre on Jefferson Boulevard was a showbiz fixture in the city, well used to figures embodying cartoonish excess – it had been the backdrop to both the crowd scenes in the original 1933 *King Kong* movie and parts of Judy Garland's *A Star Is Born*, and in 1956 it was the scene of Elvis Presley's first concert in the city. In more recent decades, it had been where Michael Jackson suffered second-degree burns after his hair ignited in the process of filming a Pepsi commercial.

The night was a snapshot of an odd, transitional period in American music. With hindsight, the sense of something stirring beneath the surface is hard to shake. Lion-haired soul crooner Michael Bolton won the Favourite Pop/Rock Album prize, beating nominees including R.E.M., a fidgety, lo-fi college rock band from Athens, Georgia, who had spent the previous decade in critical acclaim and commercial obscurity, but, with a series of polished, serious commercial juggernauts beginning with *Out of Time,* would go on to become one of the biggest bands in the world over the following decade. C + C Music Factory went home as Favourite Dance New Artist, pipping The KLF, a British pair of ageing chaos-mongers who welded together conceptual art and stadium-sized techno into a series of brilliant hit singles and legitimate art statements before deleting their back catalogue, announcing their retirement via a full-page advert in the British music press and burning a million pounds on a remote Scottish island. Show host and Oakland's pop phenomenon MC Hammer was the Favourite Rap/Hip Hop Artist on the night, but on his heels were N.W.A, whose violent, nihilistic *Straight Outta Compton* album would become inextricably bound up with the fatal riots that would consume the city for six days in April and May of that year.

But the incipient separation between the old guard and the new was perhaps most apparent in the Favourite Heavy Metal/Hard Rock New Artist category. Nominees included Alice in Chains and Nirvana, the Seattle three-piece whose second album, *Nevermind*, had been released just four months earlier. Nirvana were covered by the traditional metal press, but barely recognisable within the parameters of what that

genre had become. *Nevermind* was *sonically* heavy –
the rumbling pick-driven bass, Dave Grohl's thunder-
ous drumming and Kurt Cobain's treble-heavy, feed-
back-drenched guitar sounds contained audio traces
of everything from early Black Sabbath's doom-filled
death-trip to Journey's soaringly melodic choruses –
but everything about their presentation chafed against
what heavy metal had become. They dressed like suburban skateboarders who couldn't afford the train fare
into the city centre, and presented themselves with all
the enthusiasm of teenagers who'd been forced to get
summer jobs working at a theme park. Even the title
of their album eschewed the spark and bluster of the
best heavy metal in favour of something that sounded
like the linguistic equivalent of an adolescent pulling
the curtains shut on a bright summer's day: *Nevermind.*

But Nirvana then weren't what Nirvana would
become. In the early days of 1992, for this one night
in LA, they were the also-rans. Along with Alice in
Chains – another Seattle band who came to epitomise
grunge – they were the runners-up in their nominated
category. The previous year's winners, Slaughter (who
a year earlier had beaten Iron Maiden frontman Bruce
Dickinson and Don Dokken, and closed their speech
by somewhat strangely commanding the audience to
'visualise world peace and it'll happen'), announced
that the winners of the favourite new heavy metal

band were not standard-bearers for the new dawn of grunge, but… Firehouse.

Firehouse were from Richmond, Virginia, and had relocated to Charlotte, North Carolina, before signing with Epic Records in 1989. If they're remembered at all, it's for two songs: 'Love of a Lifetime', a deathless, first-dance-at-the-wedding ballad and the far sparkier 'Don't Treat Me Bad', their 1991 single, which reached number 19 on the Billboard Charts. 'Don't Treat Me Bad' is one of those absolutely nailed-on pieces of pop songwriting that conceals a surprisingly complicated chord structure and rhythmic gearshifts under a glossy, radio-friendly exterior. With a few changes in tempo and instrumentation it could work as a country hit, or an acoustic ballad, or a tinkling piece of lift music. It's one of those songs that will be on the second or third tier of regular rotation on classic rock radio stations all over the world until the heat death of the universe. It's a great song. The video shows Firehouse playing in what appears to be a generic Koreatown district with fire engines parked around the place, harmless explosions going off and a woman in red stilettos sporadically walking into shot before picking up a firehose and dousing the band in water. It doesn't make a huge amount of sense, but this didn't particularly mark it out in the genre, as we'll come back to later.

After Slaughter's announcement, the band took the stage. 'This is UNBELIEVABLE,' said vocalist C. J. Snare, 'totally unexpected'. An artist's impression of the band was projected on to the screen behind them – although it appeared to have been drawn by someone who had never actually seen them and had merely had the band described to them. 'We'd like to thank God, we'd like to thank our family and friends… our great record label – Sony, Epic Records and Tommy Mottola. We'd like to thank Michael Caplin, and our manager. All the people at radio, people at television and also all of our fans who supported us all the way.' Snare raised a defiant fist to the crowd. 'Thank you very much – KEEP ON ROCKING!'

Speaking in 2005, Snare was more circumspect about what that night had actually meant for his band, the genre he represented, and his career as a major rockstar. 'Really, that was like the beginning of the end.'[1]

As I write this, more than twenty-eight years after that night at the American Music Awards, Firehouse are preparing to set off on their next set of tour dates, taking in the Whisky a Go Go in Hollywood, along with less well-trodden locations like the Waukesha County Fair (with Vince Neil of Mötley Crüe), the Golden Nugget Showroom in Las Vegas and the Rock'n The Bayou festival at the Lamar Dixon Expo Center in Gonzales, Louisiana. Of the three frontmen nominated that night at the awards ceremony, C. J.

1. https://www.rockeyez.com/interviews/int-firehouse-cj_snare.html, April 5, 2005.

Snare is the only one still alive. In these circumstances, to still be running Firehouse as a going concern has to be chalked up as an achievement. The venues his band is playing are a healthy size, and he will regularly get the pleasure of older married couples telling him that they got hitched to the sound of a song that he first wrote as a young man playing solo shows in Holiday Inn hotels. His career achievements have exceeded those of 99 per cent of people who ever try to write a song or form a band.

However, for most people in the wider world, if glam metal is remembered at all nowadays, it's as the punchline to a joke, the basis for a novelty fancy dress costume, or a hilarious relic of a bygone age. There's never been a serious, critical reassessment of this period in musical history that is now treated as a bloated, hairspray-misted aberration. For glam metal and its various bedfellows, deviant offshoots and identifying names – sleaze rock, poodle rock, hair metal – music's accepted chronology records that in 1991 ('the year punk rock broke' to use the title of Dave Markey's grunge-mythologising documentary), after almost a decade of commercial dominance, glam metal was killed dead by grunge. Like some mutant branch of the evolutionary tree, it was overtaken by a younger, faster version of itself and hit a dead end, leaving behind only some rudimentary cave paintings of a stocking-clad 'bitch' and an empty bottle of Jack Daniels.

However, this is a willful rewriting of history. For

the entire 1980s, glam metal was legitimately one of the largest forces in popular music, both commercially and creatively. The music built MTV and broke open territories (Japan, Eastern Europe) that the rest of the industry then poured into. Bands pushed at the frontiers of technological production. They sold out stadiums to vast crowds of people who the music press never spoke to. Fans and artists alike died in spectacularly stupid, tragic accidents from the muddy quagmire of Castle Donington to the motorways of Florida. The genre inspired epic works of cinema from *Wayne's World* and *The Wrestler* to *The Decline of Western Civilization*. It was a legitimate cultural force that united kids like me in the suburbs of London with heroin-addled losers in California and rebellious, mullet-sporting teens in the Communist Bloc.

The music functioned as a pile-up at the end of American post-war musical culture, where the tropes and tricks of the previous forty years (cowboy blues, vaudeville, heavy rock, show tunes, punk, Laurel Canyon balladry) combined into one last smouldering heap before pop finally ate itself and succumbed to a crippling, self-referential wave of irony and repetition. Kurt Cobain referenced Boston's 'More Than a Feeling' because it was a clever, knowing wink to everything his band was overturning – David Lee Roth did an enormous star jump off the drum riser because he was signalling his silverback dominance of every other male within the stadium and it looked amazing when he did it. The bands left behind a body of songs so untouchable that they still get covered today by everyone from Mariah Carey to Taylor Swift, but the originators get no critical credit. Of course, there was also a lot of terrible music by bands like Anvil, Warrant and Tigertailz, but they're still an important part of the story.

Glam metal burned briefly and brightly, created cartoonish megastars, rehabilitated and reinvented careers, and gave us Mötley Crüe, Poison, Cinderella, Dokken, Ratt, W.A.S.P., Lita Ford, Vixen, Bon Jovi, Skid Row, Wrathchild, Slaughter and countless more. I want to tell the story of all these men and women, the story of glam metal, and the story of the music that defined both their lives, and mine.

\M/

Introduction

Britain's glam rock boom of the 1970s enters public consciousness with T-Rex's masterpiece 'Hot Love' in 1971 and sparks a genuine youth craze which spans art, fashion, delinquency, moral panic and some of the most glorious pop music to come out of the UK at any point. As much a visual phenomenon as a musical one, it was the perfect music to accompany the growth of colour television. At its more nuanced end, glam rock was a glitter-strewn riot in which the likes of David Bowie and Marc Bolan took the rock and roll iconography of their youths and injected it with a romantic futurism. The spaced-out, wide-eyed optimism of the Sixties was jettisoned in favour of a harder, more focused sound. When the cosmos was considered, it was not in terms of spiritual rebirth, but instead in the language of spacemen and rockets first spoken by Joe Meek[1] with his lo-fi recording experiments. Hair got

1. Eccentric and hugely innovative north London producer who created John

shorter, jackets got tighter and guitars became an over-driven wall of noise. It was as though the primitive rock and rollers of the Fifties had leapfrogged the subsequent decade and been reincarnated in platform heels and with a knowledge of the moon landings. David Bowie's 'Hang On to Yourself', T-Rex's 'Get It On' and Roxy Music's 'Virginia Plain' particularly contain the shuffle and reverb and barrelling piano lines of something twenty years older. With their peerless production, photogenic, androgynous protagonists and melancholic undertow, these artists represented glam's high critical watermark.

However, this was a relatively slim sliver of what British glam rock produced. Beneath this crystalline surface was something much more lumpen and thuggish but equally thrilling. Mott the Hoople were an ageing pack of touring grafters from Hereford who had consistently failed to turn the frequently violent excitement of their live shows into chart success, until superfan David Bowie passed them the masterful, elegiac 'All the Young Dudes'. The Glitter Band's compressed, thuggish terrace chants foreshadowed post-punk with whining guitar lines laid over a trucker's beat and eponymous frontman Gary leading the crowd in call and response. The Sweet were a genuinely inventive hard rock band who chafed at

Leyton's 'Johnny Remember Me' (1961) and the Tornados' Telstar (1962), before murdering his landlady and then committing suicide in February 1967.

the production line system imposed by their producers Nicky Chinn and Mike Chapman, offsetting machine-tooled chart hits such as 'Ballroom Blitz' and 'Teenage Rampage' with their own classics like 'Spotlight'. The Sensational Alex Harvey Band were a vehicle for front-man Harvey – a black-eyed former teen star from the Gorbals area of Glasgow – to mesh together the bleak, existential comedy of French storytelling singer Jacques Brel with a screaming update on the blues, and a delivery that constantly suggested an imminent explosion of physical violence. Harvey's performance of Brel's 'Next' on BBC2's *The Old Grey Whistle Test* in 1974, in which he peers down the lens from under his thick fringe while his sinister Pierrot guitarist Zal Cleminson soundtracks Brel's tale of army brothels and syphilitic infection, seems to have been calculated to unnerve all but the most open-minded viewer.

Taken together, this second tier of glam was some-thing rougher and more suburban than Bowie or Bolan. This was the sound of the hinterland between skinheads and hippies; a soundtrack for chairs being hurled round gigs in provincial theatres; platform boots giving way to Dr Martens; the juvenile nihilism of *Action* comic, Richard Allen's New English Library pulp paperbacks and the ultraviolent cinematic version of *A Clockwork Orange*. Its defining element was the transgressive power of hard-faced, working-class men daubing themselves in glitter and make-up – but in a way that seemed actively confrontational rather than personally indulgent. When David Bowie wore gold lamé, he looked androgynous and artistic; when Brian Connolly from The Sweet did the same he looked like he was daring someone to take a swing at him. And the further down the musical foodchain you went, the further this balance tipped. By the time you got to the kind of music found on Phil King's *All the Young Droogs* compilation, the sense of glam as little more than a vehicle for pissing off everyone who'd come before you is unavoidable.

But despite producing bona fide pop stars and a string of three-minute classics, glam rock never really landed in America. As the AM radio boom unfolded in a succession of lushly produced, open-road anthems, even Bolan and Bowie received a relatively muted reception. For rock audiences lapping up The Eagles, Fleetwood Mac and Led Zeppelin, British glam seemed too scratchy, too small and too unnerving. Bolan's only hit in America was 'Get It On', which just scraped into the Top 10 in 1971. 'Ride a White Swan', 'Hot Love' and 'Telegram Sam' didn't even crack the Top 50.

However, even within the confines of straight American rock, there were clearly a few artists tuning in to what the British were doing and transmuting it into something more acceptable. Aerosmith's eponymous debut was released in January 1973. While the blues – and particularly the variant deployed by the Rolling Stones and Led Zeppelin – has always loomed large in Aerosmith's music, the band had a *look* that nodded to glam – Steve Tyler and Joe Perry's teased-out hair and scarf-draped microphones gave their priapic, vaudevillian rock a deceptively feminine edge. 'Same Old Song and Dance', with its propulsive rhythm and circular vocal melody, could have slipped quite comfortably into side two of *Diamond Dogs*. The New York Dolls physically offered a through line from British glam to what came later, although, with a connection to Malcolm McLaren and a scuzzy, lo-fi sound, their greater impact was on punk rather than the subsequent eras of metal.

Seattle's Heart were largely a conventional folk-rock band with a cosmic, medieval edge, built around the astonishing vocal and guitar talents of sisters Ann and Nancy Wilson. But on 'Barracuda', they allied a rumbling rhythm track to dive-bombing, phased guitars and pushed Nancy's voice to the upper part of its register in a way that recalled one of those b-sides that The Sweet created when allowed to take control of the musical steering wheel. Meanwhile, on the East Coast figures like Blackie Lawless were moving through a succession of also-ran pure glam bands with names like Black Rabbit and Orfax Rainbow, attempting to kick-start a scene which never quite happened, while Kiss were edging the closest to codifying something like an American reading of glam.

Kiss are a difficult band to consider in the context of any overview of music, because they largely exist in their own world. Broadly, they are a fairly limited group musically, while being an exceptionally good *band*. Kiss are the product of people who have ruthlessly examined and absorbed everything that makes popular culture work and have turned it into a brand. They owe as much to the worldview and marketing of Donald Trump or a pyramid-selling scheme as they do to music. They have an amazing logo and a brilliant nose for PR stunts. They had brand recognition and a masked identity that allowed departing members to be replaced like employees with a minimum of disruption. They have an astonishingly partisan fanbase and one absolutely incredible song in the glam masterpiece 'Detroit Rock City'. Other bands hate playing with them because any bill where Kiss are present becomes a de facto Kiss show. They've not had a hit record since 1991's 'God Gave Rock and Roll to You II' and yet they are still selling out huge venues (the forty-three North American dates of their *End of the Road* World Tour in Spring 2019 grossed $58.7m). They removed their make-up in 1983 for the *Lick It Up* album and a huge amount of attendant publicity, then put the make-up back on to a mixture of acclaim and relief twelve years later. A version of Kiss will probably still be touring and playing long after all of its original members have gone the way of all flesh.

What Kiss produced musically, even in the first flush of their success, was relatively meat-and-potatoes rock music. But what they captured was the *spirit* of British glam. They sanded the edges off and made it palatable to American crowds, but they created a spectacle, and realised that this was the crucial thing that audiences were responding to. Alice Cooper, a vaudevillian garage rocker from Detroit, did something similar around the same time. At its best, Cooper's music was a sort of cold-eyed, electric reading of the blues and country – 'I'm Eighteen' doesn't convey the joy of youth, but the anger and danger inherent in someone who stands between boyhood and adulthood, and has no idea what to do with either role. But it was Cooper's stage shows which cemented his reputation, with their Technicolor riot of snakes, beheadings, axe attacks and electrocution pushing them closer to a musical than a conventional gig's stage show.[2] Audiences may not have been ready for the conceptual art-school androgyny of Bowie and Bolan, but they were ready for the pantomime spectacle of larger-than-life bands with pyrotechnic stage shows, frontmen who

2. A close, contemporaneous analogue for this kind of theatrical mass performance can be found in black music, with Detroit's Parliament–Funkadelic. Like Kiss, George Clinton's collective represented an entire genre in their own right, and created the kind of spectacle-driven live shows where you were essentially watching a vast narrative unfold with the music put into a kind of supporting role.

were glam (if not glamorous, or 'glam'), and the contradiction that came from mixing hard men with make-up, as long as there was no actual sexual ambiguity involved.

The adolescents who were watching these bands in the late Seventies would go on to form the vanguard of the glam metal explosion, while many of the key exponents of this first wave would have their careers rehabilitated and recharged in the mid-Eighties when they finally went 'fully glam'. But for now, an idea had been planted in the cultural landscape: when would it finally emerge as something new?

Chapter 1

1983: SHOUT AT THE DEVIL

As a cultural decade, the 1970s was a tough one for America. Looking back on the biggest cinematic hits of the time, two themes dominate: a desire for escapism, whether into outer space (*Star Wars*, *Close Encounters*) or an idealised memory of America's past (*Grease*). Even when films dealt ostensibly with the here and now, they contained a recurring idea of America's downfall lurking in its midst. In the likes of *Jaws*, *Taxi Driver* and *The Towering Inferno* the constant sense was that, in the most everyday situations, something completely mundane was always lurking and ready to kill you. Much of rock music broke into two similar camps: escapism and fantasy could be found in the *Jesus Christ Superstar* soundtrack (1970) and *Framp-*

ton Comes Alive (1976), but elsewhere neurosis and paranoia were the order of the day. Neil Young's *Harvest* (1972) told melancholic stories of heroin death and failed Southern states. Fleetwood Mac's *Rumours* (1977) was, sonically, the high watermark of glossy, AM rock – but dealt almost entirely in the bitter emotional fallout of the band's collapsing relationships. Even the *Saturday Night Fever* soundtrack (1978) had an edge and menace that often got lost in the wash created by its visual flair and lush orchestration. The title track's portrayal of a life in New York where the city is 'breaking', and its desperate refrain that life is going nowhere, struck a chord with millions of listeners.

This is perhaps unsurprising when the context of the years around this art is considered. The decade began with the Kent State Shootings, America already embroiled in the Vietnam War, and totemic figures of the Sixties' revolution dying of overdoses in quick succession (Jimi Hendrix, Janis Joplin, Jim Morrison in a ten-month window). The Watergate scandal, in which President Richard Nixon's administration oversaw the burgling of the Democratic National Convention's headquarters in June 1972, became a byword for presidential sleaze and corruption. The years 1973–4 saw an energy crisis triggered by the Arab Oil Embargo, which spiked petrol prices and necessitated daylight saving time being brought in four months early to conserve energy, and 1975 saw the Vietnam

War end in ignominy and American President Gerald Ford survive two assassination attempts in quick succession. In 1977, widespread rioting, arson and looting gripped New York as a city-wide blackout occurred overnight following lightning strikes on the city's key electrical substations that put TV stations off air, shut down transport networks and plunged the city into darkness. The same year, Elvis Presley died, an American icon reduced to a lumbering, cholesterol-choked parody of his former self. Before the decade was out, America would also have seen the partial meltdown of its nuclear reactor at Three Mile Island, the mass suicide of 900 members of The People's Temple (following its relocation to Jonestown in Guyana) and the assassination of openly gay San Francisco politician Harvey Milk by his former colleague Dan White.

Finally, with Iran consumed by its Islamic Revolution, the US Embassy in the capital city Tehran would be overrun by hard-line theocratic students who swarmed over the compound's gates and proceeded to take fifty-two American diplomats and civilians hostage for 444 days. Members of the embassy staff were paraded before photographers, blindfolded and with their hands bound. The subsequent rescue raid ordered by US President Jimmy Carter, Operation Eagle Claw, was intended to send a Delta Force team into the heart of Tehran to liberate the hostages; mechanical problems, fuelling issues and an enormous freak *haboob* dust storm conspired against the mission and led to it being aborted. As the craft and troops attempted to retreat, one of their helicopters crashed into a transport aircraft laden with jet fuel, killing eight service personnel. The hostages were eventually released twenty minutes after the inauguration of Carter's successor, Ronald Reagan, in return for the US unfreezing billions of dollars of Iranian assets. Carter's presidency and the entire decade ended in abject public humbling and humiliation for the world's greatest superpower.

Against this backdrop, heavy metal was at something of a transitional point. Judas Priest had spent the second half of the Seventies evolving their sound from something prog-inflected to the focused, riff-driven punishment of *British Steel* (1980), largely fixing their attention on America while punk played out back in the UK. Rob Halford's development of his leather-bound, S&M frontman persona suited their new sound perfectly. From the opening of 'Rapid Fire' onwards, Priest tore out of the speakers, sounding as inspired by the amphetamine punk of Motörhead as by anything from Deep Purple's family tree. 'Breaking the Law' – with its thumbnail sketches of life on the dole in the early years of Thatcherism, and its frustrated cry of 'You don't know what it's like' – marked *British Steel* out as too grounded in reality to be thought of as glam. But in the band's sense of theatre and the boosting of Halford's character to cartoonish extremes, they had the sense of occasion and drama that would shape the look and feel of what would come next.

Priest's fellow Midlander Ozzy Osbourne enjoyed a huge reinvention the same year with the *Blizzard of Ozz* album. Largely due to his recruitment of pint-sized guitar virtuoso and California native Randy Rhoads, Osbourne sounded re-energised and fully equipped for a new decade, with the corrosive doom of Sabbath's sound replaced with something lighter, more melodic and distinctly transatlantic. Since his work on 1973's *Sabbath Bloody Sabbath*, Ozzy's talent seemed to be buckling under the weight of his own lifestyle, and the pressure to live up to and sustain the epoch-defining work that Black Sabbath had originally released. Listening through their mid-to-late Seventies' output there's a steady sense of a talent not in decline – but steadily running out of energy. By 1978's *Never Say Die*, Osbourne's vocal tone – plaintive and naturally suited to a minor key – is like the sound of someone begging for a way out. Even on the few bright spots like the title track, the effect is roughly akin to watching a video of a hostage where they're telling the viewers they're fine but frantically signalling with their eyes that they need help.

But on *Blizzard of Ozz*, all that had changed. Osbourne himself sounds in fine voice, but a huge amount of the credit must go to Rhoads. Tiny and blond haired, Rhoads bore a passing resemblance to

Mick Ronson, David Bowie's guitarist in the Spiders from Mars, and had played in a series of bar bands around LA from the mid-Seventies, as well as recording in the first incarnation of Quiet Riot.[1] Throughout his childhood he both played and taught at Musonia, the music school established and run by his musician mother. With a huge technical expertise and improvisational aptitude, his playing on this album sounds like a quantum leap ahead of the blues-derived style that dominated most of the hard rock music of the Seventies. On opening track 'I Don't Know' alone he flits between galloping rhythm playing, spiralling lead fills and clean, arpeggiated interludes. Throughout the album his strength lies not just in the virtuosity that he so evidently possessed, but in his ability to support Osbourne's voice – an instrument that, charitably, you could describe as 'untrained'. Throughout his career, Osbourne's worst performances have shown a ten-

---

1. The first incarnation of Quiet Riot broke up in 1978 after bassist Kelly Garni hatched a 'big drunken plan' to shoot singer Kevin Dubrow dead while he was recording his vocals for *Quiet Riot II* at Record Plant studio in Hollywood. Garni had been drinking heavily with Rhoads before attempting to drive the twenty-five miles to the studio. Realising he was too drunk to safely reach the scene of his intended crime, he turned back but was pulled over and arrested by police shortly before making it back to his home. He was charged with drunken driving and felony possession for a concealed weapon. Recalling the incident in 2019 he was philosophical about his fate. 'I was kicked out of Quiet Riot because of this. I have no problems saying that. Once I started to pull a gun out, the management said, "He is out of control", which I agree to that decision that they made and have no issues with. I deserved to get fired from Quiet Riot. Totally deserved it.'

dency to lose focus, wandering approximately around the tune or behind the beat, where his keening, nasal tone sounds flat and desperate (there's a performance from April 28, 1981 of 'Crazy Train' on the TV show *After Hours* which is particularly hard on the ears). But Rhoads' playing and arrangements turned these potential limitations into bonuses: on 'Crazy Train' he propels Osbourne through the hardest sections of the vocal line, cranking out a dense rhythm track to support his frontman; on 'Goodbye to Romance' he plucks out a kind of optimistic, gentle psychedelia that harks back to the Beatles of Osbourne's childhood.[2]

What comes across most strongly is a sense of the personal bond that Osbourne and Rhoads enjoyed. Sonically, they seem meshed together creatively to the point where it's hard to imagine the same material working with either party replaced by another. Osbourne's evident affection for the musician who had largely resurrected his critical and creative standing was matched by a near-telepathic ability to work together despite the punishing levels of alcohol abuse that Osbourne was already subjecting himself to. 'I

2. In a 2017 interview to launch a campaign for the Hopes and Homes For Children charity, Osbourne talked about first hearing 'She Loves You' by the Beatles. 'That song changed my life. "She Loves You" had such an impact on me. I remember exactly where I was. I was walking down Witton Road in Aston, I had a blue transistor radio and when that song came on I knew from then on what I wanted to do with my life... I owe my career to them because they gave me the desire to want to be in the music game.'

have a lot of fond memories of Randy,' Osbourne told *Revolver* magazine in 2013. 'He lived with me for a while. We had an apartment together in London. And I always was out of my mind shitfaced and passed out somewhere. I came around one time and I heard Randy, he was having a lesson in this room with me. A classical lesson. And I come around and I heard, [*sings notes*]. I said, "That's next." "What?" "Remember that." And it became "Diary of a Madman", the song.'

The songs they produced on *Blizzard of Ozz* weren't just a leap forwards for Osbourne, they were perfectly in tune with where metal was about to get to. The big rock releases of the first couple of years of the decade, such as Rainbow's *Straight Between the Eyes* (1982), certainly had elements which were moving towards glam metal (the single 'Stone Cold' is a pretty exemplary glam metal power ballad) but they couldn't quite shake off the flourishes and swagger of a more operatic Seventies' sound. Aldo Nova's 'Fantasy' single (1982) veers close to a glam sound, but the song's keyboard lines and lush arrangements are reminiscent of the harder end of Jefferson Starship's output (plus, Nova's sensible collar-length hair meant he couldn't look fully glam metal). *Blizzard of Ozz* had a few residual elements of this Seventies' influence (the aforementioned 'Goodbye to Romance' particularly), but by 1983, Ozzy's sound had focused down into something with all the blues and swing frozen out of it for his *Bark at the Moon* album.

However, this completion of Osbourne's revival in fortunes would take place without the guitarist who had done so much to reinvigorate him personally and creatively. On March 19, 1982, Osbourne's band were en route to the Rock Super Bowl XIV festival in Orlando, where they would be headlining the Tangerine Bowl supported by Foreigner, and had stopped off overnight at a property in Leesburg, Florida. Early that morning, Osbourne's band's driver, Andrew Aycock – a trained pilot – took one of the property's '55 Beechcraft Bonanza F-35 planes and ran a short test flight with keyboard player Don Airey and tour manager Jake Duncan. Two more flights followed, this time with Rhoads and the band's hairdresser Rachel Youngblood on board. For reasons that are still unclear, during this third flight, the pilot began flying as low as possible, attempting three times to 'buzz' the static tourbus on which other members of the band were still sleeping. Osbourne's subsequent statement to investigators recounted what happened on the fourth flypast from his perspective:

At approximately 9:00 a.m. on Friday, March 19, 1982, I was awoken from my sleep by a loud explosion. I immediately thought that we'd hit a vehicle on the road. I got out of the bed, screaming to my fiancée, Sharon, 'Get off the bus.' Meanwhile, she was screaming to everyone else to get off the bus. After getting out of the bus, I saw that a plane had crashed. I didn't know who was on the plane at the time. When we realized that our people were on the plane, I found it very difficult to get assistance from anyone to help. In fact, it took almost a half-hour before anyone arrived. One small fire engine arrived, which appeared to squirt three gallons of water over the inferno. We asked for further assistance, such as telephones, and didn't receive any further help. In the end, we finally found a telephone and Sharon phoned her father.

Sharon Osbourne's statement concluded: 'I did not see the crash. All I saw was fire.' The subsequent report concluded that the plane had been just ten feet from the ground when its wing struck the bus, before it cart-wheeled into a tree and then crashed into the roof of the house. On impact it exploded, with all three passengers dying instantly. Rhoads was identified by his jewellery and Aycock through his dental records, with toxicology tests showing up only nicotine for Rhoads, but cocaine for the pilot.

The immense trauma of this loss for Osbourne and the rest of his band was cruelly heightened by its contrast with the rich seam of form he was entering. Osbourne would replace Rhoads with Jake E. Lee who had played in an early incarnation of Ratt and Rough Cutt, semi-protégés of Ronnie James Dio and his wife. The first fruits of this new incarnation of Osbourne's band, the *Bark at the Moon* album, was emblematic of a year that marked a step change in metal – the music that cut through and connected had a glossy sheen, a tight, processed sound and a spunky self-confidence. The cover saw Ozzy transformed into a moderately convincing werewolf by Greg Cannom who had previously been responsible for the key scenes in 1981's *An American Werewolf in London*. Plans to originally record at the Compass Point studios in the Bahamas were shelved after a visit to scope the location ended badly ('I was pissed, I fell flat on my face in the studio,' Osbourne told *Kerrang!*) with Ridge Farm in Surrey eventually hosting the sessions.

Despite Ozzy's disaffection with the prevailing trends in chart music ('I watched *Top of the Pops* the other week and I nearly threw up. There's this one record, I think it's called "Superman", well, I've never heard such a pile of shit in all my life.') and late jitters about the quality of the final mix, the album which emerged managed to not only replicate the propulsive, treble-laden screech and galloping attack of its predecessors, but it scored genuine chart hits. 'So Tired', a wistful ballad again drifting into a Beatles-ish psychedelia with a video sympathising with a tormented theatre-prowling hunchback, made it into the Top 20, with the far heavier title track of the album narrowly missing out on the same placing. Whatever genuine tragedies Ozzy had suffered in the preceding years – and whatever worrying signs were visible as to his future wellbeing – 1983 was a professional and creative triumph for him.

In America, the paranoia and nerves of just a few years earlier seemed to be mutating into a bolshy, overcompensating boosterism across the country as a whole. Interest rates had fallen by almost half since their 1980 peak, and while unemployment which had peaked at 10.8 per cent in December 1982 was still at 8.3 per cent, through this period almost twice as many Americans now reported feeling optimistic and positive about their economic prospects as those who felt negatively. An artificial, hyped-up optimism was in the air – one that Reagan would tap into perfectly with his 1984 election campaign proclaiming that 'It's morning again in America.' America – like Ozzy himself – had at least superficially come back from the brink.

Against this backdrop, music that was aggressive, obnoxiously loud, self-promoting, gleefully escapist and larger than life was strangely in keeping with the times, despite its countercultural trappings. Often, the artists responsible were veteran performers who had been scratching around for much of the previous decade. As well as *Bark at the Moon*, there were strong albums from Seventies' journeymen Quiet Riot (Rhoads' former band who had been reactivated for the new decade by frontman Kevin Dubrow and scored a huge hit with the anthemic title track of their album *Metal Health* and a cover of Slade's 'Cum On Feel the

Noize' which joined the cultural dots between two countries, eras and genres) and Dio, the new vehicle for Osbourne's former replacement in Black Sabbath, Ronnie James Dio. In Quiet Riot's case, at this stage, their importance wasn't just musical, but in their success in scoring a major label deal with CBS/Sony. One of the first LA area bands to be signed to such a deal after Van Halen, Quiet Riot served as a proof of concept to the other major labels circling the LA scene. Meanwhile, Ratt – whose roots went back as far as 1973 and a succession of bands with names like Firedome, Crystal Pystal and Buster Cherry, along with a revolving door of members including at one time Jake E. Lee – marked 1983 with the release of their self-titled EP and the standout track, 'You Think You're Tough'.

The song itself is a fairly unremarkable glam plod, but what's more interesting is the video. This is a perfect bit of myth-making for the band: they're seen in turn driving around LA, encountering legions of fans, gooning around at photo shoots, waving at an unconvincing Marilyn Monroe lookalike and generally living the rockstar lifestyle some way in excess of where one suspects Ratt were actually positioned in 1983. But the crucial element of the video is the guest appearances from Mötley Crüe's Tommy Lee and Nikki Sixx, along with Osbourne (both as himself, and as a particularly disconcerting middle-aged woman). Ratt guitarist Robbin Crosby would let Sixx move in with him after Sixx's relationship with Lita Ford broke down a year later, such was the close proximity of glam metal's main players. The sense is of a scene coalescing around shared networks and aesthetics and a cultural moment being on the verge of occurring. (Closing the circle further, the stocking-clad female legs being assailed by rodents on the cover of the EP belonged to Tawny Kitaen, a model and actor who would later both appear in a series of Whitesnake's videos and marry their singer David Coverdale.)

The year's first issue of *Kerrang!*[3] provides a useful snapshot of metal at the start of the glam era. Published from an office tucked down the side of Covent Garden tube station in the centre of London's West End, the magazine was still dominated by the sort of hairy, overblown rock that was sonically and culturally dragging the spirit of the Seventies over into the new decade. This bumper, end-of-year issue included a ten-page 'Deutsch Rock Dambuster!' special feature, with Accept's Wolf Hoffmann on the cover, standing

3. British rock and metal magazine, first published in June 1981. Originally, *Kerrang!* was a one-issue spin off of *Sounds* magazine, published to capitalise on the market around the New Wave of British Heavy Metal, although the first issue's cover star was Angus Young of AC/DC, with appearances not just from Motörhead, Saxon and Girlschool, but also Pat Benatar, ZZ Top and Styx. This diversity was a constant – and largely uncredited – feature of the magazine, which had a far more catholic sense of what metal fans were into than outsiders expected. The magazine would later go fortnightly, before going weekly in 1987, and throughout its lifespan has nimbly championed every new genre from thrash to emo, been a TV channel, radio station, award ceremony, website and tour. It's still going strong to this day.

legs akimbo, fist clenched and with his Gibson Flying V guitar inverted. In the readers' poll, the best bands of 1982 included AC/DC, Whitesnake, Gillan, Asia and Rainbow. The best album chart included Saxon's *The Eagle Has Landed*, Robert Plant's *Pictures at Eleven* and Rush's *Signals*. The bestsellers list of the year was similarly stuffed with the elder statesmen–like Status Quo, Meat Loaf and UFO along with reissues and compilations from Eric Clapton and Jimi Hendrix. The sense of a general stodginess pervaded. In the 'Kwotes of the Year' section, Bob Catley of Magnum stressed that 'We wear what we want and don't try and tart ourselves up to look what we're not', while Joe Lynn Turner clarified that 'There's been talk about me being a poof and wearing a wig but neither of those things are true.' A long interview with former Thin Lizzy guitarist Gary Moore and his drummer Ian Paice saw the pair griping about a culture where pop was focused on 'two people on stage with tapes and synthesisers' and radio DJs didn't appreciate them. Even Kiss were on morose form – Ace Frehley talking largely about a recent car crash which had left him with a pinched vertebrae, a broken ankle and nose, a hefty script of painkillers and an inability to wear platform heels as a result (he switched them for baseball boots). Fun – and more generally any youthful abandon – was pretty thin on the ground. In the critics' round-up page, even editor Geoff Banks sounded a weary note in his summary of what 1982 had meant to him. 'The year that I realised heavy metal was in a worse state than I thought.'

But if you looked closely there were already small shoots of potential just about visible in 1983 among new acts. Zebra's 'Tell Me What You Want' single is a proto-glam metal classic (Randy Jackson even plays a ludicrously shaped double neck guitar in the video). In that week's album charts, a few other cartoonishly colourful offerings stood out among the more workmanlike metal. At twenty-four, Hanoi Rocks' *Self Destruction Blues* looked like a glam album, although the ragbag round-up of singles from 1981 and 1982 wobbles somewhere between spindly Cure-influenced new wave ('Café Avenue') and yobby bar-stompers like the title track. Hanoi Rocks were one of those bands who were perennially a better idea and concept than musical product – even at the age of twenty, skeletal Finnish frontman Michael Monroe was a natural rockstar, with a ravaged, sleep-starved look that marked him out as unsuitable for any work beyond fronting a band like Hanoi Rocks. With the roughed-up androgyny of his feathered hair, mesh tops, black-lined eyes and tranquilised pout, the teetotal Monroe looked like a Sixties beauty who'd gone to seed after a particularly tough Seventies. Given this, his influence over the subsequent generation of metal bands was as much sartorial and attitudinal as sonic, and he's spent much of his career in musical circles whose grandeur far outpaces his actual commercial success – in 1985, Steven Van Zandt, guitarist with Bruce Springsteen's E Street Band, invited Monroe to appear on the anti-apartheid charity track 'Sun City'; his 1989 solo album featured Mott The Hoople frontman and British glam rock legend Ian Hunter; Aerosmith invited him onstage with them at Les Paul's seventy-fifth birthday at New York's Hard Rock Café; and he would later appear on stage as a guest of Alice Cooper at his live shows. Guns n' Roses were particularly enamoured of Monroe; Axl Rose appeared in the video for Monroe's 1989 solo track, 'Dead, Jail or Rock 'n' Roll', Slash appeared on stage with him in the same year as a guest, while Monroe would go on to play the harmonica solo on the track 'Bad Obsession' from 1991's *Use Your Illusion 1* album. Hanoi Rocks also had the oddity of an English drummer, Nicholas 'Razzle' Dingley from Royal Leamington Spa, who had joined the band in 1982 and enthusiastically embraced the hedonistic lifestyle enjoyed by his bandmates, setting his sights on a life far beyond Britain's musical scene. During one dressing down about his lifestyle from the band's manager Zeppo, Razzle gave an admirably succinct mission statement by way of retort: 'You know, I don't care if I fucking die. I just want to get to LA.' And with Hanoi as his vehicle, he would.

But the most significant album in that year-end

chart was only just clinging on at number 40: Mötley Crüe's *Too Fast for Love*. The debut album by the band had actually come out in 1981, but was still hanging around in the charts as a slow-burning seller at the end of 1982. *Too Fast for Love* isn't *quite* a glam metal album. Opener and debut single 'Live Wire' rattles along at a Motörhead-pace, the lo-fi barrage broken up by handbrake-turn cowbell interludes, and a three-note riff bashing away throughout. In the video, overlaid pentagram-daubed skulls float in mid air, guitarist Mick Mars vomits blood, bassist Nikki Sixx is set on fire as part of the pyrotechnic display and walls of flame rocket up from either side of the drum riser. In both the video and press shots from around the time, the band's look – stack heels, pouting lips, teased hair – is as indebted to the Seventies' shock of the New York Dolls and Alice Cooper as it is to more immediate bar-band predecessors such as Twisted Sister (indeed, the cover is an homage to Andy Warhol's cover for the Rolling Stones' 1971 album, *Sticky Fingers*). At points it feels like the band aimed for a Kiss tribute but the budget ran out. Much of Sixx's stagecraft was lifted from the theatrics that he had seen at shows by Sister, an early vehicle for Blackie Lawless, later of W.A.S.P. As 1983 got underway, Crüe hadn't quite transmuted the sleazy spirit of those earlier bands into something contemporary, but the process was underway.

Crüe's roots were in squalor, sleaze and the hard

grind of trying to interest crowds in a band who were too late for the scene that inspired them but too early for what would eventually coalesce around them. In their early photos, they just look *ill* – sunken cheeks contrasted with matted, top-heavy feather cuts, daylight-blocking aviators, and a greasy get-up of leather and lycra which they appear to have been sewn into for winter like medieval peasants. If there's any 'glamour' in this first incarnation of Mötley Crüe, it's a subversive, distorted vision of it, a mocking idea of rockstar luxury viewed from the bottom of the pile.

This made sense given Crüe's progress to date. Formed by an array of troubled adolescents (Nikki Sixx), itinerant Californians (Vince Neil), school dropouts (Tommy Lee) and semi-failed older musicians (Mick Mars), each had faced genuine difficulties and had little natural ability to work with. From 1981 onwards, they had been a Wednesday night fixture at the Troubadour in Hollywood along with Ratt, but even these $1 shows were a step up from where they had started. 'Pookies was a sandwich shop we used to play in Pasadena,' recalled Sixx in a 2016 interview with *Louder Sound*.

'We'd play anywhere.'
'But we still gave it our all, even in a sandwich shop with like 20 people there,' added Neil. 'We didn't care, we were still lighting Nikki on fire and shit like that! We had the drive. We didn't care if we didn't have any

money, because any money we made we put into our show. We lived like dogs, relying on girls to give us food and stuff. When you have no money for food, your biggest score is a girl who works in a grocery store.'

'We fucked the ugliest girl to get these hot dogs! We'd always try to figure out a way to get whatever we wanted. If we had to steal it from a chick we would. We'd size up chicks at the Rainbow: "She looks about Vince's size. That's a nice red leather jacket she has on." And we'd steal their clothes!'

What the band apparently lacked in dietary balance, chivalry or basic fire-safety awareness, they made up for in a sense of theatricality that outpaced their popularity for a time. The band gravitated towards the hundred-yard stretch of Sunset Boulevard which ran from Gazzari's to the Rainbow Bar and Grill via the Roxy, a selection of clubs which had long lost their allure as upscale supperclubs or early-Seventies celebrity hangouts and were ripe for colonisation by a new scene of bands who needed space, could bring a crowd and saw the seedy air of faded ruin around the clubs as a feature not a bug.

Unable to afford full-size amps and a PA for their early shows at the Whisky a Go Go, Crüe would instead create an illusion of scale by constructing backlit mesh scrims, podiums with flashing lights inside to elevate each band member and a drum riser that they later sold to Ratt. Spotlights were vetoed in favour of dramatic backlighting, and lengths of chain were duct-taped to the ceiling. 'We'd steal shit, build shit,' recalled Sixx in the same interview. 'It's the drive. We had no money, we just had the drive. We'd create things that make people talk about the band and the shows.' Better than anyone, Mötley Crüe understood that in 1980s America, it was more important to act the part and look the part than to actually do anything of substance. If you could create a spectacle and visualise success and scale, then everything else would follow. Their component parts weren't quite in place as 1982 tipped over into 1983, but they soon would be. While Mötley Crüe weren't fully realised at this point, they were at least an impossible-to-ignore cornerstone around which the rest of LA's metal scene – until then largely in thrall to visiting British acts like UFO, Iron Maiden and the rest of those featured in Brian Slagel's *New Heavy Metal Revue* fanzine – could start to both build itself and imitate.

Another band in a period of transformation was Def Leppard. Within the musical culture of their home city, Sheffield, they were something of a misnomer. Sheffield has arguably made more of a contribution to the development of electronic music than anywhere else in the UK – Kraftwerk played at the city's university on October 9, 1976, a show that Phil Oakey of The Human League later recalled as being 'as seismic as the Sex Pistols' gig at Manchester Free Trade Hall' from June the same year and a catalyst for a scene which went on to birth his own group as well as Heaven 17, Cabaret Voltaire and ABC. 'We hated anything that wasn't modernist', said ABC frontman Martin Fry. Later musical waves in the city included the intelligent experimental techno of LFO and the Warp Records roster, the off-kilter, occult synthpop of The All Seeing I and Moloko's sophisticated disco-house.

By contrast with this rich electronic tapestry, Def Leppard were, on the face of it, a far earthier proposition. Their 1980 debut *On Through the Night* wears its influences – and the musical loves of vocalist Joe Elliott – firmly on its sleeve. 'Wasted' and 'Sorrow is a Woman' sit in the same melancholic spot between metal and punk that Thin Lizzy had settled into around the late 1970s; the galloping drums of 'Rock Brigade' recall the roughed-up self-penned version of bubblegum glam rock that The Sweet used to slip onto their singles' b-sides. But the most notable elements on Def Leppard's first album aren't the most aggressive, but the most unexpected – the multi-tracked harmonies that open 'Hello America' and the teasing synth lines that punctuate the track suggest a band interested in pushing the boundaries of straight-ahead rock into something more sonically theatrical and technically ambitious. While the group was lumped in with the burgeoning New Wave of British Heavy Metal (NWOBHM), they clearly envisaged themselves as outgrowing that scene before too long and were already thinking at a scale markedly bigger than that of their peers. Def Leppard might have opened the *On Through the Night* tour at the 700-capacity Marquee club, but they were at least in part already composing and playing – and thinking – like a stadium act.

These tendencies weren't always universally welcomed – a portion of the crowd at that year's Reading Festival pelted the band with bottles in response to a perception that they had 'sold out' and were overly subservient to the American market.[4] By the time work began on their second album *High 'n' Dry*, Leppard were thinking even bigger – bringing in producer Robert 'Mutt' Lange who as well as working on AC/DC's *Highway to Hell* (1979) and *Back in Black* (1980) had recently crafted the glossy, synth-rich sound of Foreigner's *4* (1981). Sleeve art was handled by the legendary Hipgnosis design studio who had created everything from Pink Floyd's *Dark Side of the Moon* to T-Rex's *Electric Warrior* and Led Zeppelin's *Houses of the Holy*. Leppard weren't yet that big, but – just as Ratt would do with their video for 'You Think You're Tough' – they were projecting an illusion of where they wanted to be, and where they thought they deserved to be.

These ambitions – which at the time seemed to bor-

4. This suspicion was strongly inflamed by a cover story by Geoff Barton in *Sounds*, asking 'Has the Leppard changed its spots?' and the track 'Hello America'. Their habit of ending live sets on the *Pyromania* tour with the Creedence Clearwater Revival track 'Travelin' Band' and their status as tax exiles around this time didn't help matters later on either.

der on hubristic – would crystallise in January 1983 on the band's breakthrough album *Pyromania*. Beginning with the theatrical, bombastic, synthesised chord sequence of a grand opening theme, the album whips through a series of hook-laden tracks, most notably 'Photograph'. But as notable as the tunes themselves is the structure of the songs. Before the reprise of the final chorus in 'Photograph', the backing shudders to a halt, with Joe Elliott's voice cascading back in followed by a wall of guitars; power ballad 'Too Late for Love' is remarkably sparse, with long passages where the only support for the vocal is a single, chorus-laden guitar riff, alternating with banks of close harmony backing vocals strangely reminiscent of ABBA's bleaker moments; 'Foolin'' rides for almost a minute on an acoustic guitar line before the rest of the band arrive to slam into the chorus, and for a stadium-sized live favourite it has a remarkably stop-start feel. 'Rock of Ages' is simply odd – from its nonsensical Germanic intro phrase, through a stomping glam beat, guitar chords panning between the speakers, to a solo that woozily slurs in and out of tune and around the beat. The video – in which the band preside over a primordial moshpit, Joe Elliott staggers under the weight of a medieval broadsword before turning it into Phil Collen's guitar, a woman appears lashed to a crucifix and an owl eyeballs the camera while a cowled monk chuckles at the spectacle before him – is one of the least strange things about it.

But on the whole album, two things constantly stand out – most obviously, the band's way with an absolutely nailed-on pop chorus, which was streets ahead of any of their peers and on a par with anything you'd have found in the mainstream charts. But also their avoidance of the most obvious route to these sonic sugar-rushes. Throughout *Pyromania*, every time you think the chord change is going to drop into place, the rhythm shifts or the tune steps sideways, or the band holds out on you for a few seconds longer. It drips with self-confidence – it's the sound of a band who know how good their work is becoming, how much impact their producer is ensuring it lands with and how much bigger the listener's response will be if they make them wait for the pay-off. They'd hinted at this ability with parts of *High 'n' Dry* – notably 'Bringin' On the Heartbreak' – but it was on *Pyromania*, with its brevity, vim and texture, that it all came together. The British fans and journalists who sniped at them for pursuing mass appeal so doggedly in America had got it the wrong way round – they were simply running to get to where a band that was capable of creating music like them should be. An album which sounded like this could only ever have made sense on a huge canvas, which meant America, arenas and MTV – not low expectations, mock humility and being happy to simply sell out Hammersmith Odeon again.

Pyromania's commercial impact was immediate: 6 million copies of the album would have been sold by the end of that year, with only Michael Jackson's *Thriller* keeping it from the top of the album charts in America. 'Photograph' reached number 1 on Billboard's rock-based 'Top Tracks' chart, but crucially crossed over enough that it got to number 12 on the regular pop chart as well. The band toured solidly for twelve months, with 178 dates between February 1983 and February 1984 taking them through Europe, Australia and the Far East, as well as five months traversing North America.

The band's touring itinerary is instructive of the mentality and work ethic they had at this time – as well as obvious destinations on the coasts, they headlined in places such as Lubbock, Texas; Norman, Oklahoma; and South Yarmouth, Massachusetts. The grafter's outlook that was forged when Collen was working in a mill and Clark was in a factory back in Sheffield underpinned this road trip for them. In June 1983, eight dates had to be rescheduled after Joe Elliott's voice gave out and doctors ordered him into complete silence, but the operation rolled on. In Detroit, two nights selling 28,000 tickets per show saw them beat a record previously held by Led Zeppelin, the band who, less than four years earlier, Def Leppard had driven overnight to see play their final British show at Knebworth ('It was a religious experience, it really was... it was the biggest show I'd ever seen in my life' Elliott would tell BBC Radio's Johnnie Walker in a 2018 interview).

As the tour gained pace, Def Leppard got the attention not just of their peers, but of their heroes – Brian May of Queen joined them on stage in LA; AC/DC watched them perform in Hawaii. Leppard's penultimate show of the American tour took place in San Diego and drew 55,000 fans to see them supported by Eddie Money, Uriah Heep and Mötley Crüe. One of the few regrettable moments on the tour occurred on September 7 in Tuscon, when Elliott attempted to goad the crowd into clapping louder during 'Rock of Ages' by boasting that 'Last night we played in El Paso, that place with all the greasy Mexicans, and they made a lot more noise than that!' Drummer Rick Allen believed that he was the only person who'd heard the off-the-cuff comments, but a reporter in the venue filed the story back to the *Arizona Daily Star*. Almost three weeks later, as Leppard worked on press and promotion in Japan, word got back to the band's manager Cliff Burnstein that 'they're burning Def Leppard records and breaking them over the air in El Paso' in response to Elliott's insults.[5] 'That comment, I swear, was aimed at five Hispanic kids who were spitting at us, throwing Jack Daniels and kung fu stars at the band,' Elliott later claimed. 'It was aimed at those five kids, not at anybody else in El Paso itself. I was slag-

---

5. https://ultimateclassicrock.com/def-leppard-pyromania-tour/

ging off those five bastards... I'm a Cheech & Chong
fan, and they use [the phrase] all the time.' Elliott's
explanation fell on deaf ears, with El Paso's director
of the League of United Latin American Citizens, Joe
Loya, calling for a boycott of Def Leppard's music
and Arin Michaels, programme director for radio station KLAQ, was photographed ripping up the sleeve
of *Pyromania*. El Paso's mayor, Jonathan Rogers, called
for a citywide boycott of the band and its music in
October 1983. The issue dragged on, with civic leaders
further afield in Southern California informing Burnstein that the communities they worked with were also
aggrieved at Elliott's comments. Finally, on November 23, Elliott hosted a press conference in El Monte,
California, where he issued a fulsome apology: 'The
last thing Mexican–Americans need as they try to rid
themselves of the stereotype is for me or anyone else
to make such statements. It was stupid of me to make
such a false accusation.'[6] He also donated $15,000 of his
own money to local charities.

Aside from this one outbreak of cretinously mis-
judged 'banter', the tour was an unalloyed success.
Despite bassist Rick Savage claiming in an interview
a decade later that, 'Looking back, and hearing old
mixing desk tapes, we were fucking atrocious most
of the time!'[7] Fans clearly didn't concur. The show

6. David Fricke, *Animal Instinct: The Def Leppard Story* (Zomba Books, 1987),
p. 90.
7. http://www.deflepparduk.com/2016newssep140.html

did such good business that at the close of the North American tour, the band's live agents American Talent International took out a full-page trade ad in *Billboard* magazine to thank the band and proclaim the tour 'A SMASHING SUCCESS!' Def Leppard was an unstoppable Stakhanovite metal machine, conquering America one town at a time in matching Union Jack vests and shorts.

They also perfectly coincided their arrival in the US with the consolidation of MTV and its spread across the country's growing cable network. From 1975 to 1985 the number of cable subscribers in the US grew from 3,500 cable systems serving 10 million subscribers to 6,600 systems serving nearly 40 million subscribers. Deregulation of the market stemmed from the 1977 HBO v FCC court case, which ruled that the Federal Communications Commission was unfairly restricting cable operators in favour of broadcast networks. With many of these hurdles removed, new channels and production companies came into the market, all with reach into new geographical areas, all with airtime to fill and all with a need for visually compelling content. And for the burgeoning MTV, Def Leppard fitted the bill perfectly.[8]

---

8. One of the oddities of the MTV era was that as much as it slowed the careers of serious rock artists who weren't especially telegenic (Supertramp), it also rebooted and supercharged middling bands whose visual appeal bordered on the cartoonish. The perfect example is ZZ Top, who had already produced a decade's worth of sludgy, grinding blues-boogie before comprehensively reinventing themselves with 1983's masterpiece, *Eliminator*.

Their video for 'Photograph' (directed by David Malet[9]) saw them installed as a regular fixture on the network, supplanting Michael Jackson's 'Beat It' as the station's most requested video. But despite all of this, Leppard's success wasn't universally celebrated. *Ker-*

As well as dialling up the tempo and streamlining their sound into something more compressed and focused, the album was built on a series of flawless crossover singles, 'Gimme All Your Lovin'', 'Legs' and 'Sharp Dressed Man'. Each of these came with a promo video trading on the band's image – chest-length beards, shades, Texan 'southern gentleman' sartorial flourishes – and recurring motifs of revolving furry guitars, the band appearing in spectral form to come to the assistance of benighted rockers and the signature candy-apple red hotrod car that adorned the album's sleeve in illustrated form. Most MTV viewers would not have known of ZZ Top as a hugely credible, technically inventive mainstay of the Seventies' rock scene, led by a guitarist whose ability to jump mid-phrase from growling blues to squealing overdriven harmonics frequently gave the impression that several guitarists were on stage at once, and whose musical roots went back as far as touring in support of Jimi Hendrix with the psychedelic band The Moving Sidewalks. What they *did* know them as was a production line of hit singles with the kind of comprehensive visual identity you'd normally find in a cartoon series or an advertising campaign, making them the perfect band for the MTV era. They never quite attained the heights of *Eliminator* again – follow-up *Afterburner* was broadly considered to have leaned too heavily into a flimsy, vogueish production and suffered by comparison to its predecessor, but actually holds up very well with hindsight. The band would go on to appear in and soundtrack *Back to the Future 3*, and to this day are still touring, and still look exactly the same.

9. Prolific 1980s promo director, responsible for huge numbers of the clips that still fill VH1 to this day. His creative high watermark was David Bowie's 'Ashes to Ashes' video, in which Bowie appears as a haunted Pierrot, troubled both by intimations of the nuclear holocaust and various patrons of New Romantic hangout The Blitz. Less admirably, he also made the video for Bowie and Mick Jagger's Live Aid duet of 'Dancing in the Street' in which the two frontmen goon around a deserted warehouse while mugging furiously to the camera and gaily traducing their own reputations and legacies. Other work included most of AC/DC's videos, Iron Maiden's 'Run to the Hills', Queen's 'Radio GaGa' and 'I Want to Break Free' and the Boomtown Rats' 'I Don't Like Mondays'.

rang! had marked the start of the *Pyromania* tour with a distinctly sniffy live review, concluding that 'You could say that Def Leppard need to control their volume and come up with some more in-depth material'. Even the magazine's end-of-year round-up issue for 1983 saw the band notably absent, bar an interview with Collen and Clark which was relegated to the music gear section in the back pages and was primarily concerned with quizzing them about how much money Lange was receiving in royalties for his production work, and why the domestic metal audience took no pleasure in the band's success.

But perhaps the most revealing comment comes at the end of the interview, when the guitarist starts to explain in depth how *Pyromania*'s wall of sound was created. 'We'd put down two tracks of Les Paul for the low end, two tracks of SG for the mid-range and two tracks of Telecaster for the top end,' explained Clark. 'It sounds like there's only two guitars playing, but in some cases, there's six.' If Lange acted like a sixth member of the band, then the studio was played as an extra instrument, pushed to its limits and used to create a sound and texture that no other band in the world had at the time. 'We credited him for arrangements,' said Clark. 'He's been involved with us for so long, it's hard to see him as an outsider.' Just as the Beatles had done with George Martin and David Bowie had done with Tony Visconti, Def Leppard were blurring the lines between artist and producer, working together to create something more than a straightforward document of what their musical output sounded like.

Under Lange's tutelage, Leppard were starting to sound less like five musicians organically creating the sound of a band, and more like a solid entity whose musical offerings arrived fully formed. As the band got bigger, their flaws and imperfections were being polished away – the group and its sound was becoming bigger than any one person or element within it, with a faintly inhuman, hyperreal quality hanging in the air around the songs on *Pyromania*. Their absence from album covers made perfect sense in this context – the question was how far they could push this impulse as they went forwards. 'It turned out great, but I don't think we'll ever record like that again,' said Collen. 'On the next album we'd like to record something different. We don't wanna do Pyromania II.' At the time, he could have had no idea of just how challenging that process would be, or just how far they were going to push the boundaries of what a metal band could do, achieve and sound like.

For Mötley Crüe, 1983 was a similarly transformative year. In late May over the Labour Day weekend, their domestic profile received a huge boost when they appeared at the US Festival, a four-day festival which had begun the previous year, funded and conceived by Apple computers cofounder Steve Wozniak as a communal counterweight to the individualism that he saw as pervading society and youth culture at the time. In total, 600,000 fans turned out for the festival with the New Wave Day seeing Mick Jones' last appearance with The Clash, the Rock Day hosting U2, Stevie Nicks and David Bowie, and the Country Day including Willie Nelson and Waylon Jennings.

In the middle of all this, Metal Day saw performances from the already-huge Judas Priest, Van Halen and Ozzy Osbourne, with Mötley Crüe second from the bottom on the bill on a blazing hot day at Glen Helen Regional Park in San Bernadino. These outdoor shows were a wilder, more anarchic, blue-collar counterpoint to the modern day festival experience: the MC took to the stage to repeatedly ask the crowd to move backwards to alleviate crushing, while security sprayed the overheating front rows with water and a roughly hewn banner was passed overhead proclaiming *MÖTLEY CRÜE WE'LL TAKE A PIECE OF YOUR ACTION*. Cameras caught a young man being dragged from the crush of the moshpit by security and tottering away on unsteady legs while the restless crowd waited for the stabs of mock-classical organ music that heralded the band's arrival. Three songs in, Vince Neil tells the crowd that for their forthcoming album, *Shout at the Devil*, they need one photograph to complete the artwork. Handed a camera, he instructs everyone to raise their hand as he captures the moment for posterity. These images would go nationwide as the cable network Showtime repeated a two-hour highlights package on its station throughout the summer.

In truth, Crüe are a little out of their depth in this performance – on the large, sparsely decorated stage they seem swamped, Neil's voice is poor and the largely unknown material doesn't seem to particularly connect with a crowd of that size. Just a few months earlier they'd been kicked off Kiss' *Creatures of the Night* tour for 'bad behaviour', completing just five shows on a poorly attended schedule. But crucially, they were now in a genuinely supersized environment, on the same bill as the biggest names in metal. They weren't at a tiny club show fabricating props that gave the impression of a huge theatrical production. They had become what they already visualised themselves as – full-scale rockstars. And the release of their forthcoming album would cement that.

Released in September 1983, *Shout at the Devil* is the moment when all the disparate elements of glam metal crystallise into a whole. When the false starts and echoing traces finally come together. Where the fizz and vim of punk combine with a glossy Eighties' reboot of Alice Cooper's shlock theatricality. Where AM radio's pop sensibilities and corn-fed production is roughed up into something that rock fans could understand, champion and yell back at the stage. The album received a fairly tepid critical response – 'In short, originality is not this group's long suit. But then, who expected it to be? The whole point of bands like Mötley Crüe is to provide cheap thrills to jaded teens, and that's where the album ultimately disappoints,' wrote *Rolling Stone* – but it still sold 200,000 copies in its first fortnight.

More than a musical success, *Shout at the Devil* was a complete visual statement – as much as it *sounded* like what we now think of as glam metal, it also *looked* like it. While the album's LP cover art had a similar feel to AC/DC's *Back in Black* (1980), the cassette and 8-track perfectly showcased the band. The four band members were composited together before flaming backdrops, as though each were a character in a TV show's opening credits. The production is glossier and less ragged than on their previous album, more cartoonish and less gritty. The final line of the liner notes cautions that 'This record may contain backward messages' – another wink to the 'jaded teens' who understood full well that it didn't, but enjoyed a band deliberately provoking the authority figures who fretted about bands doing just this to lure listeners into Satanism. There was more truth in the acknowledgements' claim that 'This album was recorded on Foster's Lager, Budweiser, Bombay Gin, lots of Jack Daniels, Kahlua and Brandy, Quackers and Krell, and wild women!'

Despite this unpromising laundry list, *Shout at the Devil* was a quantum leap forwards for Mötley Crüe.

Where *Too Fast for Love* had burst open from the first bar, powered forwards at breakneck pace by its grimy punk influences, *Shout at the Devil* begins with a portentous spoken word intro over a droning synthesiser fanfare. *Too Fast for Love* rattled along with all the haste of a band who were scraping their loose change together to pay for a studio by the hour. *Shout at the Devil*'s title track swaggers in on its muscular riff, marking time before dropping into the vocals. Just listening to it you can visualise it as an opening track as the band converge on a stadium-sized stage.

While it received reviews ranging from lukewarm to derisory, *Shout at the Devil* is a remarkably even piece of work. While there aren't really any timeless standout tracks (the title track is more of a rallying cry than a song), there also aren't the longueurs which would plague many later glam metal albums. Clocking in at just thirty-five minutes, the eleven tracks are trimmed of fat and padding with the few deviations from the template (the acoustic instrumental 'God Bless the Children of the Beast') dispatched within ninety seconds. The lyrics are, by and large, absolute nonsense – 'Ten Seconds to Love' appears to be about how the protagonist is both irresistible to women while also suffering from premature ejaculation; the title track, as pointed out by American writer Chuck Klosterman, is a nominally satanic rallying cry which would make more sense if it was exhorting people to shout *with* the devil rather than at him; most of the other tracks are an assemblage of clichés and stock rebellious boilerplate.

But all of this is overwhelmed by two things. Firstly, the production, which has a genuine edge and heft, forging the ragged speed of their first album and the bombast of the prevailing mainstream rock sound into something genuinely new. The backing vocals have a multi-tracked depth, Mick Mars' powerchords chug along with a roaring growl and Tommy Lee's drums punch through the wall of noise. Most of the album sounds slower than you'd expect, and noticeably pitched down from the band's earlier work – this is music you can dance to, headbang to, cruise in a car to. Enough of its edges have been sanded off to push its appeal beyond the relatively small numbers who watched them at the Troubadour and the Whisky a Go Go.

But secondly, and more importantly, there's an absolutely single-minded sense of mission, purpose and destiny throughout the album. Everything is delivered for maximum impact – whether the calculated baiting of the moral critics who were beginning to circle around the metal scene, the pouting androgyny displayed in the face of a rock culture which was, at best, deeply uncomfortable with anything even skirting homosexuality, or the schlock-and-awe subject matter pushed in every line (sex, rape, revenge, Satanism, violence, more sex). The band's sense of scale and ambition had ballooned in a short period. 'I had ideas for the album and the tour that had to do with the mass psychology of evil behind Nazism,' said Nikki Sixx. 'I had grand ideas of creating a tour that looked like a cross between a Nazi rally and a black church service, with Mötley Crüe symbols instead of Swastikas everywhere.'[10]

The overall effect of *Shout at the Devil* is like a video nasty director suddenly being given a major studio budget and the instruction to secure an eighteen rating. The album is played completely straight, a roaring, defiant statement of belief against anyone who isn't a sworn believer, and within its own parameters, and by its own logic, it makes perfect sense. It's only when viewed critically and from the outside that the whole thing takes on a ludicrous, faintly unreal quality. In that sense, it was the perfect album for America in 1983 – and a template for a hundred bands who were about to appear.

---

10. Mötley Crüe and Neil Strauss, *The Dirt* (HarperCollins, 2001), p. 98.

Chapter 2

1984: W.A.S.P.

On a Saturday in late February 1984, viewers watching MTV would have caught a neat illustration of the dividing line that had been drawn through popular music with the advent of the station. Marshall Crenshaw's song, 'Someday, Somewhere' plays first. The song itself is fine – a Fifties-inflected lift of Gene Vincent's 'Lotta Lovin'' with a vocal line redolent of the Everly Brothers, something which feels like it drifted over gradually to America from Britain's pre-punk pub-rock boom seven years earlier. Immediately after this comes Talking Heads' 'Burning Down the House'. Now, on one level they aren't really comparable as songs – if you like jitterbugging revival rock and workmanlike songwriters who channel an imaginary golden age, then Talking Heads probably aren't the band for you. Likewise, if you're into self-consciously clever art-rock laced with sonic experiments and lashings of irony, you're probably not going to find much that floats your boat in the work of Marshall Crenshaw.

But there is a glaring, indisputable difference between the two artists, captured by their videos. In Talking Heads' clip, the video opens on a suburban home as evening turns to night, like the establishing shot of a film. The band, who five years earlier had been dressed in the suburban thrift-store standard of non-descript trousers and drip-dry workshirts are now in matching, oddly proportioned white suits. Images appear, then are reframed as projections over washed-out library footage. Band members are switched out for child-sized doppelgangers. Tricks from the video-art section of contemporary galleries – interpretative dancing, projection mapping, illusory backdrops, slow motion loops – are used liberally throughout. As the song ends the band are manipulated and dragged around the stage by controlling figures, as though they were puppets. By contrast, Crenshaw is filmed in a lacklustre live performance. The shot cuts between three fixed cameras at apparently random intervals. Crenshaw himself has an odd, waxy pallor beneath the stage lights, while his glasses catch a glare and obscure his eyes. Nothing happens in terms of narrative or visual trickery. In the wide shots, half the action is obscured by the slowly bopping crowd while everything has the muted, yellowing blur of low-quality videotape.

Now it's not that one of these artists is better, *per se*, than the other. But one of them has clearly grasped the essential truth in popular music as 1984 gets underway – if you don't communicate visually and look inventive, you can expect to have your appeal seriously curtailed.

This was a truth that would apply just as much in metal as in any other sphere of pop music. As the music press tipped over into the new year, a clear division was apparent between the bands who were thinking in 3D and those who were sticking to how they had always presented themselves. ZZ Top in matching white tuxedos and beards. Scorpions (apropos of nothing) in kendo suits. Waysted on the set of their new video with pinstripe leggings and feathered hair being mauled by a pack of replicant secretaries. By contrast, Mansfield's Savage look like they've got dressed after raiding the bags outside the local charity shop and Saxon look – as they always did – like a collection of northern PE teachers dressed up for an end-of-term performance. This is no great criticism of Saxon – they consistently traded on their resolute blokey ordinariness, never far removed from their Barnsley origins. In an interview with Belgian TV's *Pop Elektron* show in 1983 singer Biff Byford riffs like a cheerful working men's club comedian – 'We grew up on the smallest backstreets. It was so small there was no houses!' – while the band slurp at cups of tea. Their music – especially between 1980's *Strong Arm of the Law*, 1981's *Denim and Leather* and 1983's *Power & the Glory* – had anthemic moments without ever quite fully taking flight, and their attempt to effect a full major label crossover in 1985 for EMI with *Innocence is No Excuse* was a dud with Biff later admitting to *Classic Rock* that 'We got lazy and lost focus.' They never fully recovered creatively, but despite this Saxon sold solidly throughout their career (1984's *Crusader* reportedly sold 2 million copies worldwide), were a well-regarded live act, and popular enough that since 1999 following a dispute over ownership of the Saxon name there have effectively been two versions of the band touring and recording simultaneously.

But the essential truth remained: in 1984, in the MTV-driven world, the greater spoils were going to go to bands who looked more like Mötley Crüe and a lot less like Saxon. By March, *Kerrang!* was aware enough of this shift in the ground to put out a special issue titled *Vision On*, offering 'A brain-scrambling look at music videos'.

The template – both visual and sonic – set in LA by the scene around Mötley Crüe was starting to be picked up and adapted in other regions across America. From San Francisco, Night Ranger struck a winning formula combining twin-guitar workouts such as

'(You Can Still) Rock in America' with wimpy, ponderous ballads like 'Sister Christian'; Queensrÿche were from Seattle, selling 25,000 copies of their self-titled debut EP while still signed to independent 206 Records (EMI would sign them six months later); also from the city were Rail, winners of MTV's Basement Tapes talent contest and whose '1,2,3,4 Rock and Roll' classic has a similar caveman stomp to Quiet Riot's 'Metal Health'; Pasadena's Autograph scored a huge MTV-supported hit with 'Turn Up the Radio', a Van Halen soundalike which benefited from a futuristic video containing a glaring bit of product placement for PaperMate's Sharpwriter pencil.

Meanwhile, on the East Coast, reviewers were picking up on the self-titled debut album from New Jersey's Bon Jovi. Paul Suter's review in *Kerrang!* was admirably prescient – 'Jon Bon Jovi has assembled a band of classic finesse and brutal strength, most notably a shattering guitarist in Richie Sambora who's surely destined to be one of the guitar heroes of the modern age ... [the material is] blessed with a commerciality that should ensure plentiful sales and success ... truly an excellent package and one already in the running for the album of the year.' Bon Jovi's genius came in overlaying radio-friendly pop songwriting with enough attack and drama that they still felt just about like a metal act. The Juilliard-trained David Rashbaum's washes of keyboards immediately softened their sound – Saxon would never have used anything so potentially effeminate – while the band took on the fringes of Crüe's look without pushing it as far. In their first incarnation, they owed as much to the grown-out greaser look sported by Bruce Springsteen around *Darkness on the Edge of Town,* accidental pin-ups who had escaped from lives of blue-collar drudgery. In truth, Jon Bon Jovi's backstory was a little more nuanced – while raised in Perth Amboy and the son of former marines and from immigrant stock, he had started gigging with local acts while still in his teens and had a route into music through his cousin's Power Station recording studio[1] – but he'd already begun to form the workings of a model that would advance Mötley Crüe's base material into something less threatening, more adult and with wider mass appeal. Already on their debut the band were voicing the aspirations of the same bootstrapping suburban working class who fellow Jerseyite Springsteen had hymned on 'The River' and 'Born to Run'.

Bon Jovi's signature track at this time was the album opener 'Runaway'. The song dated back to June 1982 and had been through several incarnations – first as a

---

1. This familial connection saw Bon Jovi's first recorded appearance, when he supplied the vocals on 'R2-D2 We Wish You a Merry Xmas' on the Star Wars cash-in *Christmas in the Stars* album. The album credits him with his real name, John Bongiovi. With lyrics including 'If the snow becomes too deep/Just give a little beep' and what sounds like a particularly bored children's choir singing throughout, it's an inauspicious start to Bon Jovi's musical output, albeit one that got him a cheque for $180 and a credit on an RSO records release.

Billy Squier-produced demo for Jovi's band The Wild Ones, then included as a solo track credited to Bongiovi as a solo artist on the *New York Rocks 1983* compilation put together by local station 103.5FM WAPP 'The Apple'. Compared to the rest of the material on the album, 'Runaway' is clearly more accomplished. Rashbaum's opening keyboard stabs are rich with drama and anticipation; the minor key chord progression stutters into the track, a series of false starts before the whole band finally come together halfway through the fourth line. This back and forth between the solo keyboard line and the full-throated roar of the entire band gives 'Runaway' a genuine tension and depth, while the lyrics immediately showed Bongiovi as a more detailed, talented writer than most of his peers. The track is written from the perspective of a teenage girl – unusual already in metal circles – and in the opening line observes her peers, and their eyes lined in 'sable'. It's a nicely poetic line, but the use of 'sable' stands out. 'Make-up' would have scanned just as well, but he reached for something a little out of the ordinary. It's also a reference which would likely have passed over adolescent males, but been understood by female listeners.

If Def Leppard were reaching towards a wider audience in terms of their ambition and scale, Bon Jovi were doing something similar but by crossing over gender lines and creating a form of metal which didn't just welcome women in but – at least in part – spoke to them and referenced their lives. It sounds like a minor concession – and you'd struggle to portray Bon Jovi's output as feminist – but in a musical climate where other metal bands primarily showed women as ready to strip off their professional outfits and get down to their bikinis at the drop of a hat (Van Halen's 'Hot for Teacher' video), the target of phallic snakes (Whitesnake's *Slide It In* cover) or getting groped while being tattooed (Scorpions' *Love at First Sting*), Bon Jovi's output felt – both musically and ideologically – more inclusive of ordinary people, of both sexes.

This narrative nod to the kitchen-sink real lives of America's blue-collar workers that Bon Jovi wove into their material was the exception rather than the prevailing trend however in both glam metal and the wider pop culture in general. Growing in tandem with glam metal, and hitting many of the same touchpoints, was wrestling. In 1982, promoter Vince McMahon had purchased the World Wrestling Federation business from his ageing father. Over the following year, McMahon had crowded out the smaller regional federations, finally withdrawing his organisation from the National Wrestling Alliance at its AGM in 1983. Coupled with his success at getting WWF content onto syndicated TV stations nationwide, this amounted to an effective and complete takeover of wrestling in North America.

WWF's dominance was made complete in January

1984 when Hulk Hogan secured his first WWF world championship by beating reigning champion The Iron Sheik at Madison Square Garden. Hogan was the first wrestler to escape his opponent's signature 'camel clutch' move. With the fight finished in less than six minutes, veteran commentator Gorilla Monsoon declared the start of 'Hulkamania', and Hogan's reign as one of wrestling's first truly nationwide crossover figures.

Hogan was a strange-looking, somewhat unreal character, even by the standards of modern wrestling. He was impossible to place an age on – professional contact sport is typically the preserve of the young, but with his straw-like mullet and balding head, Hogan appeared two decades older from the neck up than he did from the neck down. He was clearly physically strong, but with a smooth, swollen torso which had an undefined, rubberised sheen. His bandit moustache could have been the colour it was from bleaching, the greying ravages of old age or a heavy cigarette habit. In his torn banana-yellow muscle vest, he looked like a cheap action figure of himself. He lectured young 'Hulkamaniac' fans on the need to take their vitamins, pray and believe in themselves, yet ten years later he took the stand at McMahon's criminal trial to admit to his own long history of anabolic steroid use.

Hogan was a mess of physical and social contradictions, but nobody in his fanbase cared. He was clearly a construct, removed from the usual restrictions and rules of celebrity – more rockstar or fictional character than sportsman. This blurring of the genres was amplified through his public appearances. When he fought The Iron Sheik, Hogan came into the ring to Survivor's 'Eye of the Tiger', a rousing bit of motivational soft rock from the soundtrack of the previous year's *Rocky III* film, in which Hogan had appeared – was he still playing the character at this point, or himself? And did it matter? The newly developed *Rock 'n' Wrestling Connection* franchise would further blur the lines between music and WWF, with a series of crossover bouts and storylines developed to include pop stars – Cyndi Lauper was a particularly enthusiastic participant, with a manufactured feud between the singer and wrestling manager Lou Albano[2] eventually being 'settled' in a women's wrestling bout between two of their chosen fighters, Wendi Richter and The Fabulous Moolah. *The Brawl to End it All* was broadcast live on MTV from Madison Square Garden on June 23, 1984. This set up a rematch for the following year, *The War to Settle the Score*. If any confirmation were needed that this was the front line of artifice and spectacle, the post-bout coverage was interrupted when a bemused-looking Andy Warhol wandered backstage before being co-opted into an unplanned interview with the tuxedo-clad host 'Mean' Gene

2. Albano played Lauper's long-suffering father in the promo video for 1983's 'Girls Just Wanna Have Fun'.

Okerlund. 'I'm... speechless' whispered America's pre-eminent pop artist, who in previous years had lent his approving presence to the likes of The Velvet Underground, Nico and Jean-Michel Basquiat. 'It's just so exciting. I don't know what to say.' Warhol had once remarked that he loved LA and Hollywood because 'They're so beautiful. Everything's plastic, but I love plastic. I want to be plastic.' With this in mind, it's less surprising that the WWF resonated with him.

What fans at Madison Square Garden were seeing in this odd collision between pop, art, fiction, television, vaudeville, violence and old-fashioned carnival barking was a concentrated dose of what was now needed to rise above the noise and succeed in show-business. Success primarily meant grabbing attention – just as Jimmy Carter's nuanced liberalism had been swept away by Reagan's one-dimensional optimism, if bands were going to command an audience in the saturated, Technicolor world, they would have to strike a balance between oversized pantomime performance and mainstream acceptance. Push the boundaries, but not too much.

Older bands who were sustaining a career as MTV spread and supersize became the new normal were the ones who understood this perfectly and became both more pop but also more cartoonish than they already had been. Judas Priest dialled down the social commentary and impotent rage of *British Steel* in favour of something more anthemic for their two subsequent albums *Screaming For Vengeance* (1982) and *Defenders of the Faith* (1984) and duly cracked America (at the climax of their Madison Square Garden show on June 18 fans began ripping out the cushions from the seats and throwing them on stage, resulting in the band having to pay damages and being banned from the venue for life). In 1986 *Turbo* would be a particularly divisive album with its softer lyrical content and use of guitar synthesisers. It performed far better in America than the UK and largely defined the band in many American fans' eyes. Priest's peer Ozzy Osbourne was now established enough to be selling out arenas across America, decked out in a huge fox-fur jacket and weighed down with gold jewellery. He also further ramped up his contemporary relevance by taking Mötley Crüe on tour as his support act, where Nikki Sixx found him to be 'a trembling, twitching mass of nerves and crazy incomprehensible energy… We hit it off with him from day one.'[3]

A similar reinvention was underway with Van Halen, who had been a thuggish stadium rock band with a front line consisting of hyperactive, attention-hogging singer David Lee Roth and revolutionary lead guitarist Eddie Van Halen. Van Halen's playing style was unlike anybody else's – a master of the tapping technique,[4] his guitar work was built around a frame-

---

3. *The Dirt*, p. 103.
4. Tapping: rather than the conventional way of playing a guitar in which one hand plucks the strings and the other frets the notes on the neck, tap-

work of classical scales (rather than blues), executed at a speed and complexity which frequently gave the impression that he was playing with more than six strings and more than ten fingers. Even on a slower track like 1982's instrumental 'Cathedral', the cello-like swelling and muting of the guitar's volume as he plays and the waves of echo make it difficult to work out what he's actually doing. While few could – and still can't – match Van Halen's virtuosity, his playing set the template for what one part of glam metal's sound would be: showboating, difficult to replicate and densely crammed with displays of technicality. Roth would distinguish the band from run-of-the-mill metal, defining their sound as 'Big Rock'.

However, as 1984 came around, Van Halen polished their sound just enough to ride the prevailing trends. Compared to 1982's *Diver Down*, *1984* is rich with synthesisers, the opening title track sounding more like

---

ping involves moving your plucking hand up onto the neck of the guitar and using the fingers of that hand to hold the strings against the frets before pulling them off to revert the note to that which is being played by your regular fretting hand. In short, this enables you to leap between notes which are further apart than would otherwise be physically possible with one hand, and to do so incredibly quickly. While Van Halen is widely credited with popularising the style, it wasn't invented by him – Paganini utilised similar techniques for the violin in the early nineteenth century, while footage from 1965 shows Italian guitarist Vittorio Camardese demonstrating the technique on an acoustic guitar on Italian TV. George Lynch of Dokken claimed in a 2009 interview with *The Metal Den* that both he and Eddie Van Halen had watched Harvey Mandel from Canned Heat tapping at Hollywood's Starwood club in the Seventies and duly taken their lead from him.

the swelling notes to accompany the scene when the door of the alien landing craft slowly lifts open in a sci-fi epic, rather than sounding like something to smash down the beers to at a frat house. The introduction segues into the opening notes of 'Jump', the lead single from their new album, with its hypnotic, circular riff played not on the guitar – what with the band possessing the greatest guitarist of his generation – but on the synthesiser. Eddie Van Halen's signature 'brown sound' (an ear-pricking product of humbucker pickups run at huge levels of volume and distortion) was done away with, and replaced with the fat, spongy tones of an Oberheim OB-X synth.

'Jump' was immediately easier on the ears sonically, and also lyrically. Its verse stands in sympathy with a listener who's struggling, and reminds them that others have been there before. Then, in the run in to the chorus, David Lee Roth pulls an unexpected switch and places himself in the listener's shoes. Riddled with nerves, barely noticed by the object of his affections and scarcely capable of self-aggrandisement. While this isn't exactly on a par with Bon Jovi's solidarity with runaway teenage girls, coming from David Lee Roth it's an unexpected outbreak of humility from a man whose entire public image was built on being the acme of physical and sexual self-assurance.

In that one lyrical trick in 'Jump', Roth showed his underbelly and went from doing star jumps off the drum riser and being showered in discarded female underwear to inhabiting the mind and body of an overlooked nerd with his 'back against the record machine', both literally and figuratively. The pay-off – 'might as well jump' – is both fatalistic and celebratory. *Carpe diem, we're all in this together.* The single promptly went to number 1 on the US charts, dragging its parent album along with it. Tensions had underpinned the creation of *1984* – the synth line had been written around 1981 but knocked back as being out of kilter with the band's sound, while Roth would leave in the September after the band concluded their world tour at the German leg of the Monsters of Rock festival tour in Nuremberg – but its sound and success rebooted Van Halen into a TV-friendly entity. And while the band wasn't strictly glam metal, Van Halen both took responsibility for a large part of its sound, and replenished themselves commercially by feeding on the genre's youthful energy.

A similar process – if not of reinvention then upgrading – was to be seen in Kiss. They are almost impossible to assess in the context of wider music: they are effectively a cottage industry in their own right, and largely oblivious to fashion, prevailing trends or critical consensus. They've built a vast, genuinely international fanbase, which has endured over decades and is wildly disproportionate to the amount of good music that the band has made. Even their staunchest fans – and Kiss have a very particular kind of fan who really, really likes them to the exclusion of almost everything else – would have to concede that in terms of their output they have made a little go an extremely long way.[5] The departure of key members, a reputation as patchy live performers and interpersonal feuds have done nothing to slow them down.

However, the early Eighties were one of the few times when Kiss did seem to realise that some upgrades were required if they were going to maintain their career. The *Dynasty* tour of 1979 had been beset by abandoned stage concepts, patchy attendances and cancelled shows; public appearances could be erratic, with one interview on the Hallowe'en special of Tom Snyder's *The Tomorrow Show* in October 1979 marred by Ace Frehley appearing to be drunk and Peter Criss talking about his gun collection while Gene Simmons glowers at the pair from under his make-up. In 1980 *Unmasked* was the first Kiss album in five years not to go Platinum, before Criss left in acrimony with his replacement then fired after one day by the remaining members. *Music from 'The Elder'* (1981) was a bewildering Medieval concept album, supposedly a soundtrack to an unmade film. A reordering of the track sequencing to foreground two potential singles made what narrative there was even harder to follow. Disillusioned with the decision to make the album and

5. A 2010 thread posted on Reddit asked the question: 'KISS is a terrible, shitty band. Why are they popular? Were they ever popular?' At the time of writing, the thread was running at over 900 responses to the original poster.

increasingly isolated, Ace Frehley also left in December 1982. That same year's *Creatures of the Night* album also performed badly commercially.

In this context, of stagnating record sales and line-up instability, Kiss would take a radical decision at the start of the glam era. For 1983's *Lick It Up* they would do away with their trademark make-up and adopt a harder sound with new guitarist Vinnie Vincent. Simmons recounted how the decision to go without their trademark face paint was reached.

'Let's prove something to the fans,' Paul said, 'Let's go and be a real band without make-up.' I reluctantly agreed. I didn't know if it was going to work, but I heard what Paul was saying – there was nowhere else for us to go. We did a photo session just to see what it would look like. We looked straight into the camera lens. We were defiant. I made one small concession to the fans: I stuck out my tongue, to try to keep something that connected us with the past.[6]

The grand public unmasking took place on MTV with each member introduced by host J. J. Jackson via a press shot of their usual image dissolving into a live close-up. The most immediately notable fact was how old the band looked – they had always looked strangely weary even through the greasepaint, but barefaced they looked a decade older than most of their

6. Gene Simmons, *Kiss and Make Up* (Century, 2001), p. 192.

peers. 'We made the best of it, but I was scared stiff,'[7] Simmons would say later. However, Stanley's hunch that this was the way to reboot Kiss' popularity was quickly proved right – the album was released in late September and certified gold by December of 1983, with *Kerrang!* ranking it as the third best hard rock album of the year. The title track's video was premiered on the same MTV show: the band are shown stalking a post-apocalyptic, *Mad Max*-esque landscape (apparently a scrapyard) where despite eking out an existence scrubbing their clothes over manhole covers, drinking from contaminated jerry cans and huddling around bonfires for warmth, all the women appear to be perfectly made-up extras from pay-per-view soft porn films. Whatever cataclysm has befallen society, it appears that no other men have survived.

The removal of their make-up wasn't the only shift in Kiss' presentation at this time. The cover of *Lick It Up* shows them (by their standards) pared down, with the space-age theatrical costumes traded for spray-on jeans, black leather and denim, while their sound had lost much of its bombast and focused into something harder and more contemporary. Much of the credit for this lies with Vinnie Vincent, although his tenure in the band was troubled, to say the least.

Vincent was an exceptionally talented musician who had grown up in Bridgeport, Connecticut, and devel-

7. *Ultimate Classic Rock*, September 18, 2015.

oped an early obsession with the guitar. 'I slept with my guitar as a kid and I didn't even know how to play it,' Vincent said in a 1987 *Guitar Player* interview. 'I loved the guitar more than anything and it's all I ever wanted to play.' After a peripatetic twenties playing solo shows and scoring the music for Paramount's *Happy Days* show and the *Joanie Loves Chachi* spin-off, he was called to audition for Kiss in 1982 as Frehley's replacement. Vincent has never given the impression of lacking in belief in his own abilities. 'My chemistry with the band helped put them back on top and gave them a musical credibility that they'd never had before,' he would later tell *Kerrang!*, while the tours of 1983 and 1984 were marred by frequent clashes with the band over Vincent's refusal to curtail his guitar solos to their allotted duration. 'He had no sense of what to play or when,' Stanley wrote, 'and he had no ability to self-edit.' Vincent's playing 'was like puking – it just came splattering out.'[8]

But despite this, Vincent's guitar style moved Kiss beyond their often-stodgy pantomime stomp and into something closer to the prevailing style in metal, and allowed them to pull in a younger crowd. However, his employment was terminated after the *Lick It Up* tour in March 1984 – Simmons cited 'unethical behaviour' with reports that Vincent had refused to sign the employment contract he was offered and was agitat-

8. Paul Stanley, *Face the Music: A Life Exposed* (HarperOne, 2014), p. 279.

ing for a share of Kiss' gross profits. Stanley would claim at a 1995 convention that Vincent had sold a fan an unplayed guitar, claiming it to be one of his favourite instruments and inflating the price accordingly, a transgression against the band's carefully cultivated fanbase that Stanley deemed 'totally unacceptable'. However, the band continued to develop the sound that Vincent had introduced with next album *Animalize,* released in September 1984. This would be their highest selling album since 1979's *Dynasty*, with the lead single 'Heaven's On Fire' co-written by prolific writer-for-hire Desmond Child. The video – a regrettable bit of wish fulfilment in which Kiss sit around what appears to be the executive suite of a Holiday Inn mauling at women – flags up how risky the decision to remove their make-up was. Simmons in particular suffers as his tongue-waggling routine no longer looks like the calling card of a carnival grotesque, but simply a pathological tic of a dirty old man. The whole band look even more tired than usual. However, with the album ultimately being certified Platinum in both Canada and the US, Kiss returned to the covers of the music magazines that had written them off two years earlier, and they regrouped as part of the glam metal scene. *Animalize* had done what it needed to. In metal in 1984, glam was starting to be where the money was – perhaps not coincidentally, Valentine's Day saw Joe Perry and Brad Whitford attend an Aerosmith concert and pave the way for ending their estrangement from the group. Before the year was out, the reunion *Back in the Saddle* tour would be underway and Aerosmith's commercial rehabilitation would also have started in earnest.

The potential in this new scene was being picked up on as record companies looked not just at the older acts on their rosters like Kiss, but also bands who had built up a sizeable independent following and might be able to have some edges polished off them for a wider appeal. However, for some, this just didn't work. Raven were from Newcastle, England, and originally grouped in with the New Wave of British Heavy Metal around Iron Maiden before New Jersey's Megaforce label signed them for the American market. Upgraded to Atlantic for their major label debut, their thrash edge was lost in favour of a softer sound. Follow-up *The Pack is Back* (1986) compounded all these errors and dated horribly. LA's Armored Saint were similarly earmarked for mainstream crossover, and paired with Kiss producer Michael James Jackson by Chrysalis for their major debut *March of the Saint*. 'Just way too polished', complained frontman John Bush, adding that as of 2006 the band were 'still in debt for that one'.

For these heavier bands, the alternative to a half-hearted crossover was to go it completely alone and disavow every element of the prevailing glam scene.

The exemplary act taking this route was Metallica. Drawing originally on the heavier end of the NWOBHM – Diamond Head, rather than Def Leppard – the band had first appeared on *Metal Massacre*, a 1982 compilation put together by Brian Slagel, editor of *The New Heavy Metal Revue*. The compilation served as a budget way for a slew of then-unsigned LA bands to get their first recorded material out to a wider audience.

Slagel had originally encountered Metallica's drummer before the band even existed, clocking him wearing a Saxon European tour t-shirt while hanging out in the parking lot of the Country Club in Reseda, following a show by Michael Schenker. Metallica were the last to deliver their recording, 'Hit the Lights', with Slagel using money from his job at Sears (and a gift from his aunt) to press up 4,500 copies of the compilation. The other standout name on the compilation was Ratt, and while they continued on a conventional glam trajectory, Metallica would double down on their sound and their ethos. From their first *No Life 'Til Leather* demo, through a gradually stabilising line-up, a geographically significant move away from LA to San Francisco and the tragic death of bassist Cliff Burton in a tourbus crash, Metallica developed into a one-band industry in a similar way to Kiss and Iron Maiden. Prior to 1989's 'One', they avoided the pressure to make a video which could have pushed any of their singles via MTV, and even then produced something closer to a mini film, with exerts from Dalton Trumbo's film *Johnny Got His Gun* used to tell the story of a World War One soldier reduced to an unmoving torso, unable to communicate and desperate for his own death. While later releases did move Metallica to more conventional rock territory and mainstream acceptance, through most of the Eighties they stood in opposition to the prevalent LA scene – a sort of beer-soaked, blue-collar, sonic overload of the Diamond Head and Motörhead records which had originally inspired them.

While the mainstream wasn't ready for bands as sonically heavy as Metallica at this point, there was still an appetite for shock and extremity. In a culture that was eagerly sucking up the likes of *A Nightmare on Elm Street*, *Gremlins* and the aforementioned wrestling extravaganzas, there was clearly an appetite for products that were pressing up against the boundaries of taste and decency. None of these things was genuinely frightening, or genuinely outrageous, but they gave the impression of being so. They operated within the realm of the 'safe scare', like narrative versions of a ghost train. Where much of the culture of the late Seventies had seemed genuinely tense and somehow grubby, the prevailing mood five years later was much more cartoonish. And with Kiss stepping away from the theatrical excesses of their past, a space was clear for a band to pick up the mantle of schlock and awe and deliver this to heavy metal fans. And when it came to allying shock potential with MTV hits and dialling up the bombast, one band did it better than anyone.

W.A.S.P.'s roots went back to the mid-Seventies, with Blackie Lawless relocating from New York to LA in 1975, and acclimatising to the city while living in fear in a squalid Ramada Inn on Sunset Boulevard next door to Tower Records. This was an unpromising time for a musician with Lawless' tastes: he was around the crumbling remains of the New York Dolls, gigging with their former bassist Arthur 'Killer' Kane. Lawless' first show in the city saw him and Kane perform at the Starwood alongside an early incarnation of Randy Rhoads' Quiet Riot and before The New Order, a flag of convenience for various members of the Stooges and the MC5. Disco was taking off, further reducing the relevance of hard rock in the city, while Circus Circus, his band with guitarist Randy Piper, had little to distinguish them. *Mr Cool* (1980) is an unremarkable pastiche of Alice Cooper, while the band's look – stacked heels, frizzed out hair, British glam-type clothes – is distinctly backwards looking. It feels like it's trying hard to ramp up its impact, but is essentially tired and old fashioned.

However, even at that stage, Lawless had three crucial advantages that would set him apart from his peers. Firstly, his father had worked in construction, with his son's inherited skills being put to good use building stage sets and props which would encompass fog machines, pyrotechnics, skulls, fire, smoke and mock-torture. Secondly, he was a gifted songwriter, special-ising in nagging minor-key hooks which demanded as much attention as the more obviously ludicrous elements of his presentation and perfectly suited the rasping howl of his voice – early videos of Circus Circus playing embryonic versions of later W.A.S.P. single 'L.O.V.E. Machine' show how he was develop-ing. And thirdly, he was clearly a natural frontman – with his huge black eyes, head-shaking delivery and choreographed guitar moves, he comes across in early footage like the malevolent shadow-self of Marc Bolan and sucks the camera's attention away from his band-mates at all times.

With the final line-up cemented in 1982, W.A.S.P.'s live shows quickly gained notoriety. At the Trouba-dour in 1983 they were taking to the stage beneath a flaming logo, Lawless wielding a burning torch as smoke belched out menacingly across the stage. The frontman prowled the stage with spiked gauntlets and circular blades protruding from his sleeves. After the show, he rants down the camera, blood, sweat and feathers smeared across his face, sounding part-preacher, part stolen-goods salesman.

> I tell you, I'm intense. I should have been born triplets. I got three times the intensity. Three times the sex appeal. Three times the macho of any man alive. You know

why the guys all come to these shows and you never see girls? 'Cause all the guys got their girls at home locked up. They don't want them coming out here and seeing us, 'cause they going home and getting the Vaseline out and thinking about us. That's why they NEVER come out here anymore!

The theory that women are irresistibly attracted to men in buttock-revealing leather chaps and a bladed codpiece has yet to be empirically proven, but Lawless seemed adamant.

Once signed to Capitol, W.A.S.P.'s profile and notoriety grew – and their advertising did little to play down any moral panic that was building up around the band and, particularly, their live show. 'The Mightiest Metal Show on Earth' and 'The Masters of Disaster Will Show No Mercy!' promised their posters through 1984, adding that 'The torture never stops!' Their reputation as an over the top, borderline cabaret metal extravaganza quickly grew, aided by live videos and an appearance in fantasy horror film *The Dungeonmaster*, where a live segment featuring them was filmed at The Troubadour. At this time, during centrepiece track 'Tormentor', Lawless disappeared inside a giant creaking skull before returning with an axe, a chopping block and a box labelled RAW MEAT. As the instrumental portion of the song ground on, Lawless would theatrically gorge on slabs of the meat, before popping open a giant wooden crate to reveal a topless, hooded woman tied to a rack. While he didn't appear to do much beyond daubing her in fake blood, this variously got reported as having been a live beheading, some sort of sexual torture or a full-on S&M show. Lawless later recounted that the band's notoriety at this time saw a contingent of Christian protesters infiltrating their UK shows and kneeling down to pray in the middle of the pit, a spectacle that he deemed 'Quite a surrealistic thing'.[9]

Just how good W.A.S.P. were was highlighted by contrast with their support act on these dates, Wrathchild. From Evesham in Worcestershire, Wrathchild generated a brief buzz around their *Stakk Attakk* album in 1984, but their cheap stage props, underwhelming pyro and lack of tunes made them seem like a sketch show's idea of a parody of glam metal rather than an actual band. They spent much of the subsequent four years mired in legal dispute with their label before separating in 1989 after the release of their *Delirium* album.

Thirty-five years on, W.A.S.P.'s shtick also looks almost laughably hammy – somewhere between a cheap video nasty and *The Rocky Horror Picture Show*. But their calculated assault on the moral sensibilities of America was perfectly calibrated. The band's name itself seemed to subvert the class they were attacking,[10]

9. Ian Christie, *Sound of the Beast: The Complete Headbanging History of Heavy Metal* (Allison & Busby, 2004), p. 121.

while they stood in defiance of the attacks on artistic expression being sparked by fearful incomprehension of underground culture. The murder in April 1984 of eighteen-year-old university student Mary C. Towey in her home in Oakville, Missouri, was linked to the Dungeons and Dragons' habit of her two killers, Ronald G. Adcox and Darren Lee Molitor. 'There is proof and evidence in fact that anything done within that aspect of role-playing is effective and is dangerous' said Molitor in his own defence. A sizeable campaign against unregulated 'video nasties' on both sides of the Atlantic had culminated in the UK in the Video Recordings Act 1984 which saw swathes of films from *Mondo Cannibale* to *Dawn of the Dead* seized from the shelves of video rental shops. The period also saw the start of the McMartin preschool trial in LA, a court case built on a lurid set of allegations of satanic child abuse levelled against an innocent family who ran a nursery facility. The trial would not conclude until 1990, with all charges dropped after accusations and testimonies including scenes of witches flying, children being spirited away in hot air balloons, secret tunnels, bestiality and torture with drills. America was at once both fascinated with and horrified by this kind of fantastical violence, whether it was actually existing or not.

Rather than tone down their act in the face of this outrage and panic, W.A.S.P. ramped it up, setting out

10. 'W.A.S.P.' being common shorthand for 'White Anglo-Saxon Protestants'.

their stall with the single 'Animal (Fuck Like a Beast)', the sleeve depicting a blood-soaked close up of Lawless' crotch, with a circular saw protruding from his gusset. The track would be pulled from their album to avoid a chainstore ban, but its gory profanity grabbed attention for the band and a relatively large amount of MTV support. 'It's surprising. You might have thought we might have been a little too much for MTV, but they were young, they were mavericks, and they were willing to take chances,'[11] said Lawless. Less supportive were the Parents Music Resource Center (PMRC), the DC lobbying group who would later include the band's calling card single as one of its 'Filthy Fifteen' tracks that the activists deemed most objectionable. Early adverts in the British press played up this notoriety for effect: 'THE SINGLE THEY WON'T LET YOU HEAR, IN THE SLEEVE THEY WON'T LET YOU SEE, WITH THE TITLE THEY WON'T LET US PRINT.'

The debut album (originally slated to be titled *Winged Assassins*) is a face-melting, circus-sized classic. The band's prolific gigging had honed their sound, and Lawless' ragged Seventies' glam fantasies beefed up and pushed into the red. The rollicking trucker beat of original British glam is pitched up into tracks like 'L.O.V.E. Machine', while Lawless' nasal roar merges into the sustained howl of Randy Piper's guitar on

11. *The Sound of the Beast*, p. 83.

'Hellion'. The songs have the same theatrical Broadway-musical heft of Jim Steinman's work on Meatloaf's *Bat Out of Hell*, forever sounding like chapters from a longer story. Opener 'I Wanna Be Somebody' channels the raging frustrations of male teenage angst with echoes of The Sweet's 'Teenage Rampage'. There's an irresistible immediacy to it all – Lawless constantly sings in the first person, inhabiting the frustrations and desires of his hormonal listener, despite being ten years older, on the stage and on the other side of the adolescent maelstrom. But with the punishing drum patterns of Tony Richards pushing Lawless and his bass forward, and his voice teetering somewhere between a raging outburst and a desperate cry for help, his performance is utterly convincing, despite you knowing it's just a man in video nasty drag. From the soup of 1984 – moral panics, peacocking American self-confidence, pop-art and rigged wrestling – Lawless summed up the highest goals of the aspirant glam hacks converging on LA with their own dreams: credit cards, cheap cash, fame and an early death rather than a decline into old age.

As the year drew to a close, W.A.S.P. would head out with Armored Saint and Metallica on the *Ride the Lightning* tour of North America. Three contrasting stage shows with differing fanbases. General consensus was that Metallica got the better of the other two bands throughout the run, and W.A.S.P. would eventually quit early in favour of a slot on Kiss' tour, signalling a final divergence between the glam and underground camps. 'It didn't matter what we were doing onstage,' recalled Lawless. 'It looked like two opposing armies. Sometimes we just stopped what we were doing and watched. It was a war.'[12] A war it might have been but this multi-genre bill was a significant part of the push that spread metal to every corner of the country and cemented its position as something bigger than ragged, drunken shows in a corner of LA. With the emerging theatricality of new bands like W.A.S.P., the polished regeneration of old hands like Van Halen and Scorpions (1984's 'Rock You Like a Hurricane' remains a deathless, proto-glam metal classic), Bon Jovi's arrival on the East Coast, the likes of Ratt finally getting a full release together and Kiss rolling up their jacket sleeves for an Eighties reinvention, glam metal was becoming the dominant form of rock. In 1984, the cultural energy in guitar music was to be found in spray-on leggings, under scuzzily back-combed hair and brandishing a geometrically shaped BC Rich guitar. Nothing, it seemed, could stop it.

As the year closed, a party was thrown to celebrate Hanoi Rocks' ongoing first US tour. The band were friendly with Mötley Crüe and the two groups (minus Hanoi frontman Michael Monroe who was laid up with a fractured ankle following an onstage fall in

---

12. Paul Brannigan, 'Garage Daze', *Metal Hammer* (March 2015).

Syracuse earlier in the tour) were both in attendance. At 6:38 p.m. on December 8, with the party in its fourth day, Vince Neil made a trip to a nearby off-licence along with Hanoi's drummer, Razzle. En route, Neil lost control of his red '72 Ford Pantera after swerving to avoid a parked fire engine, careered at 65mph into the oncoming traffic and smashed into two other vehicles. An hour later, concerned at how long the pair had been gone, Hanoi's guitarist Andy McCoy had also left the party along with Mötley Crüe's Tommy Lee and driven out to look for them. 'We drove past this accident,' recounted McCoy in a 2006 interview with *Metal Express*. 'I was like, *What color was the car they were driving*? Because we just passed a fucking accident with a bright red sports car. Then I saw Razzle's hat on the street.'

Twenty-four-year-old Razzle was transported to South Bay Hospital, but pronounced dead on arrival. The driver of one of the other cars, eighteen-year-old Lisa Hogan, was put into a coma for a month, with one arm and both legs broken, and would be left brain damaged and suffering from seizures. Her passenger, twenty-year-old Daniel Smithers, broke his leg and sustained brain damage. Neil himself suffered only cracked ribs and minor facial cuts.

Neil's blood alcohol level was tested at 0.17, over the legal driving limit of 0.10. However, the singer would go on to be given just thirty days for vehicular manslaughter, with ten deducted for good behaviour, plus 200 hours' community service and an order to pay compensation to the injured victims. Dee Snider of Twisted Sister was scathing in his judgement. 'Vince Neil could go and literally kill someone in a car accident. There were two other women who were in a van who were permanently crippled from that [accident] … And people are cool with that. They're like, "Yeah, all right! Rock 'n' roll!!"'[13] Hanoi guitarist Andy McCoy went further in 2016. 'It was a crime. Not only did Razzle die, two young people got crippled. And this guy sat one night in jail, got away with a misdemeanour. If he would have been a broke Afro-American guy or Latino he would have been doing life in San Quentin.'[14]

'I wrote a $2.5 million check for vehicular manslaughter [a restitution payment] when Razzle died,' Neil would later tell *Blender*. 'I should have gone to prison. I definitely deserved to go to prison. But I did thirty days in jail and got laid and drank beer, because that's the power of cash. That's fucked up.'

It was a bleak, squalid ending to what had been a stellar twelve months in metal. But more was to come before 1985 began. In England, a cold, snowy winter had set in, but the year ended on an unseason-

13. Jon Wiederhorn, 'Twisted Sister Frontman Won't Vote for His Friend Donald Trump', *Yahoo! Music* (February 2016)
14. https://www.loudersound.com/features/the-car-crash-that-killed-hanoi-rocks-razzle-vince-neil-never-apologised

ably warm day. At 12:50 p.m., Def Leppard drummer Rick Allen was driving home from the Ladybower Reservoir on the A57 in his left-hand drive Corvette Stingray with his girlfriend Miriam Barendsen. Another sports car was vying for position with Allen's on the narrow road. While trying to overtake and pull clear of it on a sharp left-hand turn, the drummer lost control of his vehicle, which flipped and collided with a dry-stone wall. The rear right hand tyre was shredded down to nothing, and the wheel folded in under the smashed wreckage of the car.

Allen was hurled through the sunroof. His seatbelt had come undone, the fabric severing his left arm as his body exited the vehicle. Two nurses and a policeman were passing the accident and stopped to assist Allen. His arm was retrieved and quickly reattached in hospital. However, by January 4 of the new year, infection had set in and the limb had to be removed once again. Allen was twenty-one years old and his drumming career, and his life as he knew it, appeared to be finished. 'It was an unbelievable feeling, an emptiness,' said bassist Rick Savage. 'I've never been close to anybody that died or had something terrible happen to them before. It was a feeling I'd never experienced.'[15]

Allen recounted the experience of that time in semi-mystical terms.

15. *Animal Instinct*, p. 8.

The only way I can describe it is that you go into a kind of survival mode where all your normal senses disappear. Whatever consciousness is there, all it's bothered about is surviving. Everything else is shut down. You just go to this place where there's no pain, and in that place you're able to decide whether you're better off dying or staying here. It's not a decision you make alone. In that state it's like you're in a communion with people that you know or have known in the past. You're disembodied, almost – it's like realising that the physical body and the consciousness are two separate entities. As I was taken to the hospital, I remember being above the ambulance and observing the whole scene, and then coming back in, a kind of integration.[16]

Joe Elliott would later tell *Kerrang!*'s Dante Bonnuto what had happened in the immediate aftermath of Allen's crash.

The arm was placed in a bucket of ice gathered from the houses nearby and Rick was in hospital [the Royal Hallamshire] within nineteen minutes, which is unbelievable. He underwent an eleven-hour operation; his arm was back on by ten to one the following morning, but infection set in and they had to take it off. His nerves are still alive though. They've got them wrapped up like spaghetti, and it's possible to have them connected in a way that can give movement to the arm. So the Steve Austin 'Six Million Dollar Man' thing is not beyond the

16. Paul Elliot, 'The Album That Almost Killed Them', *Mojo* (September 2007).

realms of possibility. Rick still feels his arm because of the nerves ... I saw him two days after it happened – it was the worst experience I've ever had.

A year which had begun with triumphant Def Leppard shows in Japan and Australia, and kickstarted a wave of supersize glam metal contenders from London to LA, ended with dead young men, permanently injured bystanders and a maimed drummer bedridden in intensive care undergoing an out-of-body experience as the old year turned to the new. Surely 1985 could only get better?

Chapter 3

1985: LIVE AFTER DEATH

Glam metal was not the only supersize, fantastical entertainment form in America that was beset by problems as 1985 got underway. In Las Vegas, Siegfried and Roy's *Beyond Belief* show was packing in audiences at the Frontier Hotel. A pair of German war babies, Siegfried Fischbacher and Roy Horn had originally plied their trade on cruise ships before being transplanted to Las Vegas in the mid-Seventies. What had originally been a reasonably conventional circus-meets-magic show had morphed into something far more fantastical by 1983 – they had taken key elements of a genre from the previous forty years and made them bigger, more dramatic and more weirdly artificial. In photo shoots, the pair reclined for their pictures in a shared home that looked like a neon jungle, surrounded by five fully sized – if somewhat despondent-looking – tigers. But by 1985, things had shifted from the unusual to the genuinely bizarre. The men looked physically different – tighter, polished, a deeper shade of bronzer-brown, outfits now shimmering in silver and black tiger stripes. Roy's shirtless chest buried under bejewelled crucifixes, both men's hair an artificial shade and flammable in texture. Between them sat a pure white tiger – the regular ones deemed no longer eye-catching enough, and these genetic aberrations required for the show instead. Fame and celebrity themselves appeared to be transforming the two men into something larger, stranger and less connected to reality.[1]

However, real life has a way of intruding on the most fantastical situations and this was the case for the pair when business associate Charles Flannery visited their home while Roy was exercising Magic, a nine-year-old Bengal tiger, in a compound in late October 1985. Flannery had known the tiger since it was a cub, but, suffering with a kidney infection, the cat became agitated. Magic launched itself into Flannery's neck, tearing his oesophagus and trachea along with a number of arteries and veins. '[It] was a playful interlude that got out of hand,' said the magicians' manager,

---

1. Apart from dealing with errant tigers, photographing Siegfried and Roy posed unique technical challenges, as Vegas photographer Robert Scott Hooper recalled on his blog. 'Seven tigers, white on white with two very tan guys… a lighting nightmare.'

Bernie Yuman, as Flannery lay in a critical condition at Southern Nevada Memorial Hospital. Magic's lesson was clear: you can get so big, and so over the top, but there will always be a price to pay for this excess, eventually.

When Joe Elliott met with Dante Bonnuto of *Kerrang!* in March 1985 he painted a picture of a band in stasis. Holed up in Wisseloord Studios outside Amsterdam, Def Leppard had a half-constructed framework of the follow-up to *Pyromania* but nothing even close to a finished article. Prior to the car crash, Allen had recorded rudimentary backing tracks for eight songs, but the recording process had quickly run into problems. First choice of producer Mutt Lange had pulled out of recording having started pre-production in the February of 1984, unable to continue working in his usual way. 'It soon became obvious that Mutt was in no state to see the whole thing through,' admitted Elliott. 'The Cars' album [*Heartbeat City*] nearly killed him; our last album nearly killed him, and the Foreigner record [*IV*] the same. I think he's just reached the stage now where to attain certain standards you're talking about grafting for a long time.' *Pyromania* had been the product of twenty-hour days, with Lange frequently sleeping on the sofa in the control room. 'You just can't do that forever, so for the sake of his health he made a wise decision not to do our album.'

The band approached a host of other potential producers, going far beyond the standard heavy metal names – Ted Templeman, Alex Sadkin, Trevor Horn, Chris Thomas, ZZ Top's engineer Terry Manning, Steve Lillywhite. 'We actually tried to get Phil Collins, who was interested but tied up with the latest Clapton LP [*Behind the Sun*].' Instead, and keen for a producer who could also input musically, the band opted for Jim Steinman, best known at that point for his grandiose arrangements and songwriting on Meat Loaf's multi-million selling *Bat Out of Hell* (1977) and fresh off working on Billy Squier's *Signs of Life* album.

It didn't work out brilliantly. 'It turned out Jim wasn't really what any of us thought he would be. In fact, I wonder how he's ever got a production credit on anything ... The guy just sat there reading *Country Life* all day and going, "Yeah, yeah, that sounds good," when it plainly wasn't. He's simply not used to recording the way we record. When we said "Listen, this is the way we work, you'd better get used to it," he tried and he couldn't. He just could not hear if something was wrong.' As well as Steinman's perceived creative shortcomings, the work ethic that had propelled Leppard out of Sheffield and around the US also proved incompatible with the American. 'We'd say "Right, we start at twelve," and he'd wander in at three-thirty. We'd stay till twelve or one in the morning, then he'd go back to his hotel and start writing songs for his *own* future projects, and he'd be up 'til nine in the morning doing that. So when he finally got round to us he'd only had five hours sleep … he wasn't there half the time.'

Steve Clark and Phil Collen were keen to offload Steinman after two weeks, while Elliott persisted, encouraged in part by tales of how arduous the *Bat Out of Hell* sessions had been before Meat Loaf's vocals were perfected. ('I just kept saying "Give the guy a chance, blah, blah, blah" … made meself look a right arsehole.') Steinman eventually made it through to November before the band finally parted ways with him, the eight existing backing tracks written off and scrapped. The relationship was further poisoned by what Elliott saw as Steinman's propensity for spending the band's money on lavish hotel suites, twelve-course meals and a desire to change the carpet in the studio. 'Which is fine, that's his personality, but when somebody walks into a studio and says that the carpet has got to go … if I'd been there I'd have decked him. Seriously! Who gives a flying shit what the carpet looks like?'

As Bonnuto left Def Leppard, they were putting a brave face on their situation. A solid body of songs were roughed out and in demo form – the list of working titles already included future releases: 'Armageddon It', 'Gods of War', 'Excitable', 'Run Riot', 'Don't Shoot Shotgun', 'Animal', 'Love Bites' and 'Women' – with the band themselves on production duties and with Lange on standby to mix. At this point, August 1985 was mooted as a release date, but, aside from production difficulties, Allen's recuperation was the great variable. 'The thing is, at the moment, his right arm doesn't work. The ball is smashed so they've had to pin it. He's got a six-inch pin as big as a poker in there ... he's being realistic – if he can't do it, he can't do it, but he's definitely gonna try.'

Technology was offering one possible route forward for Allen and the band. Bill Ludwig, Allen's kit-builder, had already alerted him to the potential of using a bespoke kit where the snare would be played by Allen's left foot while the tom tom fills would be on a pre-recorded trigger. 'With the technology available today, I don't see why he can't,' said Elliott bullishly. But the challenge remained – a brutally loud, intensely physical drummer would have to retool his entire style and drag himself back up to the standard required for tours of the length, scale and quality that Def Leppard were planning for their next album. Whatever the band told visiting journalists, as they huddled in the middle of a Dutch winter with the skeletons of half-finished songs, no producer and a drummer still in the depths of physical rehabilitation and post-traumatic stress, it was distinctly unclear that they had a future at all, let alone an upward trajectory.

The only British metal band coming close to matching Def Leppard for scale at this point were Iron Maiden. Originally grouped in with the New Wave of

British Heavy Metal, Maiden had evolved aggressively beyond the scratchy, semi-punk sound of their first two albums. Shedding original singer Paul Di'Anno, they had replaced him with Bruce Dickinson, a figure equal parts English eccentric and operatic storyteller. Dickinson's voice seemed built for projecting over ever-bigger crowds and venues, like an air-raid siren with a base note of theatricality, or Terry Thomas crossed with the four-minute warning. At this point, Maiden were deep in their imperial phase – *The Number of the Beast*, *Piece of Mind* and *Powerslave* all containing some of the most musically ambitious and thematically adventurous music in metal's history.

Maiden clearly weren't a glam band – they always kept an element of the rough-edged menace that came with their start in pubs in the East End of London, and their lyrical concerns ran through eternal touchpoints of conflict, madness, fear and Manichean tales of good and evil, rather than the cartoonish partying of glam's key bands. They were epic rather than dumb, inventive rather than repetitive, operatic rather than sleazy. But despite this, the prevailing trends were clearly impacting them to some degree. The *World Slavery* tour of 1984–5 drastically dialled up their visual impact from the preceding *World Piece* tour of 1983: the stripped-down, unadorned stage was replaced with a full theatrical Egyptian setting, with a giant three-dimensional rendering of their zombie mascot Eddie erupting from within a broken tomb behind the drum kit onto a stage flanked by walls of pyrotechnics to blast showers of sparks through his undead eyes. They took the full show behind the Iron Curtain and into Poland, Hungary and Yugoslavia, and, at various times, their support acts included W.A.S.P., Accept, Ratt, Mötley Crüe and Warrior (whose 'Fighting for the Earth' remains a minor falsetto-driven classic), a sign that while Maiden largely existed in their own bubble aesthetically – to this day, for such a huge band they are strangely uninfluential in terms of having created other bands who sound like them – they knew which bands were making the weather around them and who their crowd wanted to see on the same bill.

The tour was captured on the album *Live After Death*, which was released in October 1985, largely comprised of material recorded twelve months earlier at the Long Beach Arena. (These four dates served as proof of concept for local radio boss Fred Sands who had purchased the KNAC station at a bankruptcy auction and was duly convinced of the market for a 'pure rock' station. KNAC would go on to play a pivotal role in exposing the LA scene to a wider audience.) From the opening samples of Winston Churchill's World War Two motivational speech to the full-length musical retelling of Samuel Taylor Coleridge's poem *The Rime of the Ancient Mariner*, it remains perhaps the ultimate metal live album and a powerful document of the band parking their tanks on the lawn of the new wave of glam metallers and showing them how it was done. While the prevailing trends may have encouraged Maiden to dial up their visual presentation and theatricality, its real impulse seems to have been simply to spur the band on to reclaim their primacy.

Elsewhere, the bands who had been loosely coalescing under the glam banner throughout 1984 lost some momentum. Following Metallica's lead, the thrash scene came together as a faster, harder, no-frills counterpoint to the likes of Bon Jovi. Thrash felt more real, less playful, and a self-conscious rejection of the frivolity and success (real or projected) of glam. Thrash was a world of sweat, beer, acne and incipient violence. Exodus' *Bonded by Blood* showed two mutated Siamese twins pulling against each other, one cherubic and one devilish; Celtic Frost's *To Mega Therion* came with an H. R. Giger drawing of a horned beast eyeballing the listener while gripping a dwarfed Christ; Slayer's *Hell Awaits* depicted horned man-beasts plunging into eternal fire; Possessed's *Seven Churches* did away with illustration completely, simply opting for an inverted crucifix on a black background; Anthrax's *Spreading the Disease* showed a tormented, prone metaller being measured with what appeared to be a Geiger counter. Metallica's James Hetfield would later append a sticker to the headstock of his Jackson King V guitar, bearing the legend KILL BON JOVI.

Old stalwarts were treading water: AC/DC had begun the year headlining the Rock in Rio festival alongside Whitesnake, Scorpions and Ozzy Osbourne, but, by the middle of the year, had put out *Fly on the Wall*, a laborious trudge on a dismal par with their previous release, *Flick of the Switch*. Aerosmith were reunited with original members Joe Perry and Brad Whitford who had been away since 1981, and, while *Done With Mirrors* has been somewhat critically reassessed with hindsight, and saw Van Halen producer Ted Templeman attempting to update their sound for the new era, they ended up sounding caught between the bluesy honk of their best Seventies' work and the more streamlined sound of the younger bands they had originally inspired. *Done With Mirrors* failed to please the band, the fans or the critics, *Rolling Stone* writing it off as: 'The work of burnt-out lug-heads whose lack of musical imagination rivals their repugnant lyrics.' Kiss' thirteenth album, *Asylum*, received a mixed reception, although Gene Simmons proved his relevance with his championing (and production) of Keel and their album *The Right to Rock*. Their debut *Lay Down the Law*, with its cover illustration of a leather clad policewoman having her breasts groped was best known for a metalled-up cover of The Rolling Stones' 'Let's Spend the Night Together', but the follow-up built on the best elements of Kiss' sound and created one of the harder glam albums of the year. Simmons' production creates a markedly tougher sounding album than Kiss themselves had managed in 1985. The teachers had been outshone by their students.

If Kiss were struggling to maintain the momentum created by their unmasking, Van Halen were faring little better. David Lee Roth had left at the start of 1985, his final days in the band overlapping with his first solo release, the *Crazy From the Heat* EP. Any hope that Roth would continue in the vein of Van Halen's previous album was swiftly nixed by this selection of unlikely cover versions, including The Beach Boys' 'California Girls', The Lovin' Spoonful's 'Coconut Grove', Edgar Winter's 'Easy Street' and the pre-war standards, 'Just a Gigolo' and 'I Ain't Got Nobody'. The style veered from tropical lounge to daytime radio pop and nudge-wink showtunes. The video for 'Just a Gigolo' is a particularly horrifying misstep as Roth goons his way through multiple sets, dressed up like a bigtop ringmaster and assailed by bargain lookalikes of Michael Jackson, Cyndi Lauper, Boy George and various other figures from the pop landscape who Roth clearly felt were beneath his own level of artistry. With a lengthy set-up about the pressure on the modern artist to make a video, the aim seems to be to pass wry comment on the image-driven, flimsy world that MTV had ushered in. This would have held more water had Roth not already proven himself an intensely visual performer, perfectly suited to MTV's new paradigm and one who had just enjoyed the biggest hit of his career thanks in part to their support. Predictably it ends with him blundering into the women's changing room and hot-shoeing his way through in a gold suit and white gloves. Perhaps the ultimate judgement on this folly would be passed a decade later by Beavis and Butthead, Mike Judge's animated armchair critics, as they watched the video. 'Right now… David wishes he had his old job back.'

Roth's dig at MTV seemed doubly unfair as the channel's support of the new metal scene increased in 1985 with the launch of its *Heavy Metal Mania* slot, hosted by Dee Snider of Twisted Sister. The opening credits showed a dull suburban house on a quiet night being suddenly detonated, before Def Leppard's 'Rock of Ages' fired up over a montage of mainstream metal's greatest visual moments to date (a masked lunatic writhing in a padded cell to Quiet Riot, a headbanging front row of a crowd, Phil Collen's white-denim-clad buttocks waggling in time to his guitar solo etc.).

Elsewhere, Ratt would capitalise on their previous MTV success with second album *Invasion of Your Privacy*. Despite their look – piled up, spray-encrusted hair, heavily made-up eyes, clothes shredded to the point of indecency – with this album, Ratt pushed their sound to extreme poles throughout. The guitars sound raw and overdriven – on 'What You Give Is What You Get' they sound like they've been transplanted from a completely different production – while the body of most of the songs is a dense, overproduced chug. The standout track in terms of ambition is 'Closer to My Heart', a semi-ballad that, with its alienated lyrics and funereal pace, ends up sounding like the analogue demo for a Gary Numan track. Ratt's second album maintained their momentum throughout 1985 and saw them booked onto the Monsters of Rock bill in the UK alongside Magnum, Metallica, Bon Jovi, Marillion and ZZ Top, but ultimately it feels underwhelming. As standards rose across metal, Ratt were consistently an 'almost' band – under the make-up and hair products they looked a little too hard-faced, closer to the dragged-up bruisers who had populated British glam's first wave than the androgynous prettyboys coming through around them. They were tuneful by metal standards, but not competing at the level of their peers who were by now crossing over to the Top 10 of the mainstream charts. They looked vaguely sleazy, but not in comparison to Mötley Crüe who as well as a generally insanitary air now had the genuine taint of a pointless death forever attached to them. Ratt weren't at the same level on any front.

Somewhat less workmanlike were Dokken. Originally formed in 1979, they had first served as a kind of launch pad for members of other metal bands. Various early members had left for the likes of Ratt, Quiet Riot and an early iteration of Great White before Dokken's line-up stabilised around frontman Don Dokken, drummer Mick Brown, bassist Jeff Pilson and guitarist George Lynch. The band had strong connections to Europe, via the support of German band Accept's engineer and manager and a deal with French label Carrere. Dokken himself would also demo tracks for Scorpions' *Blackout* album while they recorded in Germany, eventually contributing backing vocals to the finished album. Until the release of 1984's *Tooth and Nail* their popularity in Europe would outstrip that in America, unlike most bands who found Europe and the UK still keener on the meat-and-potatoes tail-end of the NWOBHM.

Dokken were blessed with their singer's distinctive voice – a richly plaintive, slightly bluesy sound, redolent of Seventies' acts such as UFO and Rainbow – and Lynch's guitar skills. Unlike many other glam metal players, Lynch was technically gifted but a surprisingly restrained guitarist – on the single 'In My Dreams', he leans back into a few slashed-out chords and chiming arpeggios, sitting low in the mix beneath the close, multi-tracked harmonies. When the guitar solo comes, the impact of his liquid playing is all the more pronounced. As the vocals return, his guitar tone dissolves into them. The overall effect of Dokken's sound was a smooth, compressed, radio-friendly run of songs – while few stood out and became enduring classics, it made them a reliable, melodic entry point for glam metal in general, a gateway drug in the way that the blood-spitting, screechingly energetic W.A.S.P. most likely weren't. If you liked one Dokken song, you'd probably like all of them.

A far more divisive proposition was now found in Mötley Crüe. Already saddled with a reputation for chaotic unreliability, Vince Neil's hand in Razzle's death had tipped them from shock-rock into something genuinely squalid. The response to this was a slight shift in the band's image as they underwent the recording of *Shout at the Devil*'s follow-up, *Theatre of Pain* (one of the gophers at Cherokee studios at this time was a nineteen-year-old Slash, who lasted one day as Mötley Crüe's errand boy before absconding with $100 rather than fulfilling the band's booze order). They sounded more professional, but also a little more leaden. The careering, runaway quality of their first two albums had been replaced with something more plodding, encapsulated by their cover of Brownsville Station's glam trudge, 'Smokin' in the Boys' Room'. Something similarly enervating had happened to them physically – while looking more obviously glam, it didn't sit quite right on their ravaged faces and bodies. Frosting their skin in blusher and foundation and painting their lips a vibrant red had the opposite effect that make-up and styling is supposed to – rather than accentuating their features, it served to draw attention to the ravaging effects of two years of drug use, partying, touring and prison. It was though someone had attempted to deal with rising damp in a crumbling house by painting over it in bright pink paint.

However, the most significant development was to be found at the close of side one with 'Home Sweet Home'. It's certainly not the first metal ballad – it borrows heavily from Aerosmith's 1973 epic 'Dream On' – but works as a blueprint of the softer side of glam. A gently psychedelic piano picks out a descending intro, reminiscent of the ham-fisted style that David Bowie built much of *Hunky Dory*'s tracks around in 1971. After almost a minute of Vince Neil's vocal alongside the piano, a crashing, feedback-laden chord descends from the guitar and the drums kick in. An acoustic guitar strums in and picks up the rhythm track, massed backing vocals join in for the title's refrain, Mick Mars solos up the neck and into a screeching crescendo of notes. For the last minute, the piano line re-emerges as the musical smoke clears, joining the finale up with the introduction.

Neil's lyrics are, largely, nonsense – the video frames them as being about a response to the lonely grind of touring, and they could be about that. But equally, with their woolly depiction of dreamers with hearts of gold, people compelled to run away, exhortations to be taken to the listener's heart and a journey home which comprises a long and winding road, they could be something you sung at the end of a football season, or during an end-of-term prom, or before being deployed to the army, or while on a distant military base somewhere, or while driving back to the small town you grew up in to see the friends you thought you'd lost. Their complete lack of specificity is the song's genius and has ensured it a strange, enduring afterlife: it was remixed and overdubbed by the band for their *Decade of Decadence* compilation in 1991; Linkin Park frontman Chester Bennington re-recorded the track with members of Crüe as a charity fundraiser after Hurricane Katrina struck New Orleans in 2005; it has cropped up in the film *Hot Tub Time Machine* and the TV series *Californication*. Country singer Carrie Underwood's 2009 version was used as the soundbed when contestants were voted off the eighth series of *American Idol*. And it set the template for every other glam metal band's attempt at a track which would showcase their softer side and give them a similar shot at a crossover, radio-friendly hit. By the decade's end everyone from White Lion and Heart to Poison and Skid Row would have copied the formula.

There was no such softening apparent for W.A.S.P. in 1985. With Quiet Riot producer Spencer Proffer in charge, *The Last Command* picked up where their debut had left off, a foot-to-the-floor run through a laundry list of drunkenness, sex, revenge fantasies and adolescent delinquency. As on the debut, Lawless' voice shifted from a distracted, melancholy hum to a raging howl, with trace elements of everything from cowboy blues to punk's juvenile scream floating through it. However, while the album was commercially successful, the band had greater concerns facing them on its release.

The Parents Music Resource Center (PMRC) had formed in 1985. Comprised of four women all married to government figures in Washington DC, the committee aimed to increase the amount of control that parents had over the music that their children were listening to by enforcing the record industry to label music deemed offensive with Parental Advisory stickers at point of sale. The ultimate aim was to enforce an age-based licensing system similar to that already in place on cinema and video releases, with other measures suggested including restricting where record stores could display offending albums, lobbying television channels not to play certain videos and looking at whether the contracts of artists who breached standards of decency in live performances could be reassessed.

While metal had seemed an underground phenomenon, there was little to complain about (the moral majority's sights were never trained on, say, the white power branch of the skinhead music scene which was genuinely fomenting violence and criminality around itself) but MTV had provided a way for deliberately – if superficially – confrontational bands in a genuinely popular genre to be mainlined into homes all over the country. The women who formed this group were collectively known as the 'Washington Wives' – in truth, this nickname did a patronising disservice to an extremely effective group of political operators. Susan Baker and Tipper Gore had both worked alongside their husbands (James Baker was Treasury Secretary and Al Gore was a Democratic senator for Tennessee and future vice-president and presidential candidate in his own right) and knew how to communicate with maximum efficiency.

An early fundraising letter set out the group's mission succinctly:

Dear Friend

Just as we explained on the Phil Donahue show, the Parents' Music Resource Center needs your support. Not for the sake of the Center, but for the young people of America, perhaps your children.

Today's young people are surrounded by music, rock music. It is so pervasive that we almost forget it's even there. But make no mistake, it is there, too much of it drumming more and more destructive messages into the minds of our children.

The average teenager listens to rock music for four to six hours daily! That's more hours of rock music than hours of classroom instruction. Unfortunately, in much of that music the message is negative, even harmful.

Because too many of today's rock artists – through radio, records, television videos, videocassettes – advocate aggressive and hostile rebellion, the abuse of drugs and alcohol, irresponsible sexuality, sexual perversions, violence and involvement in the occult.

It's a cleverly worded letter. Firstly, the choice of name makes the PMRC sound like a neutral organisation – just a database of useful information for parents. They're not asking for help for themselves but for young people – young people who don't even know that they need their help. The assumptions are painted on with a broad brush – young people are surrounded by rock music (no allowance is made for the millions of young people who listened to hip hop, or followed independent bands and labels through a network of college radio stations, or liked pop, or didn't have much interest in music full stop); whatever that amount of music is, we all agree it's too much, even though there's no way of really quantifying how much they're actively listening to, bar an unsourced fact; and a blanket condemnation of rock music's content.

This last point is particularly contentious. Beyond the obvious impact of the record sleeves, very little of metal's content at this time was actually as shocking as the PMRC's letter would have led you to believe. Even the purported shock value of W.A.S.P.'s *The Last Resort* falls apart on a close reading. With the exception of the juvenile 'Ball Crusher' and 'Sex Drive' (which both read like the letters page of a top shelf magazine fed through Google Translate), much of that year's most obviously shocking album is surprisingly romantic in its imagery ('Wild Child'), mainly deploying violence in defence of a woman ('Jack Action'), or illustrative of a sensitive soul existing beneath the exploding codpiece and fake blood ('Cries in the Night' is as much a self-pitying introspective as anything that The Smiths ever came up with). Read in isolation, many of Lawless' other lyrics have a hint of the bodice-ripping novel about them.

But W.A.S.P. and the other musical artists listed on the PMRC's 'Filthy Fifteen' list[2] were caught up in a broader move against any art scene viewed as transgressive. The Meese anti-pornography commission was also established in 1985, calling for a nationwide campaign against the adult entertainment industry, while right-wing politicians like Jesse Helms and Alfonse D'Amato criticised arts funding being made available for work they saw as 'morally reprehensible' – a particular target was the National Endowment for the Arts' support for Andre Serrano's *Immersion (Piss Christ)*, a strangely beautiful, blurred photograph of a crucifix floating in a small glass tank of what is purported to be the artist's urine. As the controversy gathered around the work, Serrano would receive death threats and lose arts grants as he became synonymous with blasphemy and obscenity in his work. Later in the decade, galleries would cave to the

2. Other metal tracks listed included AC/DC's 'Let Me Put My Love Into You', Black Sabbath's 'Trashed', Judas Priest's 'Eat Me Alive', Mercyful Fate's 'Into the Coven', Mötley Crüe's 'Bastard', Twisted Sister's 'We're Not Gonna Take It' and Venom's 'Possessed'. All were categorised as referencing Sex, Drugs/Alcohol, Violence and the Occult.

pressure to cancel exhibitions of Robert Mapplethorpe's explicit, S&M-tinged photographs of male nudes.

With this wind behind them, on September 19, 1985 the Senate Commerce Committee convened hearings to test the PMRC's request that albums should be subject to the same kind of ratings and restrictions as films already were. 'We're asking the recording industry to voluntarily assist parents who are concerned by placing a warning label on music products inappropriate for younger children due to explicit sexual or violent content,' said Tipper Gore to the panel. Christian protesters outside wore matching puritan-style outfits and brandished red-and-white painted signs declaring ROCK MUSIC DESTROYS KIDS, calling to STOP ROCK and promising that THIS IS WAR.[3]

3. The musical wing of this militant Christianity was to be found in Stryper, the Orange County band who crossed a workmanlike brand of glam metal with proselytising, yellow-and-black striped clothing, guitars and stage props. Evolving out of Roxx Regime, they regularly included reference to the specific biblical verse Isaiah 53:5, pushed the number 777 as a counteracting numerology to Heavy Metal's referencing of 666, while their striped clothing, guitars, stage sets and name were a reference to the marks left on Christ's body by the whip of Pontius Pilate. *Soldiers Under Command* (1985) was decently regarded if uninspiring (to non-Christians), but by 1988's *In God We Trust*, the band had softened their sound beyond the limits of what most metal fans considered acceptable. The single 'Always There for You' is a particular low point. The band were followers of the Jim Bakker ministry – Bakker was an enormously successful televangelist who was forced to resign from his ministry in 1987 after allegations of sexual misconduct. A year later he was jailed for forty-five years for various counts of mail fraud, wire fraud and conspiracy. He was eventually released in 1994 and has since returned to televangelism. At the time of writing, his website includes a large feature on President Donald Trump's accomplishments and has an

Three artists appeared to give evidence: wholesome folk singer John Denver, art rock misanthrope Frank Zappa and Dee Snider of Twisted Sister. 'They were caught off guard, because they didn't know I spoke English fluently,' Snider would later explain. Viewed from almost thirty-five years' distance, the hearings have a faintly ludicrous aspect – oversized album covers were produced, and particularly choice lyrics were recited with little context around them to present as a *fait accompli* the idea that all this music was inherently evil.

Famed for his 'Bette Midler on acid' stage look, Snider arrived at the session wearing a ripped sleeveless t-shirt and with his cascading bleached-out curly hair bouncing over his tattooed arms. He appeared to be walking into the trap laid for him by the PMRC, but almost immediately wrong-footed the panel. 'I would like to tell the committee a little bit about myself,' he began. 'I am thirty years old, I am married, I have a three-year-old son. I was born and raised a Christian and I still adhere to those principles. Believe it or not, I do not smoke, I do not drink, and I do not do drugs. I do play in and write the songs for a rock and roll band named Twisted Sister that is classified as heavy metal, and I pride myself on writing songs that are consistent with my above-mentioned beliefs.' An

extensive shop selling dried food products for surviving the 'end times'. Stryper are not mentioned.

articulate, nuanced and intelligent teetotaller, raising a child within wedlock and believing in God was clearly not what was expected from the luridly painted pantomime dame who stomped his band through riotous tracks like 'The Kids Are Back'. Over the course of his testimony, Snider dismantled the PMRC's accusations and arguments, flagging up errors in their research, pointing out where misinterpretation had occurred and playfully suggesting that projection may be at the heart of his accusers' campaign. 'That the writer could misquote me is curious, since we make it a point to print all our lyrics on the inner sleeve of every album,' ran one particular point. 'As the creator of "Under the Blade", I can say categorically that the only sado-masochism, bondage and rape in this song is in the mind of Ms Gore.'

Snider ended his testimony on a remarkably traditional note. 'There happens to be one area where I am in complete agreement with the PMRC, as well as the National PTA and probably most of the parents on this committee. That is, it is my job as a parent to monitor what my children see, hear and read during their pre-teen years. The full responsibility for this falls on the shoulders of my wife and I, because there is no one else capable of making these judgements for us.' In conclusion, he exhorted his audience to remember that what he was creating was art, and the emotional, responsive sensations associated with this were not capable of regulation or restraint by an instrument as blunt as the law. 'The beauty of literature, poetry and music is that they leave room for the audience to put its own imagination, experiences and dreams into the words.' It was a remarkably metaphysical note to end on from a man usually seen on stage wearing pink neon cowboy boots, gruesome marionette face paint and what appeared to be the shredded wreckage of a trolley-dash through a low-budget lingerie shop.

However, even though Snider's appearance won the battle of perception, by December 1985, the Recording Industry of America would bow to pressure and agree to a programme of soft regulation, whereby they would voluntarily sticker potentially offensive releases with a black-and-white label proclaiming PARENTAL ADVISORY EXPLICIT CONTENT. Was this censorship? Not in the harsh, formal way of totalitarian societies. But it exerted a soft commercial pressure downwards on bands – major retailer Wal-Mart refused to stock PMRC-labelled releases, a major hit to smaller bands' bottom line in the days before digital distribution.

Did anyone actually find metal *frightening*? 'After all was said and done, more was said than done,'[4] said Lawless, looking back at the scandal. The hearings were a piece of theatre – an attempt to show that *something* was being done, rather than anything substantial actually being done. It was government as entertain-

4. *The Sound of the Beast*, p. 122.

ment, legislation as performance – it was no more a serious attempt to safeguard children or improve society's morals than W.A.S.P.'s live shows were a serious attempt to behead a topless woman. In an odd way, both sides mirrored each other, as agents of a culture that was becoming largely performative. The difference, of course, was that while one side of the argument had no more serious business than old-fashioned entertainment, the other one was supposed to be actually running the country. Propelled by glam's new commercial potential and visual impact, metal was now simply too big to ignore. As something inflated, overblown and self-obsessed, it might have been outraging mainstream America, but it was also perfectly in tune with it. With the PMRC's labels signalling the first signs of a crackdown on glam, the forthcoming year would dictate whether it folded under pressure or came out fighting.

Chapter 4

1986: SLIPPERY WHEN WET

The biggest musical event of 1985 had been Live Aid – the internationally broadcast 'Global Jukebox', spread across day-long festivals at Wembley Stadium in London and John F. Kennedy Stadium in Philadelphia. Originally inspired by BBC journalist Michael Buerk's reports on the famine in Ethiopia, the campaign had produced two hit singles ('Do They Know It's Christmas?' in the UK and its American counterpart, 'We are the World'), and would go on to inspire a sports-related campaign and re-recordings of the tracks. An estimated 1.5 billion people watched the broadcast in a hundred different countries over sixteen hours. But metal was largely absent on the day, bar appearances from a few old hands. Black Sabbath reformed with their original line-up – they actually sounded unexpectedly tight, although received a somewhat muted response, and looked like a relic of the Seventies rather than a going concern. Judas Priest were a bigger event given the success of the previous year's *Defenders of the Faith* album and higher US profile, but there was something incongruous about seeing them play during the day, in the sun and for an unalloyed good cause. Rob Halford is one of the all-time great frontmen in metal, but his industrial leather-perv routine seemed a little out of place under the Philadelphia sun. The crowd – and the day – was generally happier with the likes of Madonna, Tina Turner and Phil Collins, and the wider ranks of the glam metal scene didn't get a look in.

This changed the following year, thanks to an unlikely good Samaritan. Ronnie James Dio was a pint-sized vocalist whose involvement in music went back even further than Blackie Lawless'. Dio's first band, Elf, had formed in 1967, specialising in a sort of rollicking, thumbs-in-the-beltloops boogie. They were set apart from numerous other bar bands by Dio's voice – a richly fruity, operatic baritone, clearly enunciated and capable of projecting at maximum velocity over any band. Dio was clearly not glam – with his slightly dwarfish aspect, piratical looks and throwing of devil's-horn handsigns, he was never going to fit in with the Sunset Strip scene a decade younger than him. But instead, he became a kind of travelling fixer for top-tier metal bands who were on the ropes due to key members departing or creative stasis setting in. He joined Richie Blackmore in Rainbow after the mercurial guitarist had quit Deep Purple; he replaced the seemingly irreplaceable Ozzy Osbourne in Black Sabbath; and then finally fronted his own eponymous band, Dio, specialising in a myth-rich, epic brand of theatrical metal. If the world of Dungeons and Dragons had had a house band, it would have been Dio, with orcs, nazguls and morgol wraiths all rocking out in their leather jerkins to 'Holy Diver' and 'Rainbow in the Dark'.

In 1986, Dio's band members Vivian Campbell and Jimmy Bain had noticed the lack of involvement from metal musicians at a fundraising radiothon they were contributing to at the LA rock station KLOS, 'Rock Relief for Africa'. Attempting to recreate the collegiate fundraising power of the recent Band Aid, Farm Aid and Sport Aid events, the trio wrote the track 'Stars', then used Dio's reputation and pulling power to assemble a huge metal cast to perform it. The final line-up reads like a who's who of metal in 1986: Ted Nugent, Yngwie Malmsteen, Tommy Aldridge of Whitesnake, Judas Priest, Iron Maiden, Quiet Riot, Dokken, Mötley Crüe, Twisted Sister, Queensrÿche, Blue Öyster Cult, Y&T, Rough Cutt, Giuffria, Journey, W.A.S.P. and Night Ranger as well as metal satire group Spinal Tap all appeared. Lead vocals were shared between Ronnie James Dio, Rob Halford, Kevin

DuBrow, Eric Bloom, Geoff Tate, Dave Meniketti, Don Dokken and Paul Shortino. Vivian Campbell, Carlos Cavazo, Buck Dharma, Brad Gillis, Craig Goldy, George Lynch, Yngwie Malmsteen, Eddie Ojeda and Neal Schon all added guitar solos (this partly explains the song's eventual running time exceeding seven minutes). Iron Maiden's Dave Murray and Adrian Smith were in the midst of their *World Slavery* tour at the time, but still flew in to attend the main session.

The project was first publicly trailed in May 1985, originally mooting an additional London recording session and a benefit gig, plus the inclusion of Scorpions and Ratt, neither of whom would eventually make the final track. Once recruitment started in earnest, most of the original workload fell to bassist Bain, guitarist Campbell and the band's publicist Sharon Weisz, while Dio himself finished the band's *Sacred Heart* album. Rob Halford of Judas Priest was an early recruit: 'When "Do They Know It's Christmas?", the Band Aid single, and the "We are the World" record were happening, like everybody else I was sitting at home watching it all on TV, and I thought it was a shame that nobody from the heavy rock side had done something towards helping these starving people as well. I even got as far as ringing my manager in Spain to discuss the possibility of getting an event together.'[1]

1. Dante Bonutto, 'Meals of Steel', *Kerrang!* (April 1985).

The eventual recording saw all the contributors assembled together over a few sessions at the Sound City, A&M and Rumbo studios in LA. The absence of several of the old guard who had been approached for involvement – Tony Iommi, Ritchie Blackmore, Jimmy Page – made the end result lower on star power, but a more accurate snapshot of the metal scene at the time. Ozzy Osbourne's lack of involvement was perhaps for the best, given that in February of that year he had been telling an interviewer that 'Bob Geldof should start doing a few things for the junkies in this country instead of the "darkies" in Ethiopia.'[2] Dio was particularly critical of Page, who had apparently blown out a slot at the Warehouse studio in Philadelphia at the last minute. 'I don't think he could get out of bed. Yeah, that was it. In the meantime, there are children starving out there, they're fucking dying, that's the fucking point, they're fucking DYING! Yet still there were people who wouldn't contribute, who wouldn't give a tiny little piece of their talent to help feed a poor starving kid … man, you're fucking assholes, every one of you. You know who you are and, boy, I hope you sleep with yourselves fitfully every night. I think it STINKS!'[3]

While Dio's views on the no-shows from the metal community were unequivocal, it remains unrecorded

2. Dante Bonutto, 'Kommander of Khaos', *Kerrang!* (February 1985).
3. 'Meals of Steel', *Kerrang!* p. 118.

what he thought of the cover of that week's *Kerrang!*. The magazine commissioned artist Ian Gibson, then best known for his work on British comic *2000AD*, to create an image encapsulating heavy metal's response to the famine in Ethiopia. Gibson's artwork depicts a giant bleached skull resting on a parched, barren landscape, beneath a burning sun and a fiery sky. On the skull stands a musclebound, generically European man, dressed in knee-high velvet boots, a ragged purple and blue loincloth, and a faintly space-age utility waistcoat. He stares at the reader purposefully, and in his giant musclebound arms cradles a tiny, emaciated African child. The headline reads: 'LET THEM EAT METAL!'

It's safe to say that while the intentions behind this cover can't be impugned, it's a product of its time, and probably not one that would be produced today. But in a decade dominated by the simplistic, attention-grabbing and sloganeering of a rapidly expanding advertising industry, it was about as nuanced a take as one could expect. Around this time, *The Cosby Show* broke records by charging $400,000 for a single thirty-second commercial spot; Time and Warner Communications were merged into one vast conglomerate; General Electric Corp purchased RCA and via them NBC; *Vogue* began to take adverts for condoms in response to the unfolding AIDS crisis.

A curious detachment was taking place between the

way things looked and felt and the way things actually *were*. At the end of 1985, a *New York Times* headline starkly warned that 'Modest growth is all we can expect' with an economy that had been stagnant since early summer of 1984 and a Dollar that was overvalued. Gallup recorded just 7 per cent of respondents reporting that they had 'great confidence' in big business. Unemployment was down slightly on the previous year, but still at 6.6 per cent. On the surface, things had to be simplistic, aspirational and to some degree cheerfully dumb. Whatever would befall America that year – the Iran-Contra scandal, the space shuttle Challenger disintegrating seventy-three seconds after launch, killing all on board, the announcement that the previous twelve months had seen more deaths from AIDS than all previous years combined – culture needed to be simple, upbeat and big. It's no surprise that *Top Gun* was the highest grossing film of the year.

This was the case as much in glam metal as anywhere else. Separated from David Lee Roth, Van Halen returned with replacement frontman Sammy Hagar and the album *5150*, a competent, water-treading collection which bar the single 'Why Can't This Be Love' went even further than its predecessor in removing the edges and friction points from Van Halen's sound. W.A.S.P.'s *Inside the Electric Circus* was a decent enough album, although lacking in the manic energy of its predecessors – singer Blackie Lawless also had a narrow escape on the first date of the Irish leg of their world tour when his exploding codpiece backfired. 'He fell down on stage, and I thought it blew his balls off ... It was funny as hell!'[4] recalled a less-than-sympathetic bandmate, Chris Holmes. Ozzy Osbourne's *The Ultimate Sin* – despite its Dio-like fantasy cover art – saw him cross over fully to MTV-friendly status with a series of borderline ludicrous promo videos and a personal image of feathered, sprayed hair, and foundation-caked face. *The Ultimate Sin* is actually a much heavier, stronger album than it's generally remembered as being, but Jake E. Lee's guitar work and heavily melodic songs push it closer to the mainstream than anything Osbourne had previously released. In 2019, the singer would bemoan the polished quality of the album. '[Producer] Ron Nevison didn't really do a great production job,' he told *Rolling Stone*. 'The songs weren't bad; they were just put down weird. Everything felt and sounded the fucking same. There was no imagination. If there was ever an album I'd like to remix and do better, it would be *The Ultimate Sin*.'[5]

As polished as Ozzy appeared, newly emerging bands were pushing the look and style even further. Separated from Kiss, Vinnie Vincent formed the Vin-

4. https://www.eonmusic.co.uk/chris-holmes-eonmusic-interview-november-2018.html

5. https://www.rollingstone.com/music/music-features/ozzy-osbourne-box-set-interview-874037/

nie Vincent Invasion, whose eponymous debut is a masterpiece of maximalism. The excessive soloing and flamboyantly expressive playing which so aggravated his previous band members was given free reign. Vincent's guitar tone had a liquid, almost human quality, screeching up against Robert Fleischman's vocals throughout. The cumulative effect of listening to the harder tracks like 'Boyz Are Gonna Rock' and 'Invasion' (with its endless loop of divebombing feedback at the finale) is to be rendered into a state of semi-exhaustion.[6]

A sonically easier experience was provided by Philadelphia's Cinderella. The band had come through a long gestation period from 1982, with various mem-

6. Vincent's personal life has been plagued by no small amount of tragedy. At the time of writing he leads a largely reclusive existence, bar occasional appearances at Kiss conventions. In 1998 his former wife AnnMarie Peters was murdered while working as a part-time escort in Connecticut. Gregory Macarthur was convicted of her murder in 2002. In 2014, *Rolling Stone* reported from Vincent's abandoned house in Smyrna, a small town south east of Nashville, from which he had launched a series of legal battles with former bandmates while burning through hired musicians and record company money on a series of projects which always seemed to founder on Vincent's quest for absolute perfection. In 2011 he was arrested for aggravated domestic assault after his wife Diane Cusano reported herself to a police station smelling of alcohol and covered in blood. Upon entering Vincent's home, the arresting officers also found four sealed containers with dead dogs inside them. His wife claimed that the macabre situation was a result of their larger dogs killing some of the smaller ones (the pair had rescued some twenty dogs from abusive environments) and bad weather delaying their burials. No animal cruelty charges were filed, and Cusano died in January 2014 from conditions caused by her chronic alcoholism. Proposed Vinnie Vincent shows in December 2018 and June 2019 were both cancelled.

bers leaving to join fellow Philadelphians Britny Fox, Dave 'Snake' Sabo (later of Skid Row) auditioning, Jon Bon Jovi and Gene Simmonds individually trying to get them major label interest, and a permanent drummer only being found in Jim Drnec after work had finished on their debut album *Night Songs.* The cover of *Night Songs* is a perfect visual shorthand for glam metal: stack-heeled cowboy boots, leopard-print leggings and leather trousers, frock coats, draped lengths of chiffon and feathered, top-heavy hair over powderpuff faces. If an outsider imagines what they thought glam metal looked like, it's the cover of *Night Songs.* From the ground up, it's like a chronological tour of American musical styles – footwear from Alan Lomax's dustbowl recordings; garage band biker trousers; quasi-military psychedelic jackets; Aerosmith's scarves; punk's shredded t-shirts and bondage accessories; new romantic's beauty regime. Beneath a logo written in a curved, gothic typeface and bathed in purple light, the four band members posed in what appeared to be a stage set of a railway arch, with smoke machines billowing behind them. There are no instruments, or live shots or mock-documentary moments. It's all staged, all artifice, as the four pout for the camera, Tom Keifer pointing double gunfingers at the lens.

Debut single 'Shake Me' had a raucous, singalong quality (and a video depicting a modern retelling of the Cinderella myth, in which two stereotypically attractive sisters get to go to the glam metal show, while their downtrodden sibling is left at home), but it failed to break through. Second single 'Nobody's Fool' was a drastic gearshift – a fully blown, lighters-in-the-air power ballad. Their second shot at success also underlined the scale of the business which was now building around glam metal – Cinderella were fortunate enough to have, in Mercury, a label big enough to bide its time and underwrite the semi-cinematic, expensively MTV-friendly videos and studio production needed to push the band to mainstream success. Because, for all the outsider posturing of the bands, glam metal had quietly built up into a serious commercial force – even early outlier *Metal Health* had sold 4 million copies for Quiet Riot by this point; Ratt's first two albums had sold 2 million each; Dokken's *Under Lock and Key* was on its way to going Platinum. *Shout at the Devil* and *Theatre of Pain* had both sold more than 2 million copies for Mötley Crüe. All these releases raised the bar for what glam metal bands could be expected to sell and how big they could be expected to go. What had seemed like wishful projection from Def Leppard just a few years earlier was now a realistic baseline for new bands.

This was the context around 'Nobody's Fool', the sound of a band leapfrogging the scuzzy outsider phase that characterised Mötley Crüe's first album and going straight for the polished end result. The same characters appear as in the 'Shake Me' video, but the track cleaves perfectly to the template set by Def Leppard five years earlier with 'Bringin' On the Heartbreak'. A lonely gigolo's lament, a screeching metal voice pushed up to its limits to convey a broken heart as reverb-laden drums crash in behind it and a guitar solo emotes, rather than shreds, as if to say *You've broken my heart so badly, I can't even rock at full power anymore* – this is the sound of a band calculatedly aiming for arenas, and succeeding. But that's not to diminish it as a piece of work – as with the best tracks on *Night Songs*, it suggested that, while Cinderella might be an almost parodic representation of glam metal visually, their abilities and connections to a more meaningful current in American music ran deeper.

No such accusations could be levelled at another band arriving this year – Poison. The Pennsylvania band had taken Cinderella's visuals as a starting point and pushed it to extremes. Poison seemed machine-tooled to offend 'real' rock fans and dressed to start fights in bars with men who were insecure about their own sexuality. There was something almost confrontationally, aggressively feminine about their appearance – they didn't have the ironic pantomime quality of drag, or the adopted femininity of transvestitism, but instead sat somewhere between them. There was something unnerving about their look, as though they were a computer simulation of a female

– a sort of uncanny-valley idea of what a heavy metal woman might look like. Frontman Brett Michaels in particular came across like some defective prototype for Pamela Anderson, or like performance artist Leigh Bowery if he'd grown up in small-town Pennsylvania and not bothered reading any books.

For Poison, everything was surface. The same impulse that drew Andy Warhol to Madison Square Garden to watch the wrestling would have made him appreciate Poison. They were a pure distillation of a gleefully superficial culture. 'Those bands [like Poison], in their style and approach, that's what I call tits-and-ass metal,' said Rob Halford. 'Nothing wrong with that – I wouldn't expect anything else to come out of Hollywood.'[7] 'We were glam from the start,' said bassist Bobby Dall of their formation in Mechanicsburg, Pennsylvania. 'People used to throw rocks at us, but we didn't give a shit. We had a vision. We didn't care what people thought of us.'[8] Dall had first moved to LA in 1983 along with singer Brett Michaels and drummer Rikki Rockett, reasoning that if they'd moved to New York, the temptation to head home when things got tough would have been overwhelming. Having recruited guitarist C. C. DeVille who had been creating a similar concept in the New York glam band Lace, they lived in a warehouse space, parti-

7. *The Sound of the Beast*, p. 155.
8. https://www.miaminewtimes.com/music/poisons-bobby-dall-on-the-bands-glam-rock-early-days-10448800

tioned into bedrooms and a rehearsal room. The band briefly worked with Kim Fowley (writer and impresario best known for forming The Runaways), then hacked through the pay-to-play circuit common to new bands, while working everywhere from fast food restaurants to telesales to keep going. 'You rent a depressing room at Club 88, and if you can get twenty people at your show and impress them, they'll bring their friends next time and there'll be forty. We were a promotion machine,' Michaels told *Spin* in 1988. 'We got a Thursday night at the Troubadour, then a Friday, then a Friday *and* a Saturday…' However, even by the point where the band could pull 300 punters to a show, a deal remained elusive – on the grounds that while they'd mastered the promotion side of the band, songs, musicianship and general talent apparently remained beyond their reach.

When a deal was eventually signed – to Enigma, then through Capitol – their debut album did little business. First single 'Cry Tough' failed to break the Hot 100 and the album – which Michaels would later deem 'a glorified demo tape' – looked set to stall before sales kicked in around second single 'Talk Dirty to Me'. The video sums up exactly what people both loved and hated about Poison: no camera goes past without a member of the band mugging furiously to it; drum risers are leapt off in unison; the band high-kick in a chorus line; guitars are flung through the air to side-stage roadies and drum sticks are elaborately twirled; the band leap skywards to high-five in slow motion. The music itself is semi-memorable at best – an amalgamation of Eddie Cochran's semitone shuffle from 'Summertime Blues', the bouncy optimism of the Archies or the Monkees cartoon pop, and a string of lyrical clichés about drive-ins and your dad's Ford. The overall impression is of a band who have spent far longer studying the visual aesthetic of glam metal and general stagecraft rather than actually learning how to play their instruments or writing any material. Slash recalled briefly auditioning for the group after their first guitarist Matt Smith had moved back to Pennsylvania when his wife became pregnant. The future Guns n' Roses guitarist visited their warehouse space to find it already decorated with posters of the band themselves, and was subjected to more questions about his onstage footwear than his playing ability after a second audition. Even at that stage, in everything that Poison did, 'There was a tangible attention to detail.'[9] Glam metal's pre-eminent manager Doc McGhee later observed the difference between Poison and his own charges, Mötley Crüe: 'Poison … raised hell because they thought that's what rockstars should be doing. Mötley Crüe did stupid things just because they were Mötley Crüe.'[10]

9. Slash with Anthony Bozza, *Slash: The Autobiography* (HarperCollins, 2008), p. 95.
10. *The Dirt*, p. 230.

Throughout Poison's debut album, traces of post-war American music bubble up. The drum beat which opens the record and heralds 'Cry Tough' echoes Hal Blaine's three-kicks-and-a-snare which opened the Ronettes' 'Be My Baby', while the yearning chorus and its minor key shift is like a less earnest Bruce Springsteen let's-escape-this-smalltown hymn. 'I Want Action' has the glam stomp of Kiss circa 'Detroit Rock City'. 'I Won't Forget You' is the obligatory ballad, albeit one written by men who by that stage had a condom vending machine on their tourbus. 'Want Some, Need Some' is a stodgy soundtrack to motorbike cruising, like a flattened-out version of Steppenwolf's 'Born to Be Wild'. While Poison themselves seemed to be going out of their way to be as obnoxious as possible – the full-page adverts for the album branded them 'Uncensored and unanimously disapproved of by parents everywhere!' – the way that they hoovered up disparate influences and regurgitated them in their own style meant that in all honesty it's hard not to listen to *Look What the Cat Dragged In* and not hear something in there that resonates with you, even if you might not care to admit it. Even the title nods to this idea of Poison as a repository for elements of everything that had gone before them. While the obvious reading is that it's the band themselves who have arrived dishevelled and mauled at the crack of dawn, it could just as much be the music itself –

something pieced together after rummaging through America's cultural dustbin and seeing what could be recycled.

What Poison also had going in their favour was that they were proudly juvenile. Not in a pejorative sense, but in the way that they spoke to all the concerns of young life. Like W.A.S.P., Quiet Riot and Ratt, they dealt with the issues around a life of part-time jobs, consequence-free sex, generalised rage at vaguely sketched authority figures and that stage in your development where things can just be taken one day at a time. Even when glam metal did stray into more serious territory – Bon Jovi's 'Runaway' – it was always written from the perspective of the youth. At this stage, the bands celebrated and embodied life as viewed from the ground up. This mattered as mainstream pop was becoming defiantly serious and drifting into distinctly middle-aged territory. There's a very strong current that runs through much mid-Eighties' pop which is essentially the soundtrack to baby-boomers hitting the first mass wave of divorce. Phil Collins' entire solo career owes much to this, as does Don Henley's 'The Boys of Summer', Carly Simon's 'Coming Around Again' and Paul Simon's 'Graceland'. Poignant, serious sketches of suddenly being single in your forties and seeing life spiral off in a direction that you hadn't expected. Heavy metal generally, and glam metal specifically, was a glorious Technicolor counterpoint to all this, and a huge audience was standing by and receptive for it. Whatever else you thought about Poison, they weren't going to suddenly try to have an intelligent discussion with you about where things had gone wrong with their youthful hopes and dreams – they lived in the moment of your life where all is yet to come. That was a huge part of their appeal.

If Poison represented a point where glam metal was becoming culturally assimilated, the huge audiences it was starting to draw meant that it was also becoming commercially assimilated. There was money to be made from this scene. The pages of *Circus* magazine were filled with adverts for microphones and effect pedals being used by clean-cut looking young people with glam-metal hair; Vanderfluit's adverts for HOT ROCK CLOTHING & ACCESSORIES offered spiked wristbands, three-row 'pyramide' spiked belts, neon leopard-print leggings and tiger-face t-shirts; the Metal Method's cassette-based distance-learning guitar course claimed to have reached more than 50,000 guitarists in fifty-four countries; *Circus*' own music videos promised to ROCK YOUR EYES OUT, with a thirty-minute tape of W.A.S.P. live in London or fifty minutes of Queensrÿche live in Tokyo costing up to $70 in today's money. In the back pages, among the classified ads, you could see where the grubbier end of capitalism was also sniffing out the potential in glam metal. Adverts offered everything from hooky backstage passes for bands including Kiss, Ratt, Dio and

Aerosmith to fake photo ID for $6 from Cardinal Publishing Department of Jacksonville, Florida, and American Press of Colorado Springs. Two dollars got you a catalogue of 'Spandex clothes for today's rock and rollers' from Rainbow Sales in Arlington, Texas. Other listings offered bootleg live recordings, colour photographs, rock tapestries, spandex jeans and satin pants. Others just sought to contact other fans – Dustie of London, Ontario, wanted to reconnect with Myles of Boulder, Colorado ('Remember the Rainbow on Sunset Blvd. in March '85?'), while Laura of Dallas, Texas, simply wanted to hear from 'Nasty Metalmen'. The sole advert in the 'Occult' section promising 'POWER SECRETS REVEALED' turns out to be from Gavin and Yvonne Frost, the self-proclaimed 'world's foremost witches'.[11]

A sense of who was actually sustaining these business ventures can be seen in John Heyn and Jeff Krulik's short film *Heavy Metal Parking Lot*. A lo-fi piece of direct cinema filmed on the last day of May 1986, the film captures the crowds and the building anticipation outside a Judas Priest and Dokken show at the Capital Center in Landover, Maryland. There's a wild, anarchic edge to proceedings. Whip-thin shirtless men

11. Gavin Frost was a British occult author, physicist and mathematician who along with his wife founded the Church and School of Wicca. Gavin died in 2016 at the age of eighty-five, survived by his wife. Their key text, *The Magic Power of Witchcraft*, came with a cover that looked like a video nasty and promised that it would enable you to 'enjoy a life of unbelievable riches, lasting love and constant protection'.

stumble around talking about being on acid and looming military deployments. Lone metallers dance while toting supersize beers, grinning at the camera and seemingly at a show of their own somewhere. A twenty-year-old makes out with his thirteen-year-old girlfriend. A squad of adolescent males with fuzz moustaches and Judas Priest shirts bellow at the filmmakers while brandishing a portable tape deck. Almost everyone is white. One mulleted young man, in a matching zebra-print two piece, grabs the microphone and delivers his verdict on modern culture while squinting into the sun: 'Heavy metal rules ... all that punk shit *sucks*. It doesn't ... belong on this world. It belongs on fucking Mars!' One man cheerfully gestures to his custom-print t-shirt, with blocky letters picking out the legend 'FUCK OFF'.

The crowds of *Heavy Metal Parking Lot* are a record of the point when this was still an outsider's music. A crossover point was approaching fast, but if glam metal was going to maintain its momentum and reach out beyond the volatile crowd captured in Maryland, it needed an emblematic album around which the scene could coalesce and truly win over the mainstream. Europe's single 'The Final Countdown' was a huge mainstream hit, going to number 1 in twenty-five countries. A synth-laden metal updating of the sort of intergalactic voyage that David Bowie conjured up in 'Space Oddity', 'The Final Countdown' replaces that track's fragility and introspection with bombast and heroism. The album of the same title spawned other hit singles – 'Rock the Night' and the ballad 'Carrie' – and sold over 15 million copies, but never endured as a body of work. The cover art made it look like the soundtrack to a Jim Henson puppet film, while something about the band's Swedish roots meant they never seemed particularly cool. At a time when glam bands were still exuding an air of streetwise squalor, Europe's blond hair, blue eyes and healthy complexions made them appear just too wholesome. The defining album of the genre was not going to come from them.

At the start of 1986, Bon Jovi had begun work on their third record. Their second, 1985's *7800° Fahrenheit*, had been an underwhelming release which the band largely disowned in later years. With the exception of single 'In and Out of Love' there was little memorable material on it, although it at least gave the band a reason to be out on tour, where they solidified their reputation as performers, travelling Europe as headliners for the first time (1984's dates had been in support of Kiss in Europe and Scorpions in Japan) as well as supporting Ratt across the US.

Just as Def Leppard had done previously with *Pyromania*, Bon Jovi set their sights on a bigger target than any of their peers, conspicuously working in a way that maximised the chances of their forthcoming album landing as hard as possible and going beyond the limitations of a conventional metal audience. Two crucial collaborators were recruited by the band: songwriter Desmond Child and producer Bruce Fairbairn. Fairbairn had worked on *Without Love*, the 1985 album by Black 'N Blue, a Portland band who had originally appeared on the second pressing of *Metal Massacre*, Brian Slagel's 1982 compilation which had also included early appearances from Ratt and Metallica. Signed to Geffen and first working with Scorpions' producer Dieter Dierks (their first album's standout track 'Hold On to 18' is a classic in the UFO/ Scorpions vein), the band had switched to working with Fairbairn for the far more polished follow-up.

Based out of Little Mountain Sound Studios in Vancouver, Fairbairn had originally been in the group Prism between 1977 and 1982 before switching to production. He quickly gained a reputation as a methodical, engaged producer, ruthlessly focused on the quality of songwriting and arrangements, and trimming a song back to its commercial essence. 'I'm more of a pot-stirrer than someone who sits on the sidelines and waits to see what will happen,' he said. 'I like to get involved with a project right at the beginning, when the guys are still putting down their acoustic demos. At that point, I can identify those really strong ideas and encourage them, help them along, rather than wait until the last minute when it can be much more difficult to change things.'[12]

Jon Bon Jovi had been listening to other bands before starting work on his band's new album, trying to work out how to improve the underwhelming sound of their previous release. 'I had the second Black 'N Blue LP with me. By accident, I began to compare the way our compact disc sounded alongside the ordinary cut of *Without Love*. And I was stunned by how much better the latter sounded. It was quite incredible. So I called up their producer! Something just happened when we met in Vancouver to do *Slippery*. It was like a comic strip phenomenon: Kapow! We became these rockstars!'[13]

Without Love contains many of the component parts of what would become Bon Jovi's *Slippery When Wet*. The chugging bassline of 'Rockin' On Heaven's Door', Jaime St James' voice playing against the massed singalong backing vocals, and the taut, minimally melodic verses that explode into hook-filled choruses. Before Jovi's album was even completed and while the band were still holed up in Vancouver, Jon Bon Jovi knew they had something special on their hands, telling visiting journalists that this was set to be their equivalent of Bruce Springsteen's career-defining *Born to Run*. As much as the songwriting was of the highest quality, Fairbairn's production gave the band a sense of space

12. https://www.independent.co.uk/arts-entertainment/obituary-bruce-fair-
    bairn-1097061.html
13. Ibid.

and dynamics that they had previously lacked. Anything extraneous was removed. 'I'm not saying it was a mistake, but Lance Quinn's production on *7800° Fahrenheit* was very slick,' said Jovi. 'Double the guitars. Vocals everywhere... with Bruce, we're very natural sounding. He came close to capturing us live – that's the key.' However, while they may have sounded 'natural', Fairbairn's production travelled close to the artificiality of perfection. Nothing is ragged, nothing feels like an edge is being pushed at. What makes art sound exciting – but can also date it to a time – is the faint breakup that happens when equipment is pushed to its limits: the rasp of a broken speaker cone that becomes distortion; the wail of feedback overwhelming Jimi Hendrix's notes; the overdriven throb of a screaming voice pushing the recording levels into the red; a sample that is clipped and truncated because it exceeded a device's memory capacity; the breakup and saturation of colour on degraded video tape... there was no place for any of this in Fairbairn's production – no imperfection to contrast with the beauty. If Bon Jovi sounded 'natural', then a huge amount of work by all parties had gone in to making them seem so.

The album was originally planned to be called 'Wanted Dead or Alive', after the album's centrepiece ballad. 'That describes the band's attitude. We're Clint Eastwood with a guitar; rock & roll cowboys. We live nowhere, go everywhere. We ride into a town, raise hell, steal the women, then leave. Even our tour jackets were these long rider coats. It seemed perfect...'[14] However, test shots of the band in an old-time Wild West setting with photographer Mark Weiss were unsatisfactory and deemed too serious for the accompanying album. Instead, the title was changed to *Slippery When Wet*, inspired by an onstage shower-based routine in #5, a Vancouver strip club the band frequented during recording. An accompanying photoshoot planned on Bradley Beach in New Jersey failed to yield anything at first. 'We needed a few more girls,' recalled Weiss. 'So I walked across the street and pulled a few more. My assistant Danny took a walk with Tico [Torres, Bon Jovi's drummer] across the street and came back with just what the doctor ordered. An Italian hot girl named Angela. We found her – this was going to be the girl on the cover. Then I got some soap and water and started having a car wash party. The photo ended up in the sleeve of the album.'[15] 'Our testosterone was at a very high level back then,' guitarist Richie Sambora would later recall by way of explanation to *Ultimate Classic Rock*.

Perhaps conscious of the potentially limiting effect on sales of trying to get major labels – in the PMRC era – to stock an album which effectively depicted a close-up of a wet t-shirt contest, the band's label Mer-

14. Paul Gallotta, 'Bon Jovi', *Circus* (August 31, 1986).
15. https://sleazeroxx.com/the-story-behind-bon-jovis-slippery-when-wet-album-cover/

cury swiftly instructed them to come up with an alternative option. 'Jon came to my studio in New York shortly after the news that we had to come up with a new cover,' says Weiss. 'He just said to me, "Garbage bag. Spray bottle." I propped up the bag and sprayed it, then Jon wrote the words *Slippery When Wet*. "That's it, there's the cover." He didn't even wait to see the Polaroid. The next day I delivered the photo, and the rest is history.'

The artwork is remarkably low-key for such an important album. The tracks had been ruthlessly edited and sequenced, including market research sessions where the band had tested their demos by playing them for young fans at a local pizza restaurant. 'It was like a marketing test,' recalled Sambora. 'They came in and said, "Yeah, we like this one. This one gets through and that one doesn't."'[16] From the start, the album oozes confidence – the long, cod-gothic keyboard introduction of 'Let It Rock' plays out like an opening theme for a stage arrival, almost ninety seconds passing before Jon Bon Jovi's voice arrives. The lyrics are largely meaningless, call-and-response fodder – but more important are the backing vocals. Not multi-tracked and polished, but looser, the sound of a band-as-a-gang massed around one shared microphone, bellowing short riffs and phrases that a crowd could yell along with.

---

16. https://ultimateclassicrock.com/bon-jovi-slippery-when-wet/

The two standout tracks are 'You Give Love a Bad Name' and 'Livin' on a Prayer', the second and third track respectively on side one of the album. On first listen, these are the two sides of the band condensed down to their absolute essence. The first is a personal, romantic drama, a slighted protagonist warning the world at large about an alluring woman who reeled him in then broke his heart. The second is the outward-looking, social commentary – a straightforward narrative of a financially struggling couple who've just about held their lives together despite everything. While it's obviously in debt to the storytelling of Bruce Springsteen on a track like 'The River', it completely succeeds on its own terms. The opening spoken word line gives it an intimate, fairy-tale quality. A man who's had to pawn his guitar while his wife works as a waitress – this is a world away from Poison's hedonistic party music, but something which would have struck a chord with a lot of listeners as America still struggled to drag itself out of the recession that had blighted the first half of the decade. Lyrically, it's a surprisingly vulnerable, unguarded statement with the woman at its emotional centre – it's Gina's dreams of escape and the sound of her crying at night that they detail, but it's also the female voice that delivers the forceful rebuke to her wavering husband and reminds him to hold on and fight for the relationship. It's rare for male songwriters to successfully place themselves in the position of a female protagonist – more so when we're talking about a band who were about to place a close up of an amateur wet t-shirt competition on their album cover. But Jovi's appeal to a much more female audience than their immediate predecessors didn't go unnoticed. 'Because of the image, there would be a lot of women coming to see us,' said Richie Sambora. 'You came to one of our shows, there would be a lot of women there. A *lot* of women.' Dee Snider would later pejoratively term Jovi's sound at this time as 'happy metal'.

Fairbairn's production absolutely sparkles across both tracks. The *Circus* magazine writer who had visited Little Mountain Sound Studios had found him spending hours with the band over the a cappella introduction to 'You Give Love a Bad Name', tweaking the levels of each element and the exact moment at which the rest of the music follows in. 'The intro should really bust somebody's balls,' explained the producer. 'It has to jump out a little more.' Richie Sambora's guitar sound is fed through a harmoniser, giving it a plaintive, almost human quality, but for the verse the music circles around one minor chord, the guitar chugging out four notes in sequence. There's no change or movement, so when the shift eventually comes to lead into the bridge to the chorus, the impact is huge. It's a massively confident songwriting trick – to essentially demonstrate that you know your chorus will hit so hard that you can do almost nothing leading up to it so as to maximise its impact. As befits the subject matter, the chorus has a mournful, bitter feeling to it, with the backing vocals echoing the melody of the lead vocal a second later. Its narrow range and lyrical repetition makes it perfect for singing along with: a drunk, tone-deaf non-metal fan could pick this up after sixty seconds listening on the radio.

'Livin' on a Prayer' is like the optimistic twin of 'You Give Love a Bad Name'. Where the latter's chorus is angry and dour, the former's sparkles with major-key optimism. But the same motifs occur across both – the guitar line is based on the same four-note cycle; the melody of 'Livin' on a Prayer's chorus slots together with the bridge of 'You Give Love a Bad Name' perfectly; throughout 'Livin' on a Prayer' Sambora's guitar again has a humanistic, verbal feel, thanks on this occasion to being played through a talkbox, a breath-controlled synthesiser which blurs the guitar sound together with the player's voice. The end result of playing the two songs together is like looking at a piece of fabric and the pattern that it has been cut from.

In truth, these two tracks are a quantum leap ahead of anything else on the album – with the possible exception of the cowboy ballad, 'Wanted Dead or Alive'. ('Without Love' is a fairly turgid bit of water-treading; 'I'd Die for You' is a less dramatic reworking of debut single 'Runaway'.) But they have such an enormous halo effect on the rest of the record that you remember *Slippery When Wet* as being a far better album than it is. It's particularly loaded towards side one, where three of the four singles occur. But what it lacks in other standout tracks it makes up for in two ways. Firstly, it's remarkably consistent – Fairbairn's production work, Jovi's voice and Sambora's guitar sound are all immediate aural calling cards. You can drop in at any point of the album and you would know immediately that it was a Bon Jovi track. And secondly, when it comes to the lyrics it's got a simplistic, rousing energy in every other line. Jon Bon Jovi was blessed with the ability to write defiantly upbeat chorus lines that sounded like advertising copy – on his best ones, there's a genuine feeling or sentiment condensed into a few words, with maximum imagery evoked from minimum content. There's a vacuous, soundbite-heavy quality to Bon Jovi's best work that makes the songs great blank canvases – you can project almost any feeling or moment onto their sentiments. Allied to their crashing chord changes and dramatic keyboard flourishes, these believe-in-yourself exhortations could have soundtracked everything from Tampax adverts to motivational seminars.

Again, this is absolutely no criticism of the band – there's a good reason why you still hear 'Livin' on a Prayer' in bars and on talent shows to this day in a way that you don't hear 'Shake Me'. It just lined up perfectly with the spirit of the times – America was looking forwards, often against the odds, while a supercharging advertising industry pushed ever more aspirational imagery and ideas through far-reaching channels. There was a genuine whiff of death and unreliability about Mötley Crüe, while W.A.S.P. gave off a palpable menace and Poison seemed like a knowing joke. The time was right for a band who made people feel as good as the band themselves looked and Bon Jovi – in all their wholesome, machine-tooled glory – were in the perfect place at the right time. The sales duly reflected this – the album went to number 1 in Australia, Canada and the US as well as in countries across Scandinavia and Europe, and entered the Top 10 in the UK, Japan, Sweden and the Netherlands. Bon Jovi were now the biggest metal band in the world, and glam metal was the global face of all metal.

In the final few weeks of 1986, a much smaller and very different release came out to little or no fanfare. *Live ?!*@ Like a Suicide* appeared on the surface to be a live EP, put out by an independent label, and recorded by just another glam metal band – members had previously intersected in different ways with Poison, Mötley Crüe, LA Guns and Hollywood Rose, and – by the black-and-white photo on the back sleeve at least – they ticked every sartorial box (feathered and bleached hair, skin tight trousers, cowboy boots, shades).

This judgement was erroneous on every count. At the time, Guns n' Roses were already signed to Geffen Records, where they had been spotted by Tom Zutaut, the same A&R man who had first signed Mötley Crüe. Via that deal, they had taken on Alan Niven as manager. Guitarist Slash recalls how after listening to their demos, he 'Decided that we should take those takes, add a live audience track, and release it all as a live EP. He thought it was essential for us to get some product out while we still had a buzz in the industry.'[17] The crowd noise was lifted from a recording of a Texas Jamm festival in the 1970s. According to bassist Duff McKagan, 'We thought it would be funny to put a huge stadium crowd in the background at a time when we were lucky to be playing to a few hundred.'[18]

As well as the 'fake live' status of the recording, the band also conceived of styling the record as a mock-independent release, put out by the band's own label Uzi Suicide and financed by Geffen. The EP consisted of two original tracks – 'Move to the City' and 'Reckless Life', plus covers of Aerosmith's 'Mama Kin' and Rose Tattoo's 'Nice Boys'. 'They're raw, I guess – but if you ask me they still sound pretty fucking good,' said Slash with hindsight. Raw is the right word. Compared to *Slippery When Wet* there's a bubbling, aggressive undercurrent throughout the four songs. Axl Rose's voice conjures up the analogue edge of fabric being torn or metal being sliced through. The rasp and squeak of plectrums sliding the wrong way down roundwound strings catches your ear, and the high-end hiss of Steven Adler's cymbals bleeds out

17. *Slash: The Autobiography*, p. 155.
18. Duff McKagan, *It's So Easy (And Other Lies)* (Simon & Schuster, 2011), p. 123.

across the other instruments. There's a sense of nothing being quite contained, like a confined animal repeatedly pushing against the lid of its cage and bending it out of shape with every thrust, or the bolts coming loose on a machine pushed too hard. If Bon Jovi were all about the songs, Guns n' Roses – at this stage at least – were all about the *feel*. And the feel was angry, paranoid and manic.

Ten thousand copies of *Live ?!*@ Like a Suicide* were released on cassette and one-sided vinyl, with a launch party held at Riki Rachtman's club The Cathouse on La Cienga in Beverley Hills. This was the first time that live bands had been booked at the venue, with Guns n' Roses playing an acoustic set the day before Christmas Eve, supported by Faster Pussycat, Jet Boy and LA Guns. The flyer for the 'All Star Live Like Suicide Christmas Party' promised that the $5 cover charge got you this line-up, plus 'Surprise Guests (Too big to mention)', dancing from 9:30 p.m. ('To the music of Mötley Crüe, Cheap Trick, Aerosmith, Hanoi Rocks, T-Rex and More, More, More') plus the 'Gorgeous erotic dancers' of the Body Language troupe.

The EP picked up some radio play on stations like Long Beach's 'pure rock' channel KNAC, but made no great waves otherwise. At this stage, Guns n' Roses could be written off as another promising yet dissolute band in the mould of Hanoi Rocks. However, as 1986 ended, something had shifted – 1987 was going to be a pivotal year for glam metal.

Chapter 5

1987: APPETITE FOR DESTRUCTION

In 1987, MTV's early bet on the power of glam metal was proving to be a shrewd one. Videos were arriving thick and fast, usually with a familiar set of tropes, and propelling bands beyond the confines of The Cathouse, the Whisky a Go Go or Gazzari's, which were collectively functioning as a breeding ground for the new scene. These clubs were drawing in bands from all over the country and developing and multiplying them, while providing a focal point for audiences who wanted to connect with them.

The *Heavy Metal Mania* slot had run since 1985 but foundered when host Dee Snider asked – not unreasonably – for payment, only to be informed that MTV didn't have a budget. 'I was my own favourite VJ on MTV – few people can say that,' said Snider with remarkable equanimity. With *Heavy Metal Mania* ending, a new slot was proposed – *Headbangers Ball*. Originally, this was an hour of metal videos, simply implanted into an existing VJ's slot. This led to odd juxtapositions, with clean cut hosts like Kevin Seal throwing to videos by Iron Maiden and Whitesnake, while clearly knowing little and caring less for the music they were introducing.

But nonetheless, it meant that, every Saturday night, fans could be guaranteed three hours of largely uninterrupted metal videos – which, given the genre's commercial impact, still didn't seem like enough. By June 1987, six of the Top 10 slots on Billboard's album charts were occupied by metal bands. The genuine mainstream crossover that Bon Jovi had executed so masterfully in 1986 had been followed by other bands as the new year got underway. Danish-American band White Lion's second album *Pride* broke through, off the back of support slots with Frehley's Comet, Aerosmith, Ozzy Osbourne, Stryper and AC/DC, along with heavy MTV play for the single 'Wait' and acoustic ballad 'When The Children Cry'. Norway's TNT simplified and polished their sound for their third album, with single '10,000 Lovers' propelled along by an Ozzy Osbourne-like riff, but like Europe the band's Scandinavian wholesomeness counted against them.

Faster Pussycat's eponymous debut was a loose, sleazy collection of what the band termed 'alley cat rock'. Frontman Taime Downe was a co-runner of The Cathouse club along with his roommate Riki Rachtman, and the band's single 'Bathroom Wall' is a dumb classic of the place and time, reviving the spirit of Hanoi Rocks and the New York Dolls with a ramshackle sound that just about covered up Downe's vocal shortcomings. Dokken's fourth album *Back for the Attack* would become their best seller, including the single 'Dream Warriors', which appeared in the third instalment of the horror franchise *A Nightmare on Elm Street*. In the video, Patricia Arquette's character Kristen Parker is pursued through a derelict house where she's menaced by Freddie Krueger, only saved by the intervention of the band. At one point, as his guitar solo reaches its peak, George Lynch is pounced on from behind by Krueger and dragged away into a cavity wall (he keeps playing), but ultimately the band's power drives Krueger away, Don Dokken's climactic falsetto delivering the fatal blow to the hideously burned undead sex offender.

In addition to the younger acts, there was also an interesting process of reinvention going on among the bands who had first inspired the current leading lights of glam, particularly in the cases of Aerosmith and Whitesnake. Aerosmith's original look had been a huge influence on glam metal, with the sunken cheeks, beauty-gone-to-seed and silky paraphernalia seen in everyone from Ratt to LA Guns. Their grafting together of Led Zeppelin's electric blues with a raw, lascivious sleaze set a template that Eighties' bands would build on and push to further extremes. And in 'Dream On' they wrote a masterful power ballad, which a decade later echoed through the likes of Mötley Crüe's 'Home Sweet Home'. But for almost a decade they had been ravaged by infighting, drug abuse, a loss of focus and a general inability to get it together and write some songs. In 1985, an unlikely collaborative cover version of the band's calling-card funky shuffle 'Walk This Way' with Run-DMC returned Aerosmith to public consciousness, albeit with a whiff of the novelty hit about them.

However, paired with Bruce Fairbairn as producer, Aerosmith underwent a drastic return to form and favour. The same tactics that had turned *Slippery When Wet* into an all-conquering masterpiece were applied to Aerosmith and transformed them into far more than their constituent parts for the *Permanent Vacation* album. The tranquilised, bluesy honk that ran through much of their previous work was stripped out, their sprawling, loose playing condensed into something harder and more formalised. As Steven Tyler and Joe Perry were personally and professionally reunited, the production pushed them as close together as possible, with the singer's voice merging into the tones of Perry's guitar to the point where they frequently couldn't be picked apart. On the opening stabs of

'Dude (Looks Like a Lady)', this half-human-half-instrument bark pans from speaker to speaker before the chorus frontloads the track. The song hits the ground running, all the fat is stripped away, the bottom end shrinks in favour of parping horn sections, squalling guitar lines and drums that snap and pop. Joe Perry's guitar parts frequently eschew the obvious sonic attention-grabbers of metal (distortion and overdrive) in favour of a relatively clean tone knocked slightly out of phase.

The cumulative effect is of a band deep into their second decade sounding more aggressive and energised – if far more palatably mainstream – than they had done when they were actual young men. In the process, something had been cleaned up: Aerosmith were now saucy, rather than sexy, entertaining rather than malevolent, seemingly more likely to wink at a waitress than drop dead in the bathroom. But in the songwriting and production there's a pronounced sense of rebirth: 'Magic Touch' absolutely flies out of the speakers, replaying *Slippery When Wet*'s structures and melodic tricks (upbeat chorus over minor key chords, sustained guitar notes dragging just behind the beat, the delayed gratification of the big melodic drop). As unlikely as it seemed, the band who had provided so much of the source code for glam metal had been rehabilitated by the scene they spawned, and dragged into a new iteration.

The album also marked the first time that the band

had worked with outside songwriters, most notably Desmond Child who contributed to album opener 'Hearts Done Time', as well as 'Dude (Looks Like a Lady)' and 'Angel'. Child is a crucial figure in the commercial development of glam metal, cropping up throughout the story whenever floundering bands needed a sure-fire hit. His own biography describes him simply as 'one of music's most accomplished hit-makers' and even that is downplaying it somewhat. Child was immersed in music throughout his childhood in Florida, thanks to his Cuban family – his mother Elena Casals was a songwriter and published poet, while his aunt Olga Guillot was the 'Queen of Bolero'. After a brief musical career of his own in the mid-Seventies with his group Rouge (their 1979 track 'Our Love is Insane' was a club hit thanks to the endorsement of Larry Levan at the Paradise Garage, while one of his bandmates was Maria Vidal, who had a hi-NRG hit in 1985 with 'Body Rock'), Child turned to writing for other artists. His first hit was in 1979 with Kiss' semi-disco stormer 'I Was Made for Lovin' You' selling over a million copies. Child's relationship with Kiss would prove to be a fruitful one as their sound turned from glam rock to glam metal over the following decade – he co-wrote on the *Animalize, Asylum, Crazy Nights, Smashes Thrashes & Hits* and *Hot in the Shade* albums. Other artists who turned to Child included Bon Jovi ('You Give Love a Bad Name', 'Livin' on a Prayer', 'Without Love', 'I'd Die for You', 'Bad Medicine', 'Born to Be My Baby', 'Blood on Blood', 'Wild is the Wind'), Bonnie Tyler and Cher (both of whom recorded dramatic divorcee masterpiece 'Save Up All Your Tears') and Alice Cooper (the entire *Trash* album, including his worldwide comeback hit 'Poison'). Later in Child's career he would work with various solo members of Kiss, Scorpions, Skid Row's Sebastian Bach, Mötley Crüe's Vince Neil and Meat Loaf. Outside of glam metal, he proved that the tricks and styles he'd perfected with the artists of the Eighties would work just as well in mainstream contemporary pop, writing with everyone from Katy Perry and Kelly Clarkson to LeAnn Rimes and Selena Gomez. Child's name is in the credits for songs as diverse as Sisqo's 'Thong Song' to Ricky Martin's 'Livin' La Vida Loca'. For as long as there is daytime radio, TV talent shows or karaoke bars, Desmond Child will be receiving an annual publishing cheque of epic proportions.

Child's genius was to take the drama and tension of disco and copy it across to heavy metal, and in the process create a new sound which, as glam metal developed, allowed these bands to not just soften their sound for the mainstream but to capture a poignancy and universality which had previously been lacking. His typical songs have an edgy, minor key feel to them, which often contrasts with the upbeat lyrics.

In 'Magic Touch' on *Permanent Vacation*, Steven Tyler is ostensibly singing about being smitten by a new woman, but there's something bleak at the heart of the melody – it's a similar trick to that which runs through much of ABBA's material, or Phil Spector's classic girl-group productions. Joe Perry's guitars strike just off the beat, and drag vapour trails of feedback across Tyler's lines. There's still an irresistible pop core to the song, but there's clearly something more structurally serious and technically complex going on here than you'd find on 'Talk Dirty to Me'. *Pyromania* had projected forwards to how big glam metal felt it could be; *Slippery When Wet* had made this a standard reality, and raised the bar for everyone. There was no longer any projection – Bon Jovi's standout tracks had drawn a line in the sand of how good any other contenders would now have to be, and what level they had to attain. With *Permanent Vacation*, Aerosmith had proven that they could measure up to that, if not yet over a whole album, but at least in part. In the process they had created one of the rare examples of a band's second incarnation producing material that bettered that of their first.

While Aerosmith had rebooted themselves by reuniting their original line-up, Whitesnake were going about things differently. David Coverdale had formed the band in 1978, having spent the mid-Seventies in Deep Purple, where he replaced Ian Gillan.

The band's name came from *White Snake*, an album that Coverdale released in 1977 while touring as a solo artist. In their first incarnation, Whitesnake had a bluesy, pub-rock quality. While not unsuccessful – they were big enough to headline the Monsters of Rock festival at Donington in 1983 and played at the Rock in Rio festival in 1984 – they had a parochial, meat-and-potatoes quality to them. Coverdale's voice was a powerful weapon, but even on Whitesnake's best tracks – 'Fool for Your Loving' (1980), 'Here I Go Again' (1982) and 'Love Ain't No Stranger' (1984) – they could feel somewhat stodgy, and American audiences were largely nonplussed by the band as a result.

The process of reinvention began in 1984 around the *Slide It In* album when their producer and label boss David Geffen suggested that the album be remixed and overhauled for a US release to improve its chances of success. Guitar and bass parts were re-recorded, and the freshened-up version cracked the Top 40. Feeling the band were at a make-or-break point, Coverdale fully committed to America and relocated himself and the band there, beginning to write new material with guitarist Adrian Sykes. The gestation of the album was difficult – much of 1986 was written off when Coverdale contracted a serious sinus infection, and 'was reduced to talking in a whisper for six weeks'. Speaking after the infection cleared, he said, 'There was a 50/50 chance that I would not be able to sing in the same style or with the same power. I was extraordinarily fortunate. I worked with an amazing ear, nose and throat doctor, who's recently retired. He was an astonishing doctor, and a beautiful guy all around. I owe him a debt that I could never repay.' Coverdale's doctor had directed him to work with Nathan Lam, then the premier cantor at the Stephen S. Wise Temple in Beverly Hills. 'He has an astonishingly deep, basso profundo voice – which is probably why he was premier cantor in the choir. He helped me rebuild my voice,'[1] explained Coverdale. This also manifested itself in a noticeable shift in Coverdale's speaking voice, which lost its original Yorkshire accent and saw him talking more like someone who'd gone to school with Roger Moore.

With Coverdale fully recovered and his English rogue persona perfected, the band's first US-focused album, *Whitesnake*, was released in April 1987 (in Europe it would be titled *1987*). The record was A&R'd by John Kalodner who'd helped steer Aerosmith's rebirth and even crops up in the video for 'Dude (Looks Like a Lady)', with parts of the session taking place at Little Mountain Sound Studios. Producers Mike Stone and Keith Olsen had between them worked on a string of productions which shaped the softer end of rock, for the likes of Asia, Journey and

1. http://somethingelsereviews.com/2012/11/26/i-had-been-reduced-to-a-whisper-david-coverdale-on-the-sinus-infection-that-almost-silenced-him/

REO Speedwagon, as well as engineering much of Queen's 1970s' output. The finished product was far more agile and lush-sounding than the band's previous work – a sound soaked in the positivity and sunshine of California rather than the authenticity and grit of Coverdale's native Redcar, North Yorkshire. As a mark of how far the band were moving into a mainstream sound, the album's key ballad, 'Is This Love?', had originally been written by Coverdale and guitarist Adrian Sykes with Tina Turner in mind.

While the sound of the album was perfect for the time, the band was dogged by personnel issues, with the musicians who actually played on the songs either having left or been dismissed by Coverdale by the time it was released. A new, more LA-friendly version of the band was quickly assembled and press shots from before and after the record's release show a band in a period of transition. Dark hair, moody expressions and uniform black leather replaced with bleached denim, fluffy, highlighted hair, smooth, hairless chests and pouting lips. The David Coverdale who appeared on the front of *Metal Hammer* magazine around the album's release looked tanned and healthy, and appeared to be wearing a shiny blue suit jacket with the sleeves rolled up. The MTV-compliant video for 'Here I Go Again' featured walls of pyrotechnics, the new youthful band playing along and Coverdale being seduced while driving by model Tawny Kitaen (he would later marry her). Supermodel Claudia Schiffer was originally planned to be 'the Whitesnake woman', with Kitaen filling in at the last minute.

Coverdale was well aware that visual impact would be what finally got Whitesnake to break America.

I had to put on my designer's hat, because I had studied to be an art director and art teacher, so I have pretty good visual ideas. It's just being able to capture them … I have a very visual mind. And I had a great relationship with the guy [Marty Callner] who did 'Here I Go Again', 'Still of the Night', and 'Is This Love?' They were fucking huge – just ridiculous. At the time, I thought, 'Wow. This has really saved me at least five years of hard-ass touring the States.' MTV took over the world, and Whitesnake became a global entity. Whatever hotel I would go in, the TV would be on from the housekeepers being in, and it would usually be on MTV, and it was usually cartwheels on a pair of Jaguars. This was all over the world. And, for a time, I thought, 'Oh my God, we're so over-exposed,' because I'm old-school … we let the music do the talking. But if you want to succeed in this, you have to embrace a multitude of sins – as long as they don't compromise your integrity or who you are. And that was just lightning in a bottle.[2]

A similarly drastic process of reinvention was going on with Heart, a folk-rock band whose career went back to 1973. Built around sisters Ann and Nancy Wil-

2. https://consequenceofsound.net/2019/03/david-coverdale-whitesnake-here-i-go-again-video/

son, the band had created a unique sound across Seventies' albums like *Dreamboat Annie* and *Little Queen,* set apart by Ann's voice – a kind of female Robert Plant – and Nancy's intricate guitar work and flamboyant stage presence. The first half of the Eighties proved to be a difficult period for the band – constant line-up changes, an unclear identity and patchy material plagued them until 1985 when they signed to Capitol and moved towards a more contemporary soft rock sound. Their folk elements were packed away, with new arrangements using banks of glacial synths and crashing drums to foreground Ann's voice and simplify Nancy's guitar work. On 'What About Love?' and 'These Dreams' the band showed how their ear for melancholy and drama could find a new audience if they looked more like a conventional rock band. Duly, their clothes got more theatrical and the hair got bigger, and by 1987's *Bad Animals* album, the glam reboot was complete. Like Aerosmith they also benefited from a revolving door of co-writers, from Bernie Taupin to Diane Warren. In truth, while tracks like 'There's the Girl' rock, the band weren't really glam metal in any sense beyond aesthetics – but in 'Alone' they pushed the power ballad to its ultimate extremes. 'Alone' is a far more interesting track than its long afterlife as a karaoke staple suggests. Written four years earlier by the band i-Ten, in Heart's hands the gender switch pushes it into unconventional territory for a rock ballad – a woman pursuing a man (rather than vice versa), with a female protagonist who's previously been happily single. The original has a ponderous quality, with Heart's version cutting several lines and rearranging the track significantly into a genuine piece of high drama. It's borderline ridiculous, obviously – by the point in the video where Nancy Wilson is riding a black horse through a deserted forest and they're onto their third piano you pretty much give up trying to follow the narrative – but there's nothing wrong with that.

In truth, while they were more successful than at any time previously, Heart never looked entirely comfortable through the glam era – as credible musicians steeped in folk, the towering stilettos, dry-ice-heavy videos and exploding pianos of their second wave seemed like a poor fit. Rumours abounded of Ann's ballooning weight and various tricks of art direction used to make her appear thinner in videos and press shots. 'It's pretty funny when you see that stuff now,' said Nancy in a 2000 retrospective. 'It's like "god, my hair was tall, my clothes were *tight*!" My feet hurt just looking at those videos now.' Nancy comes across as one of the few people in glam who took the end of their time at the top with a degree of equanimity. 'Thank god for grunge, man. It kicked the whole thing … it cleared the decks.'[3]

3. *Top Ten Stadium Rock*, Channel 4, February 19, 2000.

That reckoning was several years away though. Since their bleak hiatus in Holland two years earlier, Def Leppard had been through a transformative creative and technical experience. At that point they were drifting, with a basic framework of demos and some song titles, but no producer. To a large degree, they were defined purely in opposition – they knew that they didn't just want the album to be a conventional follow-up to *Pyromania*, and that they didn't just want a retread of the sound that they had perfected. In their absence, the ground had shifted – the stadium-sized status and pop perfection they had tried to bring to metal back in 1983 was now relatively commonplace. The bands that they had listened to as teenagers had now revitalised themselves by moving towards the sound and style conceived by Def Leppard while bands who barely existed back in 1983 were now selling out the stadiums that Def Leppard had aimed for. In the year of *Pyromania*'s release, Donington's Monsters of Rock festival had been headlined by ZZ Top, Meat Loaf and a pre-makeover Whitesnake. By 1986, Leppard had joined the bill alongside a now-glam Ozzy, Scorpions, spoof glam band Bad News and Germany's Warlock. Warlock deserve a special mention for 1986's *True as Steel* and 1987's more polished follow-up *Triumph and Agony*, which yielded the single 'All We Are'. Fronted by Doro Pesch, they were the first female fronted band to appear on the Monsters of Rock bill.

The only non-glam outliers that day were Motörhead, but as a band they operated outside of fashion, taste or critical consensus for their entire career, and everyone loved them regardless.

It was clear from the outset that for Def Leppard to maintain their relevance and primacy, a radically different approach was going to be required to record the band following Allen's car accident. With just one arm, he was unable to tie his own shoelaces or cut a loaf of bread. Even standing up was difficult as his body's weight and balance was thrown out. While still bedridden, he had begun to explore how much of his drumming rhythms could be transferred from his arms to his feet, repeatedly listening to his favourite albums on a stereo system brought in by his brother, while tapping out patterns on a block of foam rubber placed in the foot of his bed by nurses to stop him sliding down. 'Perseverance. I guess that would be the biggest thing I learned about myself. But I suppose that had a lot to do with the strength of those around me. They really didn't give me a choice; I had to stick around and deal with it.'[4] Even once Allen had realised that technology and a new technique could largely replicate his previous style, the immediate impact was to remove a degree of spontaneity from the process. 'It was frustrating for me, as it still is, in that I can't play

4. https://www.moderndrummer.com/2011/12/def-leppards-rick-allen-per-severance/

what I think in my head anymore. I have to be more thoughtful about what I do. It used to be that I could pretty much play whatever came into my head. But now, it's slightly different. I have to think ahead a lot more about what I'm doing.'[5]

A mini tour throughout 1986 had seen Allen's electronic kit augmented by a second regular kit played by Jeff Rich, then with Status Quo, until a tiny pub gig in Waterford saw them faced with a stage too small to fit two drummers on. Allen took the plunge and played the full set alone, with the Donington show on August 16 being Leppard's full-scale return to public performance. During the band's cover of Creedence Clearwater Revival's 'Travelin' Band', Joe Elliott announced his drummer to a rapturous response from the crowd.

> My mum and dad were on the left side of the stage, plus there were all these people in the wings going absolutely apeshit, and I was sitting there crying all over my pads! I was thinking, 'Hell, I'm going to get an electric shock or something!' But I felt a lot of respect at that moment, not just from the audience, but from everyone connected with the band, because they were all watching me – checking me out. That day was unbelievable. For me, that confirmed that people were really behind me and wanted me to succeed. It was so exciting – a brilliant high point for me. I'll never forget that show.[6]

5. Ibid.
6. https://www.moderndrummer.com/2011/12/def-leppards-rick-allen-perseverance/

The rest of the band also began to approach their instruments and the recording process in a completely new way. 'The idea was that this record was not gonna come out until it was an absolute bona fide classic record,' Elliott told VH1, as the band aimed to create an album which would stand as glam metal's hit-packed equivalent of Michael Jackson's *Thriller*, but would also sound quite unlike any other piece of music recorded previously. 'We wanted to create *Star Wars* for the ears,'[7] said Phil Collen. The studio process became a laborious exercise, with countless layers of sound and individual notes being composited together more in line with the process which would become commonplace in house music, or in the densely layered sample-based side of Nineties' 'turntablism' embodied by DJ Shadow's *Entroducing* album. By the time of *Hysteria*'s release, Def Leppard were in the hole for close to 5 million dollars. The tepid performance of lead single 'W.O.M.E.N.' did little to suggest that Mercury would be seeing any return on its investment.

Essentially, *Hysteria* is a simulacrum of Def Leppard's sound. The guitars were recorded on small Rockman amplifiers as a clean signal, then processed, put together and built into singing banks of polyphonic sound by Lange during his five-month mixing session using the Solid State Logic (SSL) desk. The drums

7. https://www.guitarplayer.com/players/def-leppards-phil-collen-reflects-on-30-years-of-hysteria-on-no-guitar-is-safe-podcast

were played live, but then recorded as individual samples, slowed down to alter their tone and then fed through the Fairlight CMI synth workstation. Structures were pulled apart and rearranged so that songs would resolve in completely different ways to that first intended. Music was washed in layers of reverb and filtered through noise gates. What was essentially presented back to Def Leppard at the end of Lange's process was them, but not them. It was human, but somehow artificial. It sounded more like Def Leppard than the band themselves could have done. *Hysteria* is like glam metal's version of Magritte's 1929 painting, *The Treachery of Images*; the simple drawing of a pipe accompanied by the instruction that *Ceci n'est pas une pipe*. When you listened to *Hysteria*, you were engaging with an album that looked like Def Leppard, and sounded like Def Leppard, but in some crucial sense *wasn't* Def Leppard. The challenge for the band was then to learn how to recreate its intricate textures and polished surfaces on a vast live tour, which would turn them into the biggest metal band on earth. If *Slippery When Wet* had opened up glam metal to a female audience, *Hysteria* kept those new fans and brought swathes of new ones on board.

To date, sales of *Hysteria* have exceeded 25 million copies, while the tour similarly pushed the boundaries of what was technically considered possible. Def Leppard's manager Peter Mensch had seen Frank Sinatra

play 'in the round' at Madison Square Garden and suggested to the band that they replicate the structure
of that show. The eventual construction saw Allen's
kit built onto a revolving floor and mirrored panels
deflecting lasers around the auditorium, while thirty-
two tons of equipment were rigged into the ceiling
above the band each night and transported by eight
trucks between each date. 'It's like playing in four theatres at once,' explained Elliott in a promo video while
showing off the four front rows that this set-up gave
them. 'So you get a theatre atmosphere, within an
arena.' Pre-show, the stage set was hidden from view
by giant black scrims with the *Hysteria* artwork on,
which – after the 'Feel lucky, punk?' speech from *Dirty
Harry* had finished echoing around the arena – would
drop away at showtime to reveal the structure and the
band scattering to the four corners of the stage.

As a technical and theatrical construction it exceeded
even Iron Maiden's vast productions of that decade
(the *Powerslave* and *Somewhere in Time* tours involved
particularly ground-breaking stage sets), and audiences
responded in droves. The tour would eventually run
for over sixteen months, starting in the Netherlands
and ending in Tacoma, Washington, travelling via the
UK, Europe, Central America, Scandinavia and Japan
plus multiple legs in north America. There was still
a disparity in their popularity on both sides of the
Atlantic – their UK dates were generally in theatres

rather than stadiums – but this was Def Leppard's imperial phase. With support throughout the tour from Cinderella, Tesla, Europe, LA Guns, Queensrÿche, Loverboy and the McAuley Schenker Group (featuring former UFO and Scorpions guitarist Michael Schenker), this was a perfect snapshot of the cream of the glam metal scene in 1987. Elliott's mission to prove that his band's music could work on the same scale as *Thriller* was an unqualified success and the standard bearer for what glam had become commercially. A music which just a few years earlier had been the preserve of penniless delinquents cadging money off strippers and terrifying Congress was now the sound of mainstream America.

However, an undercurrent was stirring. On July 21, as Def Leppard recharged between dates in Holland and Ireland, Dio released their fourth album, *Dream Evil*, and glam journeymen Lion (who a year earlier had performed the theme song of the *Transformers* animated film) released their *Dangerous Attraction* album. But the most significant album released that day was the end result of Guns n' Roses' troubled, fitfully productive existence since *Live ?!*@ Like a Suicide*. For seven months, the band had burned through their advance money, trashed various rental houses and tried out numerous producers before Alan Niven and Tom Zutaut had put them in the studio with Mike Clink. The first session yielded 'Shadow of Your Love', a version of which dated back to the band's prehistory as Hollywood Rose. While the track wouldn't make it onto the main version of their album (it eventually surfaced on Japanese EP *Live from the Jungle* and on a later deluxe edition of their debut), it marked a point where the band's sound aligned with a producer's abilities. 'When we listened back, it was all there,' wrote Slash. 'It was just us, but refined; Clink had captured the essence of Guns n' Roses. Finally all systems were go. We'd spent seven months in limbo, barely playing and intermittently recording with producers who weren't right. It felt like an eternity; because of the way we lived, a few months would have decimated a lesser band.'[8]

Clink's career went back to the late Seventies where he had started as an engineer at Record Plant studios in LA, working on albums by Heart, REO Speedwagon and – particularly piquing Slash's interest – UFO, a British band first formed in 1968 and whose influence far outstripped their commercial success. A sometime vehicle for German guitarist Michael Schenker, the band existed parallel to several scenes – Seventies' blues rock, the New Wave of British Heavy Metal, the LA metal scene, punk – never quite fitting with any of them. Their superb live performances and twin-guitar attack shaped the sound of Iron Maiden, Thin Lizzy, Guns n' Roses and later acts like Queens of the Stone

---

8. *Slash: The Autobiography*, p. 166.

Age. Signature track 'Doctor Doctor' is still played as the entry music before all Iron Maiden gigs to this day.

Once in the studio with Guns n' Roses, Clink proved to be an amiable, unobtrusive presence. Liberated and inspired, the band started not just to record the demo versions of their debut album's tracks, but also to write material which would eventually crop up on their next (versions of 'You Could Be Mine' and 'Perfect Crime' date back to these sessions). Clink suggested minor rearrangements and tightened certain performances (the original demo of 'Welcome to the Jungle' is noticeably slower and looser than the version eventually released), 'but aside from that, all of those songs were captured how they were in one or two takes. It's a testament to how well things were going in the studio and how great a mood we were in.'

Holed up in Rumbo Studios and living in a rented apartment complex, the band spent their downtime wrecking their living quarters and starting fights in the bars of Canonga Park, a suburban valley neighbourhood far from their usual territory. But of more pressing concern was the issue of Slash's guitars: having hocked most of his decent gear for drug money or failed to return loan kit to companies, he was attempting to perfect the sound needed for the band's debut album with a selection of Jackson and BC Rich guitars.

9. *Slash: The Autobiography*, p. 167.

'I had a huge issue. My guitar sounded like shit coming through the soundboard of a real studio.'[10]

The guitar issue is significant. The BC Rich, more than any other, had been the signature guitar of glam metal. Through the Seventies, the brand had been known for producing high-end small runs of bespoke instruments in mildly unconventional shapes, with their popularity growing after Aerosmith's Joe Perry began playing one. But the Eighties saw them push the design envelope aggressively: ten-string models, custom paint jobs and increasingly unconventional shapes were the norm. Reverse headstocks, spiky silhouettes and novelty were the order of the day, as they became the instrument of choice for Blackie Lawless, Lita Ford, Nikki Sixx and Traci Guns. Warrant's Joey Allen had a double neck model, while Poison's C. C. DeVille played one with a body shaped like a grinning skull. But on Guns n' Roses' final day at Rumbo, Alan Niven presented Slash with a handmade replica of a 1959 Gibson Les Paul, made by Jim Foot of Guitar Works in Redondo Beach. No pickguard, two pickups, a design unchanged since before The Beatles, a flame-top finish, a solid, weighty instrument. No frills. This was the anti-BC Rich. 'The depth of the guitar's tone and the crunch of the amp come together. It just sounded *amazing*.'[11] It also set Slash apart visually, toting this

10. Ibid., p. 168.
11. Ibid., p. 174.

guitar rather than something in neon pink with a reverse headstock and angular points. It was something more serious, an anti-fun instrument. This reversion to tradition extended through the final mixing process, which in contrast to *Hysteria* was done manually on an old analogue console at Media Sound in New York.

Before the album's release, the band's management brought them to London for three shows at the Marquee, a small, historically significant club in Soho where the audience included Ian Astbury of The Cult (another band who had absorbed the prevailing trends of glam metal and reinvented themselves from a semi-cosmic post-punk band into a stadium boogie act. Astbury would book Guns n' Roses as the support for their own *Electric* tour that year). 'Those shows went over well enough that, from the start, we were never even considered part of the same league of LA hair metal bands who had come through England,' said Slash. 'We were seen as something else, which was what we'd been saying all along. Finally, it felt like we'd been justified.'[12] Every subsequent move by the band seems a conscious antagonism, a way to peel them further away from the scene around them: the original cover art was to be a Robert Williams cartoon of a giant sword-handed being leaping over a fence to attack a robot that is lurking over the body of a recently raped young woman. Faced with a wave

12. Ibid., p. 185.

of revulsion, censorship and commercial boycotts, the Williams illustration was moved to the inside cover while the outside became a painting of the five band members rendered as long-haired skulls and arranged on a cross. On the band's next trip to England a few months later, the band sat down with metal TV show *The Power Hour*. 'We didn't fit in when the band first started. We didn't fit in ever. There was LA, then there was the five of us just … crawling around in the dark,' said Slash. 'It's one of those places, it's real trendy, it goes through fads. It was hard to say we were an LA band. We were never like that – we were just us, so we really stuck out compared to everything else. I was surprised we went as big as we did, but it's just because we were really real, and people pick up on that.'

The album *Appetite for Destruction* was released on July 21, 1987 to scant response. Heart's 'Alone' was enjoying its second week of three at number 1. Just a month earlier, the top of the Billboard album charts had seen U2's *The Joshua Tree* at number 1, followed by Whitesnake, Bon Jovi, Poison, Mötley Crüe and Ozzy Osbourne. But despite metal being at a commercial high watermark, by the close of summer, *Appetite* had shifted just 200,000 copies. 'Nobody in America wanted to know about them,' said Zutaut in 2016. 'People just wanted them to disappear.'[13] The label's

13. https://www.udiscovermusic.com/stories/welcome-jungle-video-guns-n-roses/

press ads grouped them together to share a page with Tesla and their *Mechanical Resonance* album ('Two knock-out albums for August'). The band weren't getting the crucial MTV coverage, supposedly because the station was worried about being dropped from media titan John Malone's cable systems if they did so. The band's label boss David Geffen eventually intervened personally, calling MTV and brokering a deal by which the video for 'Welcome to the Jungle' would be played once, at 1 a.m. LA time on September 28, the day before the band began a European tour with Faster Pussycat ('One of those bands we hated from LA; they were exactly the kind of people we tried to avoid,'[14] said Slash).

The video had been shot over two days. The outdoor scenes were set on La Brea, intercut with live footage shot in Dale Gloria's Scream Club inside the Park Plaza Hotel. The video is a semi-autobiographical retelling of Rose's arrival in LA. Stepping off the bus, fresh-faced and lank haired, he's chewing an ear of corn and is immediately hassled by some sort of generic street low-life as he disembarks. Slash's descending guitar riff is an opening theme, but to a horrifyingly graphic news bulletin – the notes drip in delay, picking out a rhythm like gunfire before a rising siren picks up behind them. As this sonic alert sounds, the on-screen Axl is plunged into a *Clockwork*

14. *Slash: The Autobiography*, p. 205.

Orange-type existence – straitjacketed and absorbing multiple screens broadcasting police brutality and ultraviolence. Images flash past of street drunks, raised weapons, dead-eyed groupies and drug paralysis. When the band do appear there are no synchronised dance steps or jumps from the drum risers.

They look palpably dirty – people dragging themselves from dosshouses to brothels, ignoring a creeping AIDS panic while Slash was so riddled with STDs that he couldn't sleep comfortably on his stomach. '[AIDS] started a strange hysteria among rock musicians,' said Slash. 'Everyone was alarmed but most of us felt immune to the whole thing. We figured that no one needed to worry about it until Dave Lee Roth got it.'[15] It's a life where you wear make-up to cover up bruises and lesions, not to look feminine or glamorous.[16]

---

15. Ibid., p. 207.
16. Despite the bands' reported lifestyles, the AIDS epidemic largely bypassed glam metal. The most notable exception was Ratt guitarist Robbin Crosby who died in 2002. Crosby had originally left the group in 1991 after a Japanese tour. He was heavily addicted to drugs at this point, and in 1994 was diagnosed as HIV positive, having been tested while suffering from other drug-induced maladies. He didn't make his diagnosis public, and went into a depression and even more serious drug use. 'It's cost me my career, my fortune, basically my sex life when I found out I was HIV positive,' he told VH1 when interviewed in 1991 for *Behind the Music*. Around 2001 his health had worsened with prolonged hospital stays required as he developed compound conditions: surgery for back pain revealed osteomyelitis, with layers of infectious fluid pooled around his bones starving them of oxygen. Towards the end of his life, Crosby weighed 400 pounds (180 kilos), ballooning in size due to a pancreatic condition. 'Apparently my pancreas has given up and I'm not metabolising

As the video concludes, Axl has undergone a full glam metal transformation – his hair is backcombed out and he now smiles impassively at the violence on the screens rather than struggling against it. The message is that the scene coming out of LA might advertise itself as a non-stop party, but it's grounded in squalor and social dysfunction. The trappings that other bands were wearing as badges of success are repurposed by Guns n' Roses as signs of damage.

In this reading, Guns n' Roses were offering a far more honest portrayal of not just where they were, but where they had come from and where America was. The penniless, stripper-supported world of LA

food the way I should,' he explained prior to his death. 'It's real frustrating … I have a roommate that probably weighs 150 pounds and he eats a lot more than I do. It's not like I'm a pig or a slob.' In the spring of the following year he was dead, aged just forty-two, from a heroin overdose and pneumonia with complications from AIDS. In 2017, journal extracts were published on *All That Shreds* by Curt Dudley, claiming to be a personal account of Crosby's last few years and painting a bleak picture of the guitarist in his final months, pawning his guitars, borrowing money and back on drugs. On one of his last visits, Dudley claims to have found Crosby bedridden in a trash-filled apartment, half-naked and with open sores on his legs. On publication, Ratt's Stephen Pearcy took to Twitter to denounce this account as 'all BS'. 'Everybody had their different substances intake, and his just happened to be everything,' said Pearcy in an interview with *Classic Rock Revisited*. 'The one that got him was AIDS and people should be aware that dirty needles, if you choose to go that way, don't work and sex, throw a rubber on it and be careful and then party and everything else is cool. The guy was king in our eyes, he was Robbin, he was our leader, and he was my right hand man. It was terrible, it was just bad all the way around. He is a soldier we lost in the rock and roll war. He was not the first and I'm sure he will not be the last.' Drummer Bobby Blotzer posted his own tribute on the band's website: 'Never once did any of us hear [Crosby] complain about his situation. The man was put thru hell and never … ever bitched about it.'

was eulogised by many bands, but in Slash's telling it was something altogether grimmer, with runaways and dropouts vulnerable to overdose and exploitation. In his memoir, he recounts a strange Ballardian upbringing in the city with the children of late-Sixties' burnouts roaming a half-developed metropolis on their bikes, largely untroubled by parental supervision or oversight. Drummer Steven Adler recalled the LA music scene of the early Eighties and how it treated 'a cute little boy hanging out with older people', especially when those older people could supply drugs.

The next thing you know, you're completely baked, they're touching you all over and you don't know what the fuck's going on. All you know is that orgasm feels good. Anybody can make you come, and in that state, I didn't have the presence of mind to give a damn. I was used, abused, whatever. Let's get high, let's party. One time I was walking along Santa Monica Boulevard and ran into two clean-cut guys who must have been in their twenties. We started talking and they said they had some bitchin' weed back at their pad so I went with them to smoke. We arrived at this dumpy little apartment and there was another guy there, only he was in his forties, a completely scruff-looking loser. Right away, I felt uneasy. I'll spare you the details, but they hurt me pretty badly. Part of my mind just kind of shut down, and that day my reality became a bad dream. They didn't beat me up but they did everything else and it was pretty devastating. I was just fourteen at the time.[17]

Axl summed up the feel of the album to *LA Weekly* as 'depressing'. Everything about 'Welcome to the Jungle' spoke to that experience, and that loss of control, captured in Axl's closing, wounded screech.

That was the reality of life for the band and many others, and their sound, demeanour and imagery were the product of that. And the response to this single play of the video was instantaneous. By the end of 1988, the album would have sold 6 million copies and would go on to become the best-selling debut of all time. Even with over thirty years distance, *Appetite for Destruction* remains a stunning piece of work. Mike Clink's production captured all the taut menace of the band's demos and tightened the screws, so everything sounds constricted and each song filled to bursting point. The production throbs like a headache – Steven Adler's cowbell pings and rattles, while Axl Rose's voice is double tracked between his lead line and a high-pitched nasal whine, like pressurised gas escaping from a boiler. Slash and Izzy Stradlin's guitars suck up influences and tones from the past – Keith Richards' chopping chords, Billy Gibbons' squealing harmonics, Thin Lizzy and UFO's harmonies, Motörhead's rhythmic attack, Aerosmith's pervy bar-band swagger – and push them together into an unstoppable sonic attack. It's like watching a garbage compactor press-

17. Jon Wiederhorn and Katherine Turman, *Louder Than Hell: The Definitive Oral History of Metal* (Igniter, 2013), p. 129.

ing together decades of hard rock's sonic calling-cards and pushing them out in a dense, reeking block of pure matter. There are no ballads – women are there to be used, or have their decline dispassionately documented. The nearest the band come to any real sentimentality is on 'Sweet Child O' Mine' and 'Think About You'; but in each case the woman in question functions as something that transports Rose to a time before he was damaged emotionally. Even the coda to 'Rocket Queen' that ends the album doesn't quite succeed as a conventional love song. Rose seems to be talking to himself more than addressing the woman in question and in the final reckoning, acknowledging that he's failed to communicate with her.

Appetite for Destruction is a remarkably bleak, malevolent record. While they were still signed to a major label and their image was traded on – the promo sleeve of the 'Welcome to the Jungle' single distributed to radio stations exhorted DJs to 'Play this record … and don't report it,' so as to keep it off the charts and maintain its underground status – the grimness around the band was entirely authentic. *Appetite for Destruction* has an intrinsically dark energy, like it was recorded over a bad ley-line. It's a long howl of rage by people unable to articulate any emotion but impotent fury. They hate mainstream society, but also hate the scene around themselves that they are supposed to be part of. But more than anything else, they hate themselves. The pay-off line to the album's sleeve notes at first reads like an insult, but is in fact a self-rebuke. 'With your bitch slap rapping and your cocaine tongue, you get nothing done.' In due course, that line would turn out to be remarkably prophetic. But for now, Guns n' Roses had created one of the biggest albums in history, and ripped open the scene that had finally achieved critical mass around them.

Chapter 6

When people who really hate glam metal think of glam metal, what they're most likely thinking of is Poison in 1988. Having unexpectedly hit paydirt with 4 million sales of their debut album, *Look What the Cat Dragged In*, the band's follow-up was a far bigger concern. Where the debut was recorded in twelve days, their second album would see the band's label Capitol bankroll proper studio time, and draft in a big name producer – Kiss' Paul Stanley was the first choice, but after he pulled out due to scheduling conflicts, he was replaced by Tom Werman, who had previously worked with Mötley Crüe, Ted Nugent and Cheap Trick. 'It was a real budget and we had real pre-production days,' recalled drummer Rikki Rockett. 'We were like "wow, this is how it really does work. It's not an independent record – everything is the real deal!"[1]

Lead single 'Nothin' But a Good Time' came out in April 1988 and reached number 6 on the singles charts. In the video, the band look slightly less extreme than they did in their first incarnation, but all their other characteristics remain intact: formation dancing; changes of guitar on every shot for C. C. DeVille; knee-slides towards the camera and studiously choreographed footwork. There's an aggravating, hyperactive quality to the band, a cartoonish bounce which quickly makes you feel like you're trapped on a bus with excitable children who've had too much sugar and additives. This mood was always there in Poison, but it was less apparent when they were penniless upstarts. Two years of actual money, adulation and success had pushed them to new levels.

The album was released on May 3 with strong MTV and radio play for the lead single, and follow-up 'Fallen Angel' and deathless ballad 'Every Rose Has Its Thorn': the latter was written by Michaels in a launderette after he realised during a phone call that his girlfriend was cheating on him when he heard a male voice in the background. The resulting track is a sort-of-country, sort-of-glam ballad that threads together a string of imagery from the American songbook – roses, thorns,

---

1. https://www.udiscovermusic.com/stories/poison-open-up-and-say-ahh-album/

cowboys, nights, dawns – into a remarkably bland end result. The rest of the album has little or nothing that sticks out – the production is flat, the guitar solos are weary, and, outside of the singles, the band frequently resort to a kind of musical water-treading. It's like an album made from spray-painted balsa wood. Even the cover is listless – a glamour model painted in a kind of tiger-stripe paws at the camera, while a foot-long tongue lolls from her mouth and her eyes give off all the natural spark and energy of someone who's just been woken up for work after a bad night's sleep.

Obviously, none of this dented its appeal in the slightest, with the album climbing to number 2 on the Billboard charts and eventually going five times Platinum in America. The band's popularity saw them support David Lee Roth on his tour in support of *Sky-scraper*, his second solo album. Roth was a far more intelligent, complicated proposition than Poison. Avoiding the obvious concerns of his peers, Roth's album was a strangely psychedelic, keyboard-heavy affair. There was enough to keep glam metal fans on board – in Steve Vai, Roth had one of the few guitarists in America who could outreach Eddie Van Halen on a technical and creative level – but Roth was capable of an ironic detachment that eluded most of his peers. In the video for 'Just Like Paradise', Roth (an accomplished extreme sportsman) is seen free climbing around Yosemite while he is lowered onto the stage in a giant boxing ring and Vai serenades him on a triple-neck, heart-shaped guitar. For the album launch, Roth's team built a twenty-eight-foot-high mountain on the top of Tower Records on Sunset Boulevard and populated it with bikini-clad, icepick-wielding 'climberettes', while the marching band from USC blocked off the road for an impromptu Roth-themed performance. 'Traffic backs up, no shit, for three-and-a-half miles. The cops go nuts, but they love it, 'cause this is why we're all in Hollywood anyway. As the band comes around the corner to the record store, I pop out of the top of the mountain and rappel upside down to one of the platforms, waving and yelling at people on the end of the rope. And the band played in the parking lot, pedestrians backed up for miles in every direction.'[2] Roth was operating on a level that dwarfed Poison: if the key leitmotif of mainstream glam metal was artifice, then it made sense to go as big as possible. A bit of pyro and some extraneous guitars wouldn't cut it – fake mountains, marching bands and gridlocked traffic were the order of the day.

However, the problem for the bands still pushing this cartoon-sized image of life was that Guns n' Roses' unexpected success had offered a far more compelling counterpoint as *Appetite for Destruction* continued to sell throughout 1988 (a nationwide tour with Aerosmith, a performance at the MTV Video Music Awards

2. David Lee Roth, *Crazy from the Heat* (Ebury, 2000), p. 263.

and the crossover success of the 'Sweet Child O' Mine' single all boosted the band's profile). In November, as sales of the album passed the 6 million mark, *Rolling Stone* magazine would put Guns n' Roses on the cover. The journalist found the band enraged and misfiring backstage in Detroit, hurling bottles and vases at each other while kicking holes in the walls, with their hands bleeding and bandaged from slamming into their guitars on stage. They saw them as standard bearers for a society of teenagers that *USA Today* had just reported on as fraying at the edges – one in seven had admitted to a suicide attempt, 50 per cent of girls said they found it hard to cope with stress and a third said they often felt sad or hopeless. 'Nothin' But a Good Time' was perhaps ringing a little hollow with them by now.

> Kids may idolize or envy David Lee Roth, but they have little in common with him. Guns n' Roses are young enough to remember what it was like to be seventeen: Slash and Steven are twenty-three; Duff, the only married band member, is twenty-four; Axl and Izzy are twenty-six. Axl remains obsessed with the contradictions of adolescence: the unfocused rage and pervasive doubt, the insecurity and cockiness, the horniness and fear. The Gunners' songs don't hide the fact that they're confused and screwed up.[3]

Slash spent the days drinking to steady his shaking

3. Rob Tannenbaum, 'The Hard Truth About Guns n' Roses', *Rolling Stone* (November 1988).

hands and bluntly admitted to being an alcoholic, but dependent on drink to lessen his social anxiety rather than as an aid to partying.

There was something profoundly bleak about the worldview Guns n' Roses represented. They seemed closer in spirit not to any of their metal peers or musical influences, but to the blank nihilism of much of the first wave of British punk, or the burned-out end to the Sixties that had seen the utopian dreams of liberty and pleasure sour into murderous neglect and exploitation. The unsupervised LA children of the Seventies who Slash would later detail in his memoir had grown up, struck out and were wreaking their vengeance on the society that had overlooked them. Meanwhile, back in the ground zero of glam metal, the *LA Times* was reporting 'a record high in gang killings' as the crack epidemic seeped through the city fuelling 'continuing rampages by the city's street gangs' and a 25 per cent jump in gang-related homicides from the year before. As much as Guns n' Roses' success was down to their musical prowess, they'd also articulated a fearful sense that things were falling apart in America's cities – the violence, poverty, sexual exploitation and chaos that they sketched out in their songs, imagery and the dysfunction around their entire operation resonated with an increasing number of people.

A similar sense runs through Penelope Spheeris' *The Decline of Western Civilization Part II: The Metal Years*, which was released in June 1988. Spheeris' film is an unguarded snapshot of the metal scene at that point. While a few old hands dial it up for the camera – Gene Simmons talks of 'Sex and rock 'n' roll, the American way!' while Paul Stanley reclines on a bed with multiple groupies – the recurring theme is of profound insecurity and the ever-present fear of failure. Up close, the stage clothes and props look cheap and grubby – when London try to set fire to a Russian flag before 'Russian Winter', it doesn't really catch alight, while Lizzy Borden's singer has a frazzled, mushroom-shaped helmet of hair, as though someone's rubbed a balloon all over him before pushing him out on stage. Desi Benjamin, a promoter, tells Spheeris that he doesn't want to 'work until I'm sixty and die poor at seventy with a fat wife bitching at me,' while another interviewee states that 'I want an apartment with carpeting on the floor.' Aerosmith detail being just eleven months drug-free, and are blunt about addiction having destroyed them financially. '[My money] went up my nose. I must have snorted half of Peru,' says Tyler. Ozzy Osbourne shuffles around his kitchen in a leopard skin robe, trying to make scrambled eggs and spilling orange juice as he pours it while detailing how previous managers had ripped him off. Odin parades around in his bottomless leather chaps and defiantly refuses to countenance Spheeris' suggestion that he maybe won't end up as big as Robert Plant. 'It's going to happen,' he states, firmly blurring the line between optimism and flat-out delusion. The women who dance in the competitions at Gazzari's On The Strip are holding out for the prize money that might enable a down payment on a condo.

Bleakest of all is Chris Holmes of W.A.S.P., filmed as he drifts listlessly on an inflatable chair in his pool at night, illuminated by the blue flicker of the underwater lights, brushing off the risk of AIDS while recounting sleeping with four groupies at a time. 'If you can tour one year, it'll take four years off your life.' He chugs vodka straight from the bottle, the clear liquid spilling over his chin while telling Spheeris that he drinks five pints of the spirit a day. 'I'm a happy camper!' The camera pulls out to a wide shot, revealing Holmes' mother, sitting in the shadows poolside gazing fearfully at her son as he slowly poisons himself in front of her. 'I'm a full-blown alcoholic.'

This tension between the good times and the bad, the comically oversized and the grimly realistic, was manifesting across glam metal's new releases in 1988. Winger were formed around classically trained musician and songwriter Kip Winger, who had already played for a couple of years in Alice Cooper's band as his bassist. Kip appeared to be strongly modelled on Jon Bon Jovi with a good-looking, toothsome quality bordering on the cheesy. Their self-titled debut album produced the two singles 'Seventeen' and 'Headed for a Heartbreak'. With hindsight, the lyrics of 'Seventeen' seem very much of their time, with their nudge-wink proposition to a female fan whose father (and indeed the law) regards her as being too young.

Winger would later defend the song's sentiment. 'I'm perfectly at peace with "Seventeen" and I'm happy that it makes people feel good. When I wrote that song, I didn't even know that seventeen was underage. I was just taking my cue from that Beatles' line … I was completely oblivious!'[4] For obvious reasons, the latter single is the one you hear more often these days. 'Headed For a Heartbreak' is a solidly epic ballad, but the banks of glassy Eighties' synths and epic orchestration make Heart's 'Alone' sound rough-edged and experimental by comparison. Perhaps unfairly, Winger's reputation as the *ne plus ultra* of the wimpy end of glam metal was cemented by Beavis and Butthead, Mike Judge's animated couch-bound video-critiquing metallers. While the lead characters wore t-shirts for AC/DC and Metallica respectively, their put-upon, soft-boy nemesis, Stewart, was forever advertising his love of Winger. The band's standing never recovered from his endorsement.

Vixen had first been seen in 1984's low-budget comedy *Hardbodies* ('California sizzles when older rich men chase "hardbodies" in this hilarious summertime comedy'), but had existed in various incarnations first in St Paul, Minnesota, then LA since 1981. Penelope Spheeris had interviewed them for *The Decline of West-*

4. CC Banana, 'Rewind With…', *Metal Sludge* (December 19, 2008).

ern Civilization the year before they were signed to EMI. Paired with top-drawer co-writers like Richard Marx and made over to look more glam metal, the band went gold with their self-titled debut album. It's unfair to paint Vixen as a record company confection who rode a trend – they'd slogged away at the bar circuit, and proved themselves a capable live band supporting the likes of Ozzy Osbourne, Scorpions and Aerosmith. Drummer Roxy Petrucci had previously been in Madam X, who briefly included a pre-Skid Row frontman Sebastian Bach, and whose 'We Reserve the Right to Rock' and 'High in High School' are moronic, youth-insurrection classics in the Twisted Sister mould. At Vixen's best – on tracks like 'Edge of a Broken Heart' – they were capable of punchy, radio-friendly rock. It was about as soft as glam metal could get, and in a musical climate that was if not actively hostile, then not especially accommodating towards women, they had far from an easy ride. A typical *Kerrang!* cover asked, 'Can Barbie dolls play heavy metal?' While the magazine's *Ladykillers* supplement offered 'the definitive guide to women in rock' illustrated with a pair of stocking clad, stiletto-wearing legs. In the videos of Poison, David Lee Roth and Mötley Crüe, women were largely there to pole dance, bring drinks to the table or have liquids sprayed at them.

Elsewhere, Vinnie Vincent Invasion also went the

soft path with *All Systems Go*, where Vincent's pyrotechnic guitar work reigned in on ponderous, pompous ballads like 'Love Kills' and 'That Time of Year'. Queensrÿche were pushing into fully conceptual territory with their *Operation: Mindcrime* album shedding almost all glam trappings apart from on odd tracks like 'I Don't Believe in Love'. Cinderella-offshoot Britny Fox's 'Girlschool' looked and sounded pure glam metal, which secured them a tour slot with Warrant and Poison, but with its preoccupation (both in the video and lyrics) with underage girls it tends not to get played much in public these days. Ratt's tour was a big glam draw with support from Great White, Warrant and Kix, but the album *Reach for the Sky* was uninspired – singles 'Way Cool Jr.' and 'I Want a Woman' had a bouncy, novelty quality to them which felt like a weak imitation of Poison's sound. The lack of a ballad also seemed like a commercial misstep by the band, although 'Don't Bite the Hand' and 'City to City' would both be used as theme tunes by wrestlers in subsequent years. Old hands like Quiet Riot and Anvil released forgettable, water-treading albums. Ozzy Osbourne's *No Rest for the Wicked* failed to live up to his era-defining work earlier in the decade (although he scored a hit alongside Lita Ford with the strangely spaced-out suicide ballad 'Close My Eyes Forever'). Cinderella's *Long Cold Winter* was a conscious attempt to move away from the glam metal template, with a stripped-down cover and an overall sound moving closer to the blues – both the Seventies' variety of Aerosmith ('Gypsy Road'), or a more timeless bottle-necks-and-steel-guitars feel on tracks like 'Bad Seamstress Blues'. Showpiece ballad 'Don't Know What You've Got (Till It's Gone)' would become the band's biggest hit, but it never quite achieves lift-off. It plods rather than soars, and lacks the dim-witted everyman quality of 'Every Rose Has Its Thorn'. Maryland's Kix dated back through various iterations to the late Seventies, but 1988 saw them finally achieve critical mass with the ballad 'Don't Close Your Eyes', a step change from their harder rocking predecessor, 1985's *Midnite Dynamite* album. 'It became a formula,' said Kip Winger later in an MTV retrospective. 'You put out the rock song first to get your AOR base – then you did the ballad.'

A rare example of a band breaking the glam ballad template was Def Leppard, whose 'Love Bites' was a hangover single in 1988 from the previous year's *Hysteria*. The track has the same freeze-dried, mechanised feel as the rest of the album but sidesteps almost all of the clichés of the genre. There are no acoustic guitars, no orchestration, no choirs. The verse drifts past on a sequence of unfinished seventh chords, sparse, echoing percussion and trails of feedback. When the chorus eventually resolves into a singalong melody and walls of multi-layered vocals, the effect is like a huge wave breaking overhead. Def Leppard were probably the only band in metal who could have pulled this trick off at this point rather than just opting for the obvious route.

Where the wider world of metal was getting more interesting was around the edges – bands who were eschewing the ballads and mainstream appeal that the MTV template could provide. Thrash bands were evolving beyond punishing, visceral blasts of noise and stretching out into something more expansive – Metallica's *...And Justice for All* and Megadeth's *So Far, So Good... So What!* were a musical and lyrical leap beyond both bands' previous work. Living Colour were one of the few non-white hard rock bands, weaving elements of psychedelia and jazz progressions into their debut album, *Vivid*. Jane's Addiction brought an unashamed art-school sensibility to their major label debut, *Nothing's Shocking*, bypassing their Eighties' peers and reaching back to the spirit of the Velvet Underground, Can and Led Zeppelin. MTV had formalised its *Headbangers Ball* slot, assigning the show a regular host in the dubious form of Adam Curry: where previous *Heavy Metal Mania* host Dee Snider was the living embodiment of trashy cartoonish metal, Curry appeared exactly as what he was – essentially a random, clean-cut jock who had been given a box-fresh biker jacket to wear, had his hair puffed up into a leonine mane and been placed in the middle of an apocalyptic, industrial green-screen set. 'Adam was funny,' Rob Zombie of White Zombie later recalled for an MTV retrospective. 'He looked real comfortable in that leather jacket.'

The commercial blockbuster of the year was *New Jersey*, Bon Jovi's follow-up to *Slippery When Wet*. The album went to number 1 in the US, Canada, the UK and Australia. Five singles all went into the Billboard Top 10. It became the first American album to be officially released in the Soviet Union, via the state-owned Melodiya label. Musically, it's a ruthlessly exe-cuted, formidably accomplished album – but it never quite escapes the shadow of its predecessor. All the elements that drove *Slippery When Wet* are present – the atmosphere-building opening instrumental; Fair-bairn's radio-tooled production and Child's melodic handbrake turns; David Bryan's bouncing keyboard lines and breathy washes of synthesiser; the we-can-make-it ballads and the cowboy trimmings. 'Born to Be My Baby' tracks so close to the band's winning formula that it feels musically like a genetic hybrid of 'You Give Love a Bad Name' and 'Livin' on a Prayer'.

With its heritage-celebrating title, artwork spelling out their name in burnished metal as though they were a long-standing industrial institution and cus-tomised leather jackets emblazoned with the band's own name, there was an air of self-aggrandisement about the whole project. The pressure to replicate their previous album's success clearly weighed on the band – thirty-four original demos were edited down to the final twelve after Fairbairn got his babysitter to bring her friends to the studio and independently score all the tracks to work out which had the widest appeal. The commercial impact of the album is indisputable – it debuted at number 8 on the Billboard chart in the third week of September, before going to the number 1 spot a week later, eventually spending four weeks there. It went on to sell 7 million copies in the US and 5 million further copies overseas. Five singles from the album all went Top 10, with 'Bad Medicine' and 'I'll Be There for You' both reaching number 1. But its legacy is dwarfed by that of *Slippery When Wet*: where that album felt like an establishment of a new paradigm, *New Jersey* felt like an exercise in reinforcing that normality, albeit an extremely accomplished one. *Slippery When Wet* could only have been made by Bon Jovi – *New Jersey* could have been the work of any number of bands operating out of Little Mountain.

The polar opposite of *New Jersey* was to be found with Guns n' Roses. On September 7 the band won Best New Artist in a Video at the MTV Video Music Awards for 'Welcome to the Jungle', then later that month, fourteen months after *Appetite for Destruction*'s release, the album finally went to the top of the Billboard charts. By this point, the band were defining themselves in direct opposition to the scene that had birthed them. 'All we ever cared to do was top the bullshit hair metal bands that enjoyed undue success for their subpar existence,'[5] said Slash. On October 24 they appeared on *Headbangers Ball* and ended the show by destroying the set around guest host Adam Smash. Anxious to capitalise on the band's long-awaited commercial momentum, Tom Zutaut suggested rush-releasing a mini-album comprising the hard-to-find *Live Like a Suicide* EP on one side, and four acoustic tracks on the b-side (three new compositions, and a slowed-down version of 'You're Crazy' from *Appetite for Destruction*).

G N' R Lies was a commercial success (they were the only band of the decade to have two albums in the Billboard Top 5 simultaneously) but also reframed Guns n' Roses aesthetically. 'Patience' was released as a single, a tender, melancholy and unguarded ballad. The band who seemed to have spent their preceding five years using women for money, food and sexual gratification now talking in simple terms about waiting around for the time to be right with a woman you love, knuckling down and riding out the peaks and troughs of a relationship and trusting that things will come good eventually. It's a surprisingly mundane sentiment for such an unhinged band to be espousing, but it's one that, while rarely detailed in song, is the frequent reality of mature, long-term relationships.

5. Slash with Bozza, p. 237

Hang in there and we'll get through it. Musically, it avoided the most common calling cards of the metal ballad – there are no synthetic choirs, soaring strings, crashing piano chords or elaborate guitar solos. In reality, the song is barely more than a demo – a pair of acoustic guitars, Axl's voice and some backing harmonies over the coda. It has an intimate quality reminiscent of *Hitchhiker*, Neil Young's long-shelved album from 1976, which his record company knocked back on account of its unfinished feel. Throughout 'Patience' you can hear the bright clip of the plectrum against the steel guitar strings, and the breathy, sibilant quality of Axl Rose's voice. Despite its simplicity, listening to the track is a strangely intimate experience. It's got an enveloping quality, and a vulnerability to it both in the lyrics and their delivery.

The two middle tracks were more disposable – 'I Used to Love Her' a semi-joke, deliberately controversial track apparently about murdering a nagging wife, but with a dog as the actual subject of the lyric. Following straight on from 'Patience', the effect is a bit like hearing a pianist allowing the final notes of a concerto to ring out, before letting rip with a room-clearing belch. The acoustic version of 'You're Crazy' works better, the lazy tempo and stripped back instrumentation dialling up the track's inherent menace, and repositioning the lyrics so that the person Rose is denouncing is most likely himself.

The spirit of Neil Young looms again over the final track, 'One in a Million', this time the apocalyptic, paranoid tenor of 1974's *On the Beach* album. Over an acoustic guitar's strummed chords a second guitar comes in and replaces the whistled introduction, a cheap, distorted lead line buzzing like a wasp trapped inside a lampshade. Again, Rose's lyrics turn back on himself, denouncing the laziness, mental instability and misplaced value judgements that guided his decisions and lifestyle. By his own telling, he's not evil, not a pantomime villain, but something more troubling – amoral, closed down and switched off to consequences. However, this theme of the song was completely obscured by the second and fourth verses, which railed in turn against 'police', 'n*ggers', 'immigrants' and 'f*ggots'. The song trades in the most base stereotypes and imagery, linking minorities with criminality, disease, being fifth columnists and not speaking the language. The sensation of hearing the specific words is shocking, but the sentiment is anything but – it's the most tired, pub-bore bigotry, with a privileged, world-famous rockstar recasting himself as a thin-skinned victim and expressing his worldview in terms which would have seemed lazily predictable coming from a third-rate club comedian a decade earlier.

Collectively, the band have never really accounted for the sentiments behind 'One in a Million', claiming at various times that it was a reclamation of the word 'n*gger', a response to incidents of physical attack in Rose's personal life, a deliberate attempt at taboo busting or a wilful attempt at being offensive. Defenders pointed to Slash's mixed-race heritage and Rose's professional and personal friendships with the likes of David Geffen and Elton John. In the final reckoning, those verses were an epic piece of self-sabotage by Rose: the acclaim afforded to Kurt Cobain a few years later when he shifted Nirvana to a stripped-down sound for the band's *MTV Unplugged* performance could and should have been Rose's, but the controversy around those few lyrics all but obliterated everything else on *G N' R Lies*. When faced with a chance to publicly excel, he sought a way to undermine himself and fulfil his belief that the world was stacked against him. In 2018, when the deluxe 'Locked n' Loaded' edition of *Appetite for Destruction* was released, it included everything from the band's recorded history and the Sound City sessions which went on to become *Appetite for Destruction*, along with other demos, cover versions, lithographs and a book of photographs. 'One in a Million' was quietly scrubbed from history and wasn't included on the release.

However, one incident would overshadow everything else that year, even 'One in a Million', for Guns n' Roses and metal in general. On the third Saturday in August, Castle Donington hosted the annual Monsters of Rock festival. As an overview of the year in metal it had a decent glam contingent – Kiss were second from the top of the bill, ahead of David Lee Roth. Also appearing were Megadeth, proggy German metallers Helloween and headliners Iron Maiden, then touring their *Seventh Son of a Seventh Son* album, with its arctic apocalypse-themed stage set. The line-up was considered the strongest since 1984's triple whammy of AC/DC, Van Halen and Ozzy Osbourne, and 107,000 spectators were expected at the racetrack venue. The weather had finally cleared after heavy rain in the days leading up to the event.

When the bill had been programmed, Guns n' Roses' position as the second act of the day made sense – for context, this had been the slot occupied by Cinderella the previous year, and joke act Bad News the year before that. However, in the interim period, 'Sweet Child O' Mine' had been released – a number 1 in the US, it had also gone to number 4 in Ireland and number 6 in the UK. By one estimate, 35,000 fans arrived to buy tickets on the day itself, swelling the crowd beyond the size of previous years. Despite the band's lowly position on the bill, in pre-gig interviews backstage Axl Rose was churlishly dismissive of his fellow performers. '[Iron Maiden] doesn't have anything to do with rock and roll as far as I'm concerned. What they do is what they do, I hope never to be like that. I hope it's not catching.'

As soon as the band's performance started, the crowd surged forwards in waves. On several occasions, Rose asked the audience to take a few steps backwards to relieve the pressure at the front of the stage. The situation was exacerbated by the wet conditions underfoot on account of the previous days' weather and the fact that the arena was arranged so that the ground was sloping down towards the stage. Empty cider bottles were refilled with urine by fans further back from the pit and hurled overhead, raining down on the band, security and fans alike. Warned by the stage management that a serious crowd control situation was developing, the band played 'Patience' and an improvised blues jam to slacken the pace, but as they followed on into 'Welcome to the Jungle' – preceded by Rose telling the crowd that 'I know this concert's survival of the fittest…' – the crowd surged again. As the band closed the set with the final notes of 'Sweet Child O' Mine' ringing out, Rose gave his parting shot over the PA: 'Don't kill yourselves.'

What none of the band knew was that two young men were already dead at that point. Eighteen-year-old Alan Dick and twenty-year-old Landon Peter Siggers had been pulled unconscious from the crowd, their bodies found beneath four inches of mud after thirty injured spectators had been removed from the crowd by security. 'At first I did not realise that they were people,' wrote head of security Mick Upton in his report into the incident. 'The pressure load on these two victims was such that we had to dig under them with our bare hands to turn them over. We managed to extract both of them from the mud but they appeared to us to be lifeless. Suddenly the band started to play again and crowd conditions made it impossible for us to examine them in any detail. We evacuated the victims to St John ambulancemen and they were removed to hospital. But they were found to be dead on arrival.'

A later coroner's inquest would record a verdict of accidental death, praising the efforts of the security team on the day and noting that 'Their efforts undoubtedly saved lives.' Future events were limited to 72,500 spectators, and it would be two years before Donington hosted another Monsters of Rock.

Nineteen-eighty-eight was a year of extremes. Glam metal's commercial dominance was complete, with bands scoring genuine crossover hits and drawing mainstream audiences to their shows, while older bands were reanimating in the wake of these younger acts' success. But beneath the hedonism, something grim was seeping out. However upbeat the likes of Bon Jovi sounded, violence, disease, paranoia and racism were all in the air and had manifested in the shape of Guns n' Roses. A year of huge commercial gains was ultimately overshadowed by bigoted doggerel and a day at a gig that had left young men dead and many others injured and traumatised. Music which just a few years earlier had been the preserve of penniless outsiders was now a huge commercial juggernaut and, as the lesser lights of *The Decline of Western Civ-*

ilization were finding out, if you weren't hitting the big time you were quickly left behind. In that sense, it couldn't have been more in tune with mainstream America. However much bands wanted to jump on the glam metal bandwagon, the contradictions inherent in the music were stretching it to breaking point. Something was going to give.

Chapter 7

1989: PUMP!

'"DEATH THREAT" OZZY SENT TO BOOZE CLINIC! BAN ON SEEING WIFE! HELL OF DRY-ING OUT!'

Uncommonly for Britain's biggest tabloid newspaper, the headline of the *Sun* actually downplayed rather than sensationalised the story that it was reporting at the start of September 1989. On Saturday the third, after recording an interview at Capital Radio (where the writer Mick Wall had found him 'a mess. Eyeballs popping out of his skull, his face a mask of sweat; his mind drifting in and out of conversation'[1]), Ozzy Osbourne and his wife/manager Sharon had returned to Beel House, their home in Amersham just outside

1. Mick Wall, *Appetite for Destruction* (Orion, 2010), p. 174.

of London, to celebrate their eldest daughter Aimee's sixth birthday. Ozzy was drinking heavily (Russian vodka, his drink of choice at that time) and an argument broke out between the couple over dinner. This continued and worsened until late in the evening when the singer attacked his wife, with her phoning for the police in fear of her life. Ozzy was arrested, and spent the following thirty-six hours at Amersham police station before a Monday morning appearance at Beaconsfield Magistrates Court. Bail was granted on the conditions that he check into a residential alcoholic rehabilitation programme, not attempt to contact his wife and not return to the family home. He was returned to Huntercombe Manor, an alcohol treatment facility where he had stayed on two occasions previously.

Osbourne had been drinking to 'blackout' point for a year previously. When interviewed for Sky One at the Moscow Music Peace Festival a few months earlier in July he was open about his proclivities and how they informed his lifestyle. 'I've got to be honest with you – if I was living here full time I'd be dead of alcoholism. Sniffing car tyres, anything to get out of it. No wonder there's such an alcohol problem here, there's nothing else to do.' The festival bill was put together by Doc McGhee, then manager of both Bon Jovi and Mötley Crüe, with a line-up including both bands, Osbourne, and McGhee's other charges Skid Row, Scorpions, Cinderella and local bands Brigada S and Gorky Park all appearing at Central Lenin Stadium.

The show was conceived by McGhee as a groundbreaking cultural expedition into the Eastern Bloc, a two-day show that would function as the Soviet Union's answer to Woodstock. However, it also operated as a kind of community service for McGhee, who on April 25 had walked away from court with a $15,000 fine and a five-year suspended prison term after the conclusion of a case dating back to 1982, when he had been arrested over the suspected smuggling of 40,000 pounds of marijuana from South America into the US. By the time the case came to court, he had built his legitimate career and business empire, and Jon Bon Jovi argued as a character witness that McGhee could contribute more to society with restorative action than with a jail term. 'A man with his knowledge and commitment to the music industry can do so much good as a public servant,' he wrote in a submission to the judge.[2]

With this in mind, the show was arranged quickly with proceeds due to go to the Make A Difference Foundation, McGhee's anti-substance addiction initiative, while also promoting drug abstinence in the Soviet Union.[3] Because of this, there was an imperative

2. https://ultimateclassicrock.com/doc-mcghee-convicted-marijuana/
3. A CIA report in October 1986 stated that while the scale of drug abuse in the Soviet Union was relatively small compared to that in America, the government was preparing to crack down on it aggressively. Widespread

on all performing artists to stay clean and sober for the duration of the trip, although the fact that Osbourne had already wet himself before the plane touched down behind the Iron Curtain suggests that this edict was being taken more seriously by some artists than others. 'It was all bad from the moment we stepped on the plane,' recalled Tommy Lee. 'There was a so-called doctor on board, who was plying the bands who weren't sober with whatever medicine they needed. It was clear that this was going to be a monumental festival of hypocrisy.'[4] Upon disembarking, Richie Sambora and Tom Kiefer both talked about being advised to bring their own toilet paper to a country still under the privations of Communism. For their first night in the city, all the bands had dinner not at any Russian restaurant, but at the local outpost of the Hard Rock Café, with Nikki Sixx confessing that he thought that the trip had been heading for Poland. 'The C chord in America is the same thing as the C chord in Russia or anywhere else. So this is a message from youth to youth, basically,' said Richie Sambora to an attending MTV film crew. Cinderella were somewhat less culturally sensitive on their pre-show jaunt around the city, gathering around an organ and knocking out an

drug use among Russian troops stationed in Afghanistan during the war of 1979–1989 had imported the habit back into the country, but particular concern was fuelled by its popularity among 'privileged youth from Russian ethnic backgrounds – the USSR's future leaders'.

4. *The Dirt*, p. 226.

impromptu version of 'Gypsy Road' in mocking, cod-Russian accents. The event was a mixed success for McGhee – while his bands were exposed to a vast new audience, clashing egos and arguments over running order led to Mötley Crüe's Nikki Sixx yelling that 'we didn't fly all the way to Russia to be an opening act while Bon Fucking Jovi gets to headline for an hour and a half' before cornering his manager backstage and knocking him over 'like a broken Weeble'.[5] The band fired McGhee shortly afterwards. One of the few positive outcomes of the festival was that it inspired Scorpions to write 'Wind of Change', the 1990 multi-million selling whistling-filled tribute to Glasnost, which was number 1 in countries across the continent.

Osbourne's own performance at the festival, with a band consisting of Tommy Aldridge, Zakk Wylde and his former Sabbath bassist Geezer Butler, was – as was commonplace at the time – an experience which he seemed only fitfully engaged with. The band themselves sounded tight and aggressive, honed by fourteen months prior touring – Wylde had followed Rhoads and Jake E. Lee in Osbourne's line of exceptional guitarists – while their frontman meandered around the beat and sporadically connected with the tune that he was aiming for.

Back in England, still drinking heavily, the pressures from the tour and Osbourne's own personal demons

5. Ibid., p. 227.

built until the domestic incident, which culminated in Osbourne coming to in a filthy police cell with human faeces on the walls and scratches all over his face. 'I'm a chronic alcoholic and I'm in a chronic phase … I suppose I was pissed and I took it a little too far and threatened to kill her,'[6] he said in the aftermath of the attack. His wife later recounted the flashpoint, where following their argument her husband came downstairs in his underpants, sat on the sofa opposite her, and said 'We've come to a decision – we're very sorry, but you're going to have to die, there's no other option,' before jumping on his wife, pinning her down with his full weight and trying to strangle her. She managed to press a panic alarm, and when she regained consciousness he was gone.

Osbourne painted a bleak picture of a life of touring – insane highs, followed by crashing periods of boredom, low-level resentment at his wife's work commitments (she was also managing the Quireboys and Lita Ford) and the added side effects of being injected with steroids to keep him physically able to perform. Underlying problems were exacerbated by a disconnection from his children who he could only see sporadically and an inability to relate to people who weren't in his bubble of touring. Drinking saw him terrifying his family, while withdrawing from alcohol would send him into spasms and seizures, and he fore-

6. *Appetite for Destruction*, p. 180.

saw an indefinite stay in the rehabilitation facility as his only immediate future. 'I just wanted to have a few drinks and mellow out,' he told Mick Wall. 'But I just go crazy with booze now. Today, when my children left me, that was enough for me to want to stop. They were all crying, looking out the back of the Range Rover, and my heart broke. And being in a place like this, it's kind of lonely, you know?' Sharon Osbourne dropped the case soon after, but the overall picture was dismal: one of the world's biggest metal stars, padding around a secure facility like a tranquilised circus animal, smoking out of the window to avoid the attention of the staff and climbing the walls with boredom.

As Ozzy was descending into the violent depths of alcoholism and addiction, Aerosmith were coming back the other way. The creative rebirth that had started with 1987's *Permanent Vacation* continued in 1989 with *Pump*. This was the band's tenth studio album and yet another product of Bruce Fairbairn's operation at Little Mountain Sound Studios. It shares many of the characteristics of the other hits coming out of there – primarily a sense of focus, energy and dogged pursuit of as many musical hooks as possible. Its overall sound is rougher-edged than that of *Permanent Vacation* and the songs more consistent.

The opening to the first track, 'Young Lust', foregoes Fairbairn's customary stage-setting introductory passage and flies straight into the first crashing chords, a skull-pounding drum tattoo and then the first chorus. Ravaged by years of drugs, in-fighting and – more importantly – underwhelming albums, Aerosmith didn't have the luxury of Bon Jovi of being able to tease and seduce the listener. They had far too much to prove, and whatever goodwill listeners might have had towards them probably evaporated somewhere around side one of 1982's *Rock in a Hard Place*. While *Permanent Vacation* was a good album with moments of genius that had partially rebuilt the band's reputation, Aerosmith were right to be insecure. They were now a decade older than most of their peer group, many of whom would have been fans of theirs originally but were now lapping them commercially. With *Pump*, Aerosmith had everything to prove.

As an album, *Pump* succeeds admirably in this mission. 'Young Lust' is crammed with ideas, working through pace changes, sudden stops, and moments when the band drop out and just leave Joe Perry's guitar whining away behind Steven Tyler's voice. At that moment, the bass tones are backed off completely, a high-pass filter leaving the guitar sounding like it's hissing out of a tiny practice amp. It's a strangely intimate moment, as though the tape has caught Perry and Tyler, reunited, somewhere back in time, sketching and jamming out a loose idea. Moments later, the full force of the band returns, but it's a brief glimpse behind the musical curtain: a way of saying that, for all the density and bombast of the studio, if you take everything away and strip Aerosmith down to their barest bones, this is what they do and this is how well they do it.

'Young Lust' ends and rather than the customary dead air between tracks there's only a second's breath before 'F.I.N.E.' begins. An audio cue that they need to get this out of themselves so badly that they can't even waste the three seconds of dead air and empty grooves in between the songs. The track begins with the guitars bending and grinding upwards through microtones, gradually working towards the starting pitch of the song, like a rock climber grasping for a fingerhold somewhere above them that will allow them to explosively pull themselves up. Again, the song is crammed to bursting point – horn sections, falsetto cries, muted, crunching chords that strum out the same rhythm as the drum breaks, and, behind the vocal bridge, the woozy glissando of a slide guitar playing long, languid notes that slowly drift across the song before the rhythm kicks back in and normal service is resumed. It's relentless, multi-layered and overflowing with ideas.

A brief vocal interlude precedes 'Love in an Elevator', a hoary old set-up skit that ends with Steven Tyler's rascally chuckle and a spiralling riff that mimics the sensation of elevators descending on their cables. While the album delivered six singles, this is probably the best known and seems to sum up where Steven

Tyler's head was at both lyrically and emotionally. Aerosmith are associated with double entendres, but there's nothing 'double' about most of the material here: 'Love in an Elevator' appears to be, as far as one can tell, about having sex in a department store elevator. The tracks are viscerally horny – they drip with references to lust, love, illicit sex, putting clothes back on, taking clothes off, oral sex, lingerie, condoms, masturbating with a noose, prostitutes (or, as Tyler terms them, 'ill-gotten booty'). The cover art depicted two trucks piled together as though one was mounting the other. Tyler told interviewers that, after years of his libido being wiped out by drug use, since getting clean he had dedicated himself to making up for lost time and he certainly seems mentally fixated on the pursuit of the opposite sex throughout in a way that would seem excessive in a man twenty years his junior, or even an unneutered stray dog. While other more serious concerns do occasionally intrude – 'Janie's Got a Gun' was an unexpectedly sombre closer to side one, dealing with the revenge killing of a father by his daughter after years of abuse – the pace and ferocity of the album barely relents.

Closer 'What it Takes' is a melancholy, beautifully constructed ballad again co-written by Desmond Child: with a video depicting a wild saloon bar fight and a lilting accordion playing throughout it strayed into the mega-selling area of modern country, and pointed to a potentially more grown-up future for the band. But *Pump* was overall a defiant reclaiming of territory by Aerosmith from all the younger bands who had imitated and outshone them for the preceding five years.

This was particularly apparent when considering the other new arrivals and new releases of the year. What had been a trickle, then a steady flow of glam metal releases, was now turning into a flood as record companies sought to cash in by either signing any band who might turn out to be the next Bon Jovi, or seeing which of the older artists on their roster could be given enough of a stylistic makeover so that they might benefit from some of the halo effect around glam. Alice Cooper's booze-impeded wilderness decade finally ended when he scored a worldwide hit with Desmond Child's co-write 'Poison' and its parent album, *Trash*. Danger Danger's 'Bang Bang' single (and the album of the same name) was popular on MTV and the band constantly seemed to be opening up for the likes of Alice Cooper, Warrant and Kiss, but it's featherweight pop with a superficial metal makeover. Pretty Boy Floyd's *Leather Boyz with Electrik Toyz* nodded back to Slade in terms of its spelling with a sleeve depicting the band as giants shooting a pyramid of lightning bolts down onto a night-time cityscape, but the music was a trashy, anaemic version of W.A.S.P.'s sound. France-to-LA transplants XYZ's *Inside Out* was produced by Don Dokken, but was an unmemorable plod through a range of glam clichés (dustbowl video, Dokken-alike vocals, tapping guitar solo); Bang Tango's 'Someone Like You' showcased frontman Joe Leste's voice – which ranged from a pompous croak to a Steven Tyler-scream – but would prove to be a one-hit wonder. Tesla had been around since 1981 but by 1989 aligned perfectly with prevailing trends on 'Love Song', a ballad denuded of almost all glam metal elements, and built around a ninety-second acoustic guitar introduction which sounded like the instrumental music that might play at a medieval re-enactment banquet, as the first suckling pig was carried in with an apple in its mouth and a dwarf in fool's motley danced a jig. Philadelphia's Britny Fox's second album *Boys in Heat* was, at its best, as good as AC/DC's most average material of the decade and after this album they would embark on a seemingly never-ending series of line-up changes. The most unfairly overlooked act of this crop were Vain, a vehicle for Bay Area producer-turned-vocalist Davy Vain whose *No Respect* album was a scrappy, attention-deficit session that channelled early Mötley Crüe and gained good critical reviews, but failed to generate much in the way of sales. The band were dropped by their label two years later.

One exception to this procession of ho-hum releases was Mötley Crüe themselves, whose *Dr Feelgood* album was a far more accomplished work than any of their previous releases. Coincidentally, it was recorded with

Bob Rock in Vancouver at exactly the same time that Aerosmith were creating *Pump* in the studio next door. Fresh from rehab, Mötley Crüe shared therapist Bob Timmons between themselves and Aerosmith, as the perfectionist Rock drilled them through a painstaking process to actually fulfil their potential as a band and capitalise on a period when drugs and alcohol weren't impeding their abilities. The end result – especially buzzsaw classic 'Kickstart My Heart' – was a powerful rejoinder to critics who saw Mötley Crüe as a triumph of theatrical style over musical substance. On October 3, Tommy Lee's twenty-seventh birthday, he received a fax from his bassist: 'HAPPY BIRTHDAY, TOMMY. YOU HAVE A NUMBER ONE ALBUM.'

However, one new release outclassed not just *Dr Feelgood*, but all of the other new releases in 1989 – the debut album from Skid Row. Founding guitarist Dave 'Snake' Sabo was a teenage friend of Jon Bon Jovi and had played in an early line-up of the band, making an uncredited appearance on the *New York Rocks* compilation version of 'Runaway' before Richie Sambora was recruited. Formed in 1986, the band largely came under the wing of Bon Jovi – their manager Doc McGhee also represented them and secured them a deal with Atlantic Records in 1988 which led to them working with producer Michael Wagener. Wagener was a German producer and mixer and a storied figure in glam metal: he produced White Lion, Warrant, Stryper, Dokken and Great White, and engineered German band Accept. He had mixed Mötley Crüe's *Too Fast for Love*, but was diverse enough to also work with much heavier bands, mixing Megadeth's *So Far, So Good... So What!* and Metallica's *Master of Puppets*. 'He was the dad overseeing a bunch of kids running around in the sandbox, making order out of chaos,' says Sabo. 'He was a huge factor in that record being what it is, because he extracted those performances out of us. They didn't just happen – they were pulled out of us by Michael. When we felt we were there, he'd go, "Well, it's close – but I know you've got one more in you that's better."'[7]

Under Wagener's production, Skid Row perfectly straddled the two diverging strains from glam metal. When they finally found Sebastian Bach (formerly of Kid Wikkid and Madam X) they had a pretty-to-the-point-of-feminine frontman with an octave-hopping voice and a fizzing sense of ill-disciplined chaos coming off him in waves. With 'I Remember You' the band proved that they could write radio-friendly, lighter-raising ballads which would transcend the confines of a metal audience as well as anyone. But the whole sound of the album was filled with ragged edges and surprisingly heavy playing. Bach was a huge fan

7. https://www.loudersound.com/features/the-story-of-skid-row-glamglamglam-metals-last-hurrah

of Rob Halford, and even on the softer tracks, where his voice goes up to its tonal limits, there's a screaming edge reminiscent of Judas Priest. Visually, the band downplayed their original look into something harder and less cartoonish. 'It was Jon Bon Jovi who saw our pictures,' says Bach of their original image.

> We did a photo session, and me and Snake and Rachel, we all had huge hair. Nobody's ever seen that photo session, but Jon Bon Jovi just freaked out and said, 'You guys can't look like this. It's ridiculous.' Jon was taking us on tour, so we left the hair spray at home. It made it a lot easier to get ready for a show. I remember being confused, because everybody else was like the Vinnie Vincent Invasion – glitter and the biggest hair and makeup and color, and Skid Row came out black-and-white. I remember saying, 'It looks like a mistake – you can't even see us. It's just, like, shadows.' But it was absolutely perfect. There was no wrong moves made with the first Skid Row record.[8]

The album endures as a classic – a self-mythologising riot that perfectly captures the ignorant exuberance that originally made glam metal fun, while binding it to something heavier and genuinely edgy. The screaming guitar tones and sense of swing around the drums hark back to Van Halen's golden era or Twisted Sister's best work. There's an element of social com-

8. https://archive.blabbermouth.net/news/sebastian-bach-says-jon-bon-jovi-thought-skid-row-looked-ridiculous-in-bands-first-photo-shoot/

ment to tracks like 'Youth Gone Wild' but it's seen entirely through a personal lens, and devoid of analysis or any bigger picture: it's just a snapshot of life's unfairness as it would be experienced by an unthinking adolescent with long hair and a surfeit of testosterone. The randy energy of 'Big Guns' and the chest-beating of 'Making a Mess' are genuinely exciting, but the track that truly elevated the band was '18 and Life'. Nominally a ballad, it opens up on a slowly picked out minor chord before Bach delivers a Springsteen-worthy tale of Ricky, a wayward youth who accidentally shoots a friend dead when drunk and is sentenced to life imprisonment as a result. The lyrics are curiously old-fashioned, steeped in the language of American misadventure, moral panics and historic delinquency – switchblades, gasoline, six-shots, the wild one. The imagery could have come from *West Side Story* or a James Dean film or a Raymond Chandler story.

However, the delinquent buzz that made Skid Row exciting and prevented them from being Winger or Cinderella came with its own dramas and challenges. The band were briefly kicked off the Bon Jovi tour on account of Bach's constant onstage profanity; he wore a t-shirt onstage and in a photo shoot bearing the legend *AIDS Kills Faggots Dead*. And, finally as the year ended, after being hit in the head with a bottle during a rendition of 'Piece of Me' at a show opening for Aerosmith at the Civic Centre in Springfield, Massachusetts, Bach hurled the item back into the crowd, breaking the nose of an innocent female fan. He then dived headlong into the pit, kicking another fan in the head before being dragged back out by security. Bach was arrested after the show, let out on $10,000 bail and later sentenced to three years on probation.

His personality was clearly an issue, but further friction arose on account of the mentor-cum-management relationship that Bon Jovi had originally had with them. Bach claims that his band's growing popularity – and better merchandise sales – led to tensions between the two throughout Jovi's 1989 tour on which Skid Row were the support act. A dressing down for Bach's onstage profanity reportedly culminated in Jovi telling the younger man 'I'll fucking own you', before things eventually came to a head at Rupp Arena in Kentucky. Bach claimed that he had been doused with freezing cold milk by Jovi's road crew seconds before he took the stage, leading to him verbally attacking the headliners from the stage (referring to the frontman as 'Bon Blow Me'). After the show, a sixty-strong group of Jovi's road crew and family came after Bach, throwing punches and threatening him. Accounts of the fracas vary, although Bach's contextualisation of it was unequivocal: 'Look, I'm a twenty-two-year-old fucking Metallica freak on speed. I'm psychotic. I can drink four bottles of whiskey before I go on stage. Jon is a thirty-one-year-old Bruce Springsteen fan with a fax machine. He gets pissed on one drink. Who do you think is gonna win a fight?'[9] Further damage was done to their relationship by a business dispute stemming from Jon Bon Jovi and Richie Sambora's ownership of much of Skid Row's publishing, the consequence of the deal the younger band originally signed to get them started in the industry. With their debut's unexpected success, what was originally seen as something akin to a consultancy fee soon multiplied into a significant fortune.[10] The deal was relaxed following the Rupp Arena incident, although a gagging order signed by Bach as part of the deal occluded the exact details, but it would be 2006 before Bach and Bon Jovi were fully reconciled after a surprise meeting at a London hotel bar where Bach was hanging out with Axl Rose.

At the time, the drama around Skid Row did them no harm at all – they were seen as a far cooler prospect than peers like Enuff Z'Nuff, with their rainbow tie-dye and peace-sign trousers. Every news story about Skid Row's chaotic gigs or baiting of their former mentors strengthened their image as a juvenile counterweight to the reinvention of artists old enough to be

9. https://www.loudersound.com/features/skid-row-it-didn-t-matter-what-we-did-it-wasn-t-our-time-anymore
10. 'Nobody thought that we would become a big band,' said Bach to French TV in 2012. 'That happens all the time in the music industry. Jon was like, "We'll take you on tour, but if you guys make it big," then he gets a cut of it. So I was bitter about that for a while, but then I realised that we probably wouldn't have made it as big, or maybe at all, if he didn't take us.' Sambora returned his share of the publishing to the band, while Bon Jovi kept his, prolonging the dispute until their reconciliation.

most listeners' parents, and set them up as a genuinely dangerous prospect in the way that Mötley Crüe had once been before succumbing to druggy torpor. Even relatively lukewarm reviews didn't count against the band, with the album going to number 6 in the US Billboard charts and the '18 and Life' single reaching number 4 in America and number 12 in the UK. 'I Remember You' was a soaring ballad, set apart by Bach's heartfelt, screaming delivery and Dave Sabo's harmonic-drenched guitar solo, and rightly became a mainstay of American proms.

In all these contradictions and warring impulses, Skid Row embodied a wider confusion about American identity. Glam metal had originally represented a sort of aspirational everyman dream that the most unlikely contenders – penniless, anti-social, semi-delinquent men from the least glamorous corners of America – could, by little more than force of personality, succeed in the most traditional terms and gain money, women and power. That as rebelliously as they presented themselves, the American dream would allow them to win, and win big. Just as Reagan's bumptious optimism had sustained America's self-belief in defiance of the actual state of the country throughout the 1980s – the AIDS crisis, the crack epidemic, the corruption of the Iran-Contra affair – glam metal had grown into an embodiment of a positivity culture. Prior to Guns n' Roses, this stadium-sized, party-all-the-time, no-tomorrow rock was the perfect soundtrack for a culture that needed to prove it was the biggest and the best. But in 1989, America's key reason for needing to keep up this façade began to disintegrate as a series of revolutions, upheavals and regime changes swept through the countries of the Communist Bloc and its satellite states elsewhere. Regimes were ended and replaced with a kind of democracy and, most symbolically, on November 9 the Berlin Wall was breached and stormed by vast crowds of protestors as soldiers stood down and allowed the free flow of people from east to west for the first time in decades.

This was a moment of ostensible victory for the west, America and everything it embodied. Yet in removing America's key adversity, it also necessitated a period of greater self-awareness. New president George H. W. Bush opted not to immediately visit Berlin, lest it be seen as triumphalism. 'What would I do? Dance on the wall?' he asked. Finally freed from projecting outwards against a perceived near-equal enemy, America was left to contemplate the state of its own existence. W.A.S.P.'s *The Headless Children* saw the band move away from the blood-spurting, high-octane camp of their earlier albums and towards a slower, more doom-laden sound and something more like social commentary.[11] The cover depicted a proces-

---

11. For a band who originally came across as a novelty turn, W.A.S.P. have proven to be a remarkably consistent act. *The Crimson Idol* (1993) was a critical and commercial success, and a rare example of a band forged in the glam era managing to transition beyond the genre, and the twenty-fifth

sion of dictators, religious fanatics, Klansmen and mur-
derers before a gaping, flame-licked hellmouth – but
crucially, they appear to be walking out of, rather than
down into, the abyss.

Guns n' Roses' worldview was similarly darkening.
On 'Paradise City', Rose had depicted what he saw
as – beneath the pomp and exaggeration – the reality
of America's ragged existence, with Captain America
reduced to a pitiful, clownish figure. As the new year
began, Rose would take to wearing a lurid pair of Stars
and Stripes cycling shorts on stage. Stripped to the
waist, eyes closed, breath pumping through his nos-
trils like an exhausted thoroughbred and sweat greas-
ing his pale skin, he was an unlikely standard bearer.
But, by his cold-eyed reading of the country, the self-
loathing, paranoia and aggression that consumed Rose
made him the perfect flag waver for it. Just as Jimi
Hendrix had marked the end of the Sixties and its
utopian dreaming with a feedback-strangled retelling
of the *Star Spangled Banner*, Rose touted the Stars and
Stripes not as some swaggering patriotic gesture but
a reclamation of the flag as a symbol of everything
that raged within him. With his racism, misogyny,
seething anger and barely contained violence, Rose
was a product of his country. And whether the country

anniversary tour of the album in 2018 saw them selling out dates across the
UK. Blackie Lawless' voice – and hair – remain impressively intact.

liked it or not, he was holding up a mirror to them and forcing them to look closely at what stared back.

Chapter 8

1990: STICK IT TO YA!

Throughout 1990, Jason Becker was recording with David Lee Roth. Having parted company with Steve Vai at the end of the *Skyscraper* tour in 1989, the former Van Halen frontman had continued his tradition of pairing off with boundary-smashing guitarists who had completely changed the way the instrument was played, both technically and creatively. While LA's Guitar Institute of Technology was producing a steady stream of hyper-technical shredders, Roth required the same combination of attributes that had been found in his original wingman Eddie Van Halen, and that had made the guitarist such a formidable prospect – not just the ability to play hard and fast, but to *swing*, function as part of a band and push the instrument to talk in a way that nobody else had done before.

Becker was just twenty when Roth recruited him, but seemed remarkably unfazed by the huge shoes into which he was stepping. An audition at Roth's father's house at the end of 1989 saw the young man nail the Van Halen tracks 'Hot for Teacher' and 'Panama' along with Roth's solo cover of 'Just a Gigolo'. Becker was already a relatively seasoned player – born in 1969, as soon as he started to learn the guitar he was spotted as being an uncommonly talented child. His father Gary, a painter, originally attempted to teach his five-year-old son the guitar formally. 'He was bored and never came back for lesson two,' he recalls. Home video footage from school concerts and bedroom jam sessions show a happy, relaxed young man, with waves of dark curls bouncing as his whole body wrung notes from his guitar. By the age of fourteen he was playing Bach's *Fugues* note-perfectly on the electric guitar.

His talent was quickly spotted by outsiders – in 1986, Shrapnel Records' boss Mike Varney heard Becker's demo tape and paired him with Marty Friedman in Cacophony, a kind of speed-guitar supergroup. 'He just melted me,' recalled Friedman of his first meeting with a younger, better-looking, more talented guitarist whom he might have had every reason to dislike. The pair were at the forefront of the largely instrumental 'shred' guitar scene, which had seen a new wave of guitarists like Steve Vai, Yngwie Malmsteen and Joe Satriani develop an ultra-fast, supremely technical style of guitar playing that drew as heavily on classical music as on traditional rock. Becker was from this tradition, but had much greater ambitions and prospects, as veteran music writer Alan di Perna – who interviewed Becker several times for *Guitar World* magazine around this period – remembers. 'The thing I liked about him was that he came out of what I sometimes term the "shred ghetto". And a lot of those players just remained in that world – they can produce these virtuosic flurries of notes, but they can't really cross over into mainstream rock, but Jason had shown a great ability to do that. Shred players often can't master the sort of looser, bluesy, swagger and panache of more classic rock, but Jason nailed it. He was so clearly destined for more than just doing clinics in guitar shops.' Becker's biggest concern at the time seemed to be a lack of problems. His father recalled him phoning home from tour and fretting that '[His bandmates] are always bitching about their parents. I don't have anything to say.' 'He was worried he'd got no character,' added his mother. 'I said, "Don't worry. It'll come. Bad things'll happen."'

One night, around the time he started working with Roth, Becker was woken up by an intensely painful cramp in his left calf. The pain persisted for the rest of the night and the next morning the same point on his leg felt tired and 'lazy'. For the following four months, the nagging muscular fatigue persisted. What Becker didn't – and couldn't – know was that this apparently trifling discomfort was the first obvious sign of an illness which in short order would see him robbed of movement, speech, independence and his career. Essentially, his central nervous system was downing tools, and refusing to pass on the signals that his completely healthy brain was sending to the rest of his body. Diagnosed with Amyotrophic Lateral Sclerosis – known in America as Lou Gehrig's Disease and the most common form of Motor Neurone Disease – Becker was given just three to five years to live by doctors.

This diagnosis would be cruel enough for anyone. For a man barely into his twenties it was particularly bleak. But for someone who was already one of the most acclaimed musicians of his generation, a child prodigy who had just been hired for one of the most prestigious gigs in American rock music, it was an incalculably spiteful turn of events. All evidence suggested that the young man would be dead by twenty-five, and would see out his days in a hospital, his completely sentient mind trapped in a mechanised, useless body. Throughout recording sessions for Roth's forthcoming album, *A Little Ain't Enough*, Becker was secretly spending mornings at the hospital, undergoing gruesome procedures ranging from spinal taps to biopsies. By the time recording successfully finished, he was using the lightest guitar strings possible due to his weakened hands. He was forced to admit his condition to the band, pull out of the worldwide arena tour to promote the record, and move back home with his parents to Richmond. The entire family struggled with the diagnosis. As Gary Becker bluntly stated: 'It just stabbed me in the heart.'

Becker's decline was terrifyingly fast. Jesse Vile's 2012 brilliant film of the guitarist's life, *Not Dead Yet*, documents the young man frantically trying alternative therapies and experimental drug treatments (at one point even having his mercury fillings removed), while becoming dependent on sticks, then confined to a wheelchair, his hair thinning, his voice failing and his muscles wasting away. A pitch-black comedy reared its head at points – Becker would exaggerate his disabilities while being filmed and feign dying in front of his relatives, telling them that they had to get used to it. But before long, the severity of Becker's condition was obvious. By 1992 he could barely speak; by 1997 he was completely paralysed.

Becker wasn't alone in glam metal in being laid low. Adam Curry was dispensed with by *Headbangers Ball*, and unceremoniously replaced with Riki Rachtman, a completely inexperienced newcomer, who landed the job thanks to being owner of The Cathouse and a close friend of Axl Rose who accompanied him to his audition.[1]

---

1. With his mane of hair – which had a tendency to frizz under the studio lights – a downtrodden, put-upon demeanour and, by his own admission, extremely limited interviewing skills, Rachtman wasn't an obvious anchor

Following his appearance in *The Decline of Western Civilization*, Chris Holmes of **W.A.S.P.** spent another eight years as an alcoholic, amassing DUI convictions and growing increasingly miserable about his role in a band which he felt had become a solo vehicle for an overly controlling Blackie Lawless. 'I was drinking 'cause I was an alcoholic,' he told Canadian YouTube channel *The Metal Voice* in a 2015 interview. 'And it was also being in **W.A.S.P.** being treated the way I was being treated all the time. You got to understand if somebody uses reverse psychology on you to hold you down so you don't shine like they do. I was always held down all the time, anything I did I was always in trouble and you get tired of that. Every bad thing that happened to **W.A.S.P.** was my fault, which most of the time it wasn't.' It eventually took Holmes until February of 1996 to get sober. Poison's C. C. DeVille's drug and alcohol use culminated in him coming onstage with the band at the 1991 MTV Awards, starting before they had been introduced, and then playing the wrong song ('Talk Dirty to Me' instead of 'Unskinny Bop') before unplugging his guitar mid-set. Attempting to read an autocue of links, he barked semi-coherently, gripping co-host Julie Brown as if trying to stay afloat, his shock of neon pink hair highlighting his

for the station to hire. However, his deep connections with the scene built up at The Cathouse and a genuine personal relationship with many of its leading lights gave the show a credibility that Curry had been unable to deliver.

deathly, sweat-soaked pallor. He was asked to leave the band shortly afterwards, and in summer of 1992 he was recorded ranting down the phone at Brett Michaels having called into a radio show on which his estranged singer was appearing. A week later, DeVille was invited along by the same show to give his side of things on air, but, perhaps fittingly, he turned up late and missed his slot.

Steven Adler was faring little better in Guns n' Roses, mired in cocaine and heroin addiction and struggling to engage as the rest of the band began work on the follow-up to *Appetite for Destruction*. His final appearance with the band was at the Farm Aid benefit on April 7 – as he came onstage, he took a running jump at his drum kit, but with his depth perception scrambled, landed in a crumpled heap several feet short (the gig was more notable for being the first public performance of 'Civil War', the first track from what would eventually become the *Use Your Illusion* album a year later). In 1996, an overdose on a cocaine and heroin speedball caused Adler to have a stroke and two heart attacks, and left with his face partially paralysed. In 2011, he gave an unvarnished assessment of his fall from grace to *Rukus* magazine: 'From having hundreds of friends, to getting kicked out of the band by my best friend – and a guy who I was doing the drugs with! – it left me with no-one to turn to,' said Adler. 'I was very sad and lonely. My wife left me, and I didn't blame her. It's hard to watch someone you love trying to kill themselves. That's what I was doing.' Also in 1990, Def Leppard's Steve Clark was put on a six-month leave of absence by the rest of the band on account of his prolific drinking. After one bender in Minneapolis led to the guitarist being found unconscious in a bar and admitted to hospital, his blood alcohol level was measured at 50 per cent higher than that recorded in Led Zeppelin's John Bonham at the time of his untimely death.[2]

Glam metal – which had meant to be about a neverending party, and life within a consequence-free, adolescent bubble – was taking lumps out of its main protagonists.

Jason Becker's problems were obviously of a different magnitude to those of his peers and not self-inflicted. But he also found the most ingenious response. With his condition declining but still desperate to make music, Becker had his friend Mike Bemesderfer devise a software programme connected to a visor-mounted sensor. Becker could click a virtual keyboard by moving his chin, altering the velocity of each note and gradually assembling them into entire pieces of music. 'A lot of it comes from the positivity of his upbringing and his family in general,' said Jesse Vile when asked what he thought motivated Becker to keep going. 'He still has lots of love for friends and family, and for creating music. The fact that he still wants to go on and he's not ready to say goodbye is the number one driving force.' His 1996 album *Perspective* was the result of this exhausting compositional process, with his epic ten-minute composition *End of the Beginning* going on to be performed by the Oakland Symphony Orchestra and the Diablo Ballet in 1999. On its release, Eddie Van Halen appeared on video with Becker to describe him as having been 'just one of the best ... rock and roll guitarists on the planet'.

At the time of writing, Becker's condition, while chronic, appears stable – a painstaking care programme by his family and friends has kept him as healthy as he can be and vastly extended his life expectancy. Meditation, spiritual interests and his remote compositional work has kept him together psychologically, while an ingenious non-verbal communication system based on flickering eye movements allows him to 'talk' with those around him. There's an obvious poignancy to seeing Becker now, physically reduced by his disease, and comparing him to the slowly degrading VHS footage of a happy, handsome figure, bathing in the adulation of a crowd of metallers while the notes subside from another pyrotechnic guitar run. His work on *A Little Ain't Enough* (and especially the title track) marked the last truly great work that David Lee Roth produced and offers a tantalising glimpse of where Becker's talent could have gone. But something life-affirming still shines through the guitarist's continued existence. 'It's a much bigger reason than anybody out there knows, why he's still here,' concludes his mother in the film. 'But he's still here.'

Bon Jovi's *New Jersey Syndicate* tour had turned into a gruelling, globe-spanning trek for the band. Fourteen months' worth of shows had taken them from Ireland to Mexico, criss-crossing continents en route. Their high-octane live sets began with Jon Bon Jovi being blown through the floor of the stage in a wall of pyrotechnics, took in acoustic interludes and saw catwalks extending out over the crowd to allow the band to breach the boundaries of the stage. On the tour's completion, Jon Bon Jovi peeled away to work on a solo album, the soundtrack to modern western *Young Guns II: Blaze of Glory*.

The title track works over the same ground as 'Wanted Dead or Alive' from four years earlier – bar a few minor modulations, the chord sequence is a close fit, while both songs adopt the imagery of the open plains and the wild west to paint the protagonist as a heroic loner. The cowboy motifs are laid on even more heavily in Jovi's solo track – the drums beat a military tattoo in the background, Jeff Beck's guest appearance brings with it an overdriven slide guitar solo, the additional percussion shakes out a reptilian, scuttling sound. It's a deliberate grasp for 'classic songwriter' territory – a push beyond the concerns of those Bon Jovi tracks that spoke to teenage babysitters in pizza parlour listening sessions and into those of middle-aged Marlboro men. Combined with post-tour fatigue, this air of earnestness gives the whole album a wearying feel. Metaphors are creaky and laboured, the songwriting aims for authentic cowboy pastiche but can't shake off the production techniques of the period and so feels like an academic exercise. Interviewers encountering Jon Bon Jovi around this time found him sullen and brooding, alluding to disagreements with Richie Sambora and still fuming over negative reviews that he had received years earlier. The youthful, chest-beating energy which had propelled Bon Jovi through their two multi-million selling albums was nowhere to be seen. Similarly middle-aged was Damn Yankees' 'High Enough', a power ballad from Ted Nugent and members of Styx and Night Ranger that came complete with a video that looked like a Hallmark channel afternoon movie.

Excessive seriousness wasn't an accusation that could be levelled at Wales' Tigertailz at this time. First formed in 1983, it took them until 1990 to release their second album, *Bezerk*. They stuck close to the Poison model: camera-mugging enthusiasm, bubblegum pop melodies, dayglo presentation and the same mixture of hyperactive excitement and wall-climbing exuberance that you'd expect to find three days into a junior school holiday when nobody's eaten anything bar Skittles and chocolate and collective discipline is starting to break down. Interestingly, when you listen to a track like 'Love Bomb Baby' without any visual accompaniment, there's almost nothing that actually defines the track as being 'metal'. Tigertailz's studied devotion to the glam metal template ended up turning them into a purely visual spectacle. It's hard to see how this could have been pushed any further without descending into out-right ridicule (although Nelson, a freakishly Aryan-looking pair of platinum-haired ultra-soft rocking siblings, attempted it with the video for 'After the Rain' in which the pair come to life on a poster, lead an unhappy teen away down a hole in the space-time continuum and help him to undergo a Native Ameri-can shamanic ritual after which he experiences a Nel-son gig).

In response, among new metal bands, a slight muta-tion was occurring with several largely disavowing the Eighties as an influence and reaching further back to something that felt more 'real'. While not strictly glam metal, The Dogs D'Amour, The Black Crowes and Quireboys all looked back into the 1970s' source mate-rial of Aerosmith and The Faces and conjured up an alternative narrative of where metal might have gone if the theatrical blues side of those bands had won out over the chaotic booze-fuelled partying side. The Dogs D'Amour had been around in various incarna-tions since 1983, specialising in a scuzzy, beatnik form of druggy blues. Self-mythologising and dissolute, the band looked like Hanoi Rocks if they'd been buried alive and then dug up a year later, making the moderate success of 1989's *A Graveyard of Empty Bottles* and 1990's *Errol Flynn* even more noteworthy.

The Black Crowes had the feathered hair, velvet jackets and midriff-split polka-dot shirts of their fully glam peers but their debut album *Shake Your Money Maker* was created within a very different frame of reference. From the Elmore James-referencing title and their cover of Otis Redding's 'Hard to Handle', the band injected the basic model of the white American rock guitar group with something older, looser and more African-American. With hindsight, this sounds pretty tame – it was only 'black' in the sense that the Rolling Stones' early Seventies' material diverged from the white rock template by adding in gospel-tinged backing singers and a horn section. But glam metal was, as a genre, incredibly white, so any deviation from this was noteworthy. There was little overt racism in the scene – indeed, very little of anything which was in any way overtly political – which is partly why Axl Rose's bigoted lyrics on 'One in a Million' had become such an issue. It was just an incredibly homogenous world, and where it linked back to the original blues, it was always through the secondary form in which it had been assimilated by later white artists rather than the African-American pioneers: slide guitars appeared, but from country rather than the Delta; railroad songs and travelling blues came from dustbowl cowboys, not itinerant cotton pickers; rock and roll's chords were fed down the line from Elvis and Duane Eddy, not Little Richard.

England's Quireboys mined a similar path – essentially a very close pastiche of Rod Stewart's original band The Faces (right down to its cheerily colloquial title), their debut album *A Bit of What You Fancy* was a great honky-tonk pub rock record which essentially used glam as a Trojan horse to secure them Sharon Osbourne's management, a major label deal with EMI and a support slot with Guns n' Roses on their second trip to the UK in 1989. They kept this dual identity up through the recording and release of their debut, working with Rod Stewart's musical director Jim Cregan as producer and supporting the Rolling Stones, but also touring with LA Guns and appearing at Monsters of Rock alongside Whitesnake and Poison when it returned after a year off with a reduced capacity and new crowd safety measures in place. Also on the bill that day were fellow British band Thunder who traded in an even more meat-and-potatoes version of metal than the Quireboys: their debut album, *Backstreet Symphony*, was a solid effort which ticked all the boxes (big ballad, rocked-up cover version, anthemic title track) and they were a very tight live band, but even their look – black leather jackets, more relaxed hair, plain blue jeans, no make-up – suggested a band, and a scene, slowly tiptoeing away from glam metal's aesthetic excesses and groping for something more 'real'. Their drummer and comic foil, Gary 'Harry' James, was actually bald, which seemed about as non-glam as it was possible to get.

Even some of glam metal's staunchest advocates were backing away from the genre and the associations that came with it. George Lynch's new outfit Lynch Mob's debut *Wicked Sensation* was notably harder sounding than his Dokken output, but without Don Dokken's wallpaper-loosening voice it lacked the impact of his previous band's best work. Kiss were preparing for a vast tour with a stage set replicating their *Hot in the Shade* album. 'There's lasers and bombs, and this sphinx that talks, which was forty feet tall last I heard,' Paul Stanley told *Kerrang!*, while denying that the shows would see him return to wearing make-up and explaining that the expanded set list would focus less heavily on their recent work. Britny Fox's frontman 'Dizzy' Dean Davidson also spoke to the magazine as he launched his new project, Black Eyed Susan, but stressed that 'it's definitely not Britny Fox, it's real down to earth', while laying into his former bandmates: 'They're fake. I could really tell you some shit but I'm not going to. What's the point? Let them keep the name. I don't need them … As for Michael [Kelly Smith]'s image, well I just got tired of that … I toned things down, he kept at it. There he was, lookin' like he should be in Tigertailz or some glam band.' Poison's

Flesh and Blood album received positive reviews, but critics mentioned how much of the material sounded like off-cuts from the previous album while nodding to a similarity to Bryan Adams' blue-collar AOR on 'Ride the Wind'. In April 21's *Kerrang!* Axl Rose ranted at length about wanting to assault Vince Neil ('I wanna see that plastic face of his cave in when I hit him ... guns, knives or fists, whatever you wanna do, I don't care...') while talking about the ballads he was writing and his love of ELO's Jeff Lynne. In return, Neil wearily observed that 'It was like rock and roll had suddenly turned into the World Wrestling Federation.'[3] This disillusionment with success was noticed by Mötley Crüe's former manager Doug Thaler post-*Dr Feelgood*. 'The combination of the new sobriety, the stress from their marriages, and the attainment of a level of success beyond what they had ever imagined began to work a change in the band. Fear, exhaustion and mood swings set in.'[4]

While the upper reaches of the metal charts were still glam-heavy around this point – albums from Lita Ford, Heart and Skid Row, singles from Dirty White Boy and Tigertailz – an increasing number of bands were being covered in *Kerrang!* who appeared to be the polar opposite both stylistically and sonically. New Seattle four-piece Soundgarden looked like Sabbath-

3. *The Dirt*, p. 233.
4. Ibid., p. 248.

listening stoners, talked about their love of British comic *Viz* ('Finbarr, Tina's Tits, I really like the Pathetic Sharks,' said guitarist Kim Thayill) and mocked the tropes of glam's visuals, joking that if they ever did 'one of those girl videos' they'd have their podgy, dishevelled road manager Gunny Junk dancing in a cage with masking tape over his nipples. Even Jack Russell of Great White was keen to stress that 'we're not a glam or a hairspray band that gets press on our image, we've done everything with our music.' Meanwhile, a small singles review deemed slovenly Seattle grunge band Mudhoney 'the hippest band in the world right now'.

Still cleaving defiantly to the glam metal template was *Stick it to Ya*, the debut by Slaughter. Vocalist Mark Slaughter and bassist Dana Strum had formed the band after jumping ship from Vinnie Vincent Invasion together. Sticking with Chrysalis records, the two boosted their line-up to a four piece and recorded the album in summer of 1989, releasing it in January 1990. The sleeve depicted a large-breasted woman in a swimsuit, pinned to a fairground knifeboard in an image created by Glen Wexler – the model was Laurie Carr, *Playboy*'s Playmate of the month from December 1986 and at that time the wife of Robbin Crosby from Ratt (in their wedding photo the pair are dressed in formal wedding attire, while Crosby stands behind his wife, reaching around to cup her breasts with both hands). The album was a commercial success, but listening to it gives the constant nagging sense that you're listening to ideas that you've heard somewhere in the very recent past. 'Eye to Eye' opens the album with the mechanised noodling and reverberating drum breaks that kicked off Dire Straits' 'Money for Nothing', before a vocal comes in closely matching Joe Elliott's verse on Def Leppard's 'Rock of Ages'. 'Burnin' Bridges' sounds like Ratt's 'Round and Round'. 'Up All Night' (with its video created by future Hollywood titan Michael Bay) echoes the riffing strut of Van Halen's 'Runnin' with the Devil'. This continues throughout the album – 'Spend My Life' is Bon Jovi, 'She Wants More' is AC/DC's 'Whole Lotta Rosie' played backwards. None of these are bad reference points, but it seemed a damning judgement on a genre not even a decade old that one of the biggest albums it produced that year was already recycling its past.

It's arguable that this was simply a logical conclusion to where glam metal had been going since 1983. Since Mötley Crüe had grafted together Kiss, Motörhead and the New York Dolls, glam metal had been a giant cultural whirlpool, pulling in disparate elements from throughout the history of white guitar music and piecing them together in a vast work of assemblage. All music builds on what has gone beforehand and cherry picks elements of it, but glam metal seemed to take the culture clash element as far as it could go. The biggest element was plucked from each previous epoch, inflated, had the brightness turned up and was then squashed together with everything else. None of it had to make sense next to the other because each element was simply there for its own sake: Bon Jovi could tell Bruce Springsteen narratives on one song then pretend to be cowboys the next; W.A.S.P. could be a pantomime horror show that terrified middle America, but also dress up as American football players. As glam metal aged, this process accelerated. The snake began to eat its own tail and Slaughter ended up churning back ideas and sounds from closer and closer to the present day.

Even glam metal's best artists were no more 'real' than the wrestlers that the WWF had created and sent out into rigged bouts throughout the decade. But this didn't make them any less brilliant – Andy Warhol's great creative innovation had been the realisation that anybody, and anything, could be art, as long as it was delivered with maximum conviction and maximum spectacle. This shift in perception had underwritten pop culture from that point on, with a move away from traditional technique and an acceptance of 'fame' as a kind of talent in its own right. This was a world where objects and happenings were as important as the members of bands themselves – Poison's videos, Def Leppard's stage set, Blackie Lawless' exploding codpiece. All these objects contained a kind of star power in the way that Warhol's soup cans and screen prints did. The same fascination that drove him to attend Wrestlemania – with all its artifice, hype, exaggeration and ironic glamour – would have made him understand glam metal. But the problem with something that is built on hype and inflation is that sooner or later it reaches its limits and either bursts, or collapses in on itself. When something arrives fully formed and larger than life, it can't get any bigger.

A harbinger of the genre's collapse may have been sensed by Warrant. Formed in 1984, the band's 1989 debut *Dirty Rotten Filthy Stinking Rich* is best remembered for the ballad 'Heaven'. Musically, 'Heaven' is a fairly standard construction – a strummed acoustic introduction and a pared down vocal, with the chorus arriving like a wall of fireworks going off in the sky. But the song is elevated by Jani Lane's understated vocal and a surprisingly tender lyric – it's set up as a tale of blue-collar love, in the same lineage as Springsteen's 'The River' or 'Livin' on a Prayer'. The protagonist looks at a photo of the woman in front of a ramshackle house, and beyond that to the factory where he used to work. The memories, like the photo, are faded, but are returning to him gradually. The hint is that he might be much older – the photo being black and white dates the image and suggests a much-longer-lost love. So while the chorus celebrates their relationship, there's a nagging, melancholy undercurrent – is the relationship still alive, or is he bereft, endlessly replaying it in his head and pretending to himself that a long-gone feeling is still shared by his ex? The timezones are unclear throughout the song, and the suspicion that he's simply reliving a feeling that's gone resurfaces. Memories come back not as a comfort, but as a torment, and his promise that he won't be giving up on the relationship sounds more like a delusional threat than a comfort. The end result places the track closer to the rueful nostalgia of Don Henley's 'The Boys of Summer' than to most metal ballads.

However, their 1990 follow-up completely eclipsed this track and the impression it made on the public. There are a few great tracks on the *Cherry Pie* album, especially 'Uncle Tom's Cabin', a swampy, rocked-up murder ballad about a corrupt policeman covering up a killing in a small town and the retribution that stems from the crime. Unfortunately, however, the lead single from the album wasn't this, but the title track – as cretinous a slice of glam juvenilia as ever existed, from the cover art (a waitress dropping a slice of pie which hovers in front of her crotch) to the video (the same waitress getting hosed down by firefighters, more pie getting dropped, comedy false teeth, more sexual innuendo, etc.). It was a sort of image-defining work of such awful magnitude that it had an enormous halo effect on the band's entire output. It was the kind of song you'd hear blasting from frat houses and on the deck of a booze cruise at Spring Break. It made Tiger-tailz and Wrathchild seem considered. While the song was a big commercial hit for a relatively unknown band (number 10 on the Billboard charts) it seemed to sum up everything about a scene that was becoming wearingly bloated. The presence of Lane's friend, Poison's C. C. DeVille, supplying the guest guitar solo on 'Cherry Pie' raised further eyebrows about Warrant's own musical abilities.

A few months later, Warrant were in the UK to promote the re-release of 'Cherry Pie' and were booked to appear on *The Word*. This went out every Friday night on Channel 4 and was a riotous, self-consciously edgy magazine show, trawling British subculture for stories to feature and juxtaposing them with a surreal mixture of in-town celebrities on promotional junkets, a worse-for-wear studio audience and live bands. As a PR gimmick, someone had given out promotional cherry pies to the audience to celebrate Warrant's appearance. The band hadn't even reached the first chorus before the baked goods began to rain down on Lane. Protected only by his cowboy hat and biker jacket, he struggled to reach the highest notes as he batted away a hail of paper plates, broken pastry and stewed fruit. Back in LA, *Screamer* magazine might still be filling its covers with the likes of Bang Tango, LA Guns and Mr Big. But in Britain at least, Warrant had just received an intimation of where the new decade was heading.

Chapter 9

1991: USE YOUR ILLUSION

On January 17, 1991, America's bombing campaign
of Iraq began, supported by a coalition of thirty-five
countries. Over 100,000 sorties would be flown
between that day and the end of February with 88,500
tons of ordnance dropped on the country following
its invasion of Kuwait. The war was unusual in that
it played out in seemingly real time on the emerging
rolling news channel, CNN. The same cable TV technology that had pumped the noise and colour of glam
metal into American homes less than a decade earlier
was now disseminating a different kind of spectacle.
Night vision shots streaked green with tracer fire,
embedded journalists' voices crackled down radio lines
from inside the Rashid Hotel and data-strewn eagle-
eye footage showed the aerial overview of how coali-

tion bombs were flattening military and civilian infrastructure. American general Norman Schwarzkopf became an unlikely household name, while the supersized SUVs that rolled through desert roads would soon become a coveted mode of domestic transport back at home.

The public was watching war in more detail and in closer proximity than ever before. Yet there was something illusory about it all. For the most part, what was being seen was a reconstruction of events, filtered from embedded reports, carefully released media pool footage and military-approved interviews. None of these things were 'false' but they were presented as discrete elements, before being shaped into a viewer-retaining narrative. Odd visceral moments broke through – most notably, Ken Jarecke's photo of the grimacing, charred body of an Iraqi soldier, burned alive while trying to escape through the windscreen of his truck – but inconvenient details were largely suppressed (that particular image of Jarecke's was removed from the Associated Press' newswire in America before it was published). What reached the public was, for the most part, a clinical reimagining of the war, built up from its component parts and shaped into something which both resembled the truth, but wasn't the truth. Viewers were steadily fed spectacle, noise, bombast and a photofit picture of American supremacy: in that sense, glam metal had converged almost completely with the news, politics and public life. What had been birthed less than a decade before as a squalling carnival of outsider spirit was now marching in lockstep with mainstream America and its cultural norms.

Creative bright spots were few and far between in glam metal this year: Skid Row's second album, *Slave to the Grind*, roughed up the sound of their first, and its best moments – the lead single 'Monkey Business', the borderline-thrash of the title track and closing ballad 'Wasted Time' – matched that record's anthemic power. The band seemed to have sensed the prevailing trends with this semi-reinvention, and when they set out to tour the album, support came from Pantera and Soundgarden, rather than anyone from the glam metal stable. Alice Cooper's anti-drug anthem 'Hey Stoopid' failed to match up to the success of 'Poison', but its rollicking, fuzzed-out boogie brought back memories of his *School's Out* heyday. The track was further boosted by backing vocals from Ozzy Osbourne while a double guitar attack from Joe Satriani and Slash gave it an added edge (albeit one that didn't completely chime with the song's lyrics in Osbourne and Slash's case). Trixter's 'One in a Million' was an MTV favourite but was so soft that it was essentially the sound of a boy band with the addition of long hair and artfully ripped clothes. White Lion's *Mane Attraction* album was an overly-serious, ballad-heavy collection which included a re-recording of their 1985 debut 'Broken Heart'. Van Halen's *For Unlawful Carnal Knowledge* was a dense, wearying plod, leavened only by the motivational spark of single 'Right Now' (which in turn sounded like something from the AM rock of ten years earlier rather than anything groundbreaking). Stryper, Mötley Crüe and Ratt all marked time with compilations and round-ups. Poison similarly stood still with *Swallow This Live*, an album most notable for including a lengthy and entirely uncalled for C. C. DeVille solo spot, titled 'Guitar Solo', which *Guitar World* would go on to rate as the worst guitar solo of all time.[1]

As the Gulf War continued, both Winger and Cinderella cancelled tours of Europe. In Winger's case, this was because guitarist Reb Beach's brother was called up for active service and Beach elected to stay at home with his family. Cinderella had already played their first UK shows when they issued a statement explaining that 'Due to increased tension in the Middle East

---

1. From December 2008's *Guitar World*: 'Remember when you were in high school and your novice shredder best friend kept insisting he'd "almost nailed" Eddie Van Halen's "Eruption" solo, and you'd be stuck in his room wanting to kill yourself as he tried to play it again and again? That's a little what listening to C. C.'s jaw-dropping nine-minute solo spot is like. Only instead of your friend going "No, wait!" and starting over every time he fucks up, there's an arena full of idiots loudly cheering him on. And just to show you the breadth of his chops, C. C. also throws in a messy attempt at some "Hot Club"-style gypsy jazz licks (Django Reinhardt would surely be envious of the tres magnifique tones C.C. coaxes from his pointy-head-stocked axe), a touch of polka, some searing Miami Vice blues bends and, of course, several more dive bombs and two-handed tapping runs whenever inspiration fails. Completely devoid of taste, structure or steady tempo, this should be required listening for budding guitarists everywhere. Surely they can't do any worse.'

and concern over ability to maintain security throughout Europe for the band and personnel, the band returned to America.' Great White took a similar line, their statement telling critics that 'We have no doubt there will be some macho blowhards who will make a big noise about flying in the face of danger, but rock n' roll is not supposed to be a game of chicken with terrorists.' Little Angels switched the title of their latest album from *Spitfire* to *Young Gods* and amended their logo so instead of showing a devil riding a missile he was now sat astride a globe. Winger's 'Miles Away' was adopted as an anthem by US servicemen in the Gulf – less sentimentally, reports emerged of pilots blasting Van Halen's 'Why Can't This Be Love' to fire themselves up ahead of bombing raids.

Elsewhere, other problems that had accumulated throughout the Eighties reached their terminal conclusion. Early on January 8, Def Leppard's Phil Collen was phoned by his manager Cliff Burnstein with news of Collen's co-guitarist Steve Clark. Clark's leave of absence from the band – an attempt to see him confront and deal with his alcoholism – had been unsuccessful and Clark had died in his sleep on a sofa in his home in Chelsea, west London. He was just thirty years old. The coroner's report suggested that having cracked a rib while drunk, Clark had been prescribed valium and codeine for pain relief, but instructed not to drink while taking them. He disregarded this advice and a swelling on the brain ensued, claiming his life while he slept. Clark's berth in the band had been kept open while he went into rehab in anticipation of his relatively swift return, but during his time in the centre in Tucson, Arizona, he began a relationship with another patient – Janie Dean, a recovering heroin addict. In Phil Collen's recollection, once this relationship began the pair relapsed and, once engaged, enabled each other's worst impulses. 'In a way Steve didn't have much choice in the matter,' wrote Collen. 'He was surrounded by drink most of his life. Steve's dad was a taxi driver and I think Steve was always trying to prove he was worthy of his rock star status … Steve had to prove his manhood to his dad all the time, that he had the values of a Sheffield steelworker underneath his golden splendor.'[2] Collen briefly tried to quit the band, but was talked back into it by Joe Elliott. Collen then embarked on a process of relearning Clark's guitar lines, performing a sad kind of musical séance. Alone in the studio, listening to the half-finished parts Clark had created on their demo tapes, Collen worked at replicating his friend's style and tone and turning his ideas into finished songs. 'It was just me and Steve in that room. It felt almost as if there was a ghost in there with me as I played his parts over and over.'[3]

The constant subject of discussion throughout the

---

2. https://loudwire.com/def-leppard-steve-clark-death-anniversary/
3. https://www.loudersound.com/features/phil-collen-adrenalized-extract-steve-clark

year was when Guns n' Roses' full follow-up to *Appetite for Destruction* would finally emerge. A delay to the album meant that its accompanying world tour had already begun some four months before the album itself was out. This created an odd situation where elements of the album were common knowledge – the title, its underwhelming artwork in yellow-and-blue colour schemes and some of the material. One widely circulated bootleg contained largely piano-and-voice demos for the tracks, suggesting that the follow-up was going to slip the bonds of metal entirely and end up somewhere closer to early Seventies' Elton John in sound and feel. A steady stream of news stories accompanied the enormous shows: constant late arrivals, usually attributed to Rose; the singer challenging fans to fights for perceived infractions; meandering sets running over three hours in length, taking in instrumentals, half-finished cover versions and acapella sections. Songs being stopped and the band leaving the stage due to crowd issues. More late arrivals. Baiting of named journalists by Rose and the encouragement of the crowd to jeer the mention of them (snatches of this undignified pantomime eventually ended up being used on the track 'Get in the Ring' on *Use Your Illusion II*).

It seemed inevitable that eventually the wheels would come off in a serious way. Finally, on July 2, as the band played at Riverport Amphitheatre in

Missouri, their performance of 'Rocket Queen' was derailed as Rose, clad in cycling shorts, a cowboy hat and a strangely cropped shaggy fur coat – which made him look like something from the Henson Creature Workshop – spotted a fan taking photos in the crowd and instructed security to remove their camera. Unsatisfied with their response, Rose dived into the crowd, took the camera, flailed around against various fans and security before being deposited back on stage. 'Well, thanks to the lame-ass security, I'm going home' he declared, before hurling down the microphone with an echoing crunch and leaving the stage. As the band followed Rose into the wings, a full-blown riot broke out. Plastic seats were torn out and hurled like Frisbees at security guards' faces. With the stage stormed the video screens were pulled down. Fans swung from cables while a sixty-ton lighting rig threatened to topple over from above them. Fires were started outside the venue and turf was ripped up. The chaos lasted for over three hours and resulted in forty fans and twenty-five police officers being injured, most of the band's equipment being looted or destroyed and Rose being charged with incitement. 'The band just grabbed the vintage guitars they had and that was it,' recalled Guns fan and concert attendee Bryan Pollard in *The Riverfront Times*. 'People were rolling out 4×12 cabinets and monitor mixing boards. That part was just hilarious. It was some sort of white-trash Fellini film.' The band nodded to the incident in the liner notes of their next album: 'Fuck you, St Louis.' A lone voice of disquiet was guitarist Izzy Stradlin. 'When something like that happens, you can't help but think back to Donington. What's to stop us from having some more people trampled – because the singer doesn't like something? Like, what's the point? What are we getting at here?'[4]

The finished version of *Use Your Illusion* was finally scheduled for release on September 17, 1991. A month earlier, the Monsters of Rock festival took place – bar Mötley Crüe, the line-up was glam-free, with even Nikki Sixx grousing pre-festival about a desire to be taken more seriously. 'The controversy follows us, and … I'm getting a little tired of it. We're not a circus act, y'know?'[5] Headliners AC/DC showcased their latest album *The Razor's Edge*, another in a succession of records by the band which paired a couple of very good singles with a lot of forgettable ballast. The top draw of the day were Metallica, who just that week had released their eponymous fifth album, an almost entirely black-wrapped record, a move away from their thrash roots and progressive experiments, and towards something slower, heavier and more self-consciously epic with Bob Rock as producer. The band were head to toe in black clothing, playing black guitars – it was a far cry from the previous year when

4. https://www.loudersound.com/features/izzy-stradlin-in-too-deep
5. Stefan Chirazi, 'Decadence Dance', *Kerrang!* (August 10, 1991).

Thunder, Quireboys, Poison, Aerosmith and Whitesnake had played.

The *Use Your Illusion* tour arrived in London on August 31 at Wembley Stadium, the country's flagship football stadium and an imposing concrete structure built in 1923. A pair of ornamental towers flanked the front entrance, like vast ice cream cones, with the open roof offering no protection from the elements to fans who would be crammed onto the pitch from lunchtime onwards. On a hot, dusty afternoon, the bill opened with Nine Inch Nails, Trent Reznor's one-man industrial nihilist-pop project. Second support were Skid Row. Greased in sweat and stripped to his lace-up leather trousers, Sebastian Bach delivered a profanity-packed set, peaking – in direct contravention of an order from the local authority – with 'Get the Fuck Out', having first read out a letter from Brent Council ordering the band not to play the track. 'And if they pull the show after that, there's going to be 80,000 fist-throwing motherfuckers right in front of me, man!' he beamed at its conclusion (the council duly cancelled Skid Row's forthcoming headline show at Wembley Arena, necessitating its relocation to London Arena on the far side of the city in November. At that show, Bach blew through the venue's curfew, resulting in thousands of fans being stranded in the then un-redeveloped Docklands district after they missed the last trains home). 'That type of posed toughness was so dumb,' Skid Row's bassist Rachel

Bolan later conceded. 'How did a kid that went to prep school end up such a rebel?'[6]

Guns n' Roses eventually took to the stage as the sun set over the stadium. Now minus Steven Adler and with new drummer Matt Sorum who had previously played with The Cult, the set was an odd mixture of material familiar from *Appetite for Destruction*, new tracks that were semi-familiar from bootlegs and cover versions ('Live and Let Die' which had previously been released on the *Days of Thunder* soundtrack, snatches of Grand Funk Railroad's 'Bad Time'). Rose wore a t-shirt with the word MARTYR crossed out on it, and on 'Mr Brownstone' his voice oscillated between his familiar rasping scream and a strangely fruity, more studied tone. The most familiar of the new tracks was 'You Could Be Mine', which had been released in the June of that year as part of the soundtrack to *Terminator 2: Judgment Day*. James Cameron's modern sci-fi masterpiece told the story of John Connor, a delinquent boy on the run while two futuristic robots – one benign, one evil – battle for control of him. The song's chorus reused the pay-off line from *Appetite for Destruction*'s liner notes – 'With your bitch-slap rapping and your cocaine tongue, you get nothing done.'

The release of 'You Could Be Mine' was a major event – *Kerrang!* devoted an entire double page spread

6. https://www.loudersound.com/features/skid-row-it-didn-t-matter-what-we-did-it-wasn-t-our-time-anymore

to reviewing the track and its b-side, 'Civil War'. The first track arrives on an off-kilter, hammering drum pattern, underpinned by a restless, repetitive bass line fed through a chorus unit to give it a wobbling, unstable quality. Slash's guitar line comes in playing a straining minor key riff, repeating on itself in ever-decreasing circles before the tune abruptly shifts to an audio echo of the vocal progression that opens up the Beatles' 'Twist And Shout'. As with the climax of the guitar solo in Quiet Riot's 'Metal Health', the overdriven tone of the guitar gives it a strangely human quality and melts it together with Rose's nasal, plaintive voice. It's a sound at once both emotive and inhuman. As the lyrics progress throughout the track Rose's opening bravado is stripped away and inverted. By his ranting crescendo, his sights seem to be trained at once on a partner, his band mates and ultimately himself, and the patterns of self-destruction that had marked every phase of the band's life up to that point. The inclusion of idiotic racist lyrics, the picking of fights with other bands, the ability to turn successful shows into life-threatening riots and the paralysis that had gripped the band since their last album – all elements in a slow commercial and creative suicide attempt.

The final line – an exasperated howl against a man's failure to grow up, learn or progress in any way – is the ultimate self-admonishment of everything about Rose himself at that time. A raging, artistic intellect, locked in by the expectations of a genre which was on its last legs, desperately trying to create a piece of work which would either destroy the world of commercial metal or force it to abandon his band. Through the bootlegs and the live shows there were intimations of what this would entail, but the eventual release of *Use Your Illusion I* and *II* was still a head-spinning moment for the band's fanbase. MTV News reported that 1.5 million fans had queued up at record stores across America to buy the simultaneously released albums. 'Success made it take a long time,' Slash explained to the channel, before acknowledging other delaying factors. 'And the associated drug problems that ensued.' Geffen Records had taken advance orders for an unprecedented 4 million copies of the albums, double the previous record total clocked up by Michael Jackson's 1987 release, *Bad*. Three thousand branches of the Wal-Mart and K-Mart chains opted not to stock the album citing its explicit content, but around a thousand stores opened on the stroke of midnight – Slash sneaked into the Tower Records outlet on Sunset Boulevard where he had once worked to observe the frenzy through a two-way mirror. Ozzy Osbourne turned up at stores in Manhattan to sign autographs and promote his own new album, *No More Tears*. Between 12:01 a.m. and 2 a.m. more than half a million copies of the two albums were sold in total. Volume one eventually sold 685,000 copies in its first week of release, and volume two sold

770,000, with the band occupying the top two slots in the Billboard charts simultaneously.

Taken in its totality, *Use Your Illusion* is a sprawling, unfocused work. A selection of tracks like 'Right Next Door to Hell' and 'Perfect Crime' could have slotted in to *Appetite for Destruction*, sharing their sense of profane, neurotic energy. Those driven by Izzy Stradlin such as '15 Years' slow down and work a looser, more bluesy groove like early Seventies' Rolling Stones. But around the edges, the album starts to push off in unexpected directions – 'Don't Cry' dated back to the band's earliest shows and is the closest to a conventional power ballad, but with a gorgeously weary, psychedelic quality to it, the sound of the comedown after an apocalyptic explosion of rage. It's a remarkably pared-down track with few of the standard tricks employed by metal bands on these songs. Leading into the final chorus, the tempo slows for one bar, pulling back off the beat as if the band are summoning up their energy before the final push for the finale. 'November Rain' went to the other extreme, laying on saccharine backing vocals, synthesised orchestras, pianos and an epic coda in a pursuit of Elton John-like grandeur. The video tipped things over into the preposterous – a cinematic staging of the marriage of Rose and his then-girlfriend Stephanie Seymour, including helicopter tracking shots, an appearance from *Headbangers Ball* host Riki Rachtman as an extra, a mock funeral,

Slash playing a guitar solo on top of a grand piano. The final track on volume two was the most divisive – 'My World', nominally an eighty-six-second rap by Rose over a mechanised drum loop, his voice distorted and choked. The sense was of someone who'd been listening to his support group Nine Inch Nails' experiments in machine-driven pop, and even some hip hop (Rose had worn a Public Enemy t-shirt on stage at various points in the tour), but had taken completely the wrong lessons away about what made each genre work. Izzy Stradlin later claimed that he hadn't even known 'My World' would be on the album until he heard the finished product.

At its best, *Use Your Illusion* showed how a band could break the confines of a genre and stretch themselves musically and creatively into an entirely new space. 'Locomotive (Complicity)' works with the elements of funk that bands like Living Colour, 24-7 Spyz and Jane's Addiction were transfusing into metal at that point but avoids the embarrassingly stiff pastiche that bands like Extreme produced when they tried to loosen up. 'Estranged' is a nine-minute epic with a glimpse of the Isley Brothers' 'Summer Breeze' in its guitar line. 'Civil War' is a post-Gulf War update of the protest song, trading in the sad impotence of the Sixties' folk singers for a raging howl against a culture where night vision footage of Tomahawk missiles flattening cities had become primetime entertainment. If the political music of Rose's childhood was the sound of pure spirits standing aside from the carnage and observing, 'Civil War' was what you got when the onlookers had been completely corrupted and tarnished by their own country's behaviour and the resulting destruction. America had 'won' the Cold War and uplifting scenes of blossoming democracy were beamed out from the former Eastern Bloc. But at home at least, the landscape Rose surveyed was one of corruption, hatred and festering aggression, as much in his own band as in society at large.

However, the hardest criticism one can make of *Use Your Illusion* is that over its meandering length, all too often it fails to provoke any of these feelings or inspire these thoughts. Far too much of the album eventually just trudges by: the imbecilic chest-beating of 'Get in the Ring'; the workmanlike crash of 'Shotgun Blues'; the country plod of 'You Ain't the First'. At its best, *Use Your Illusion* imagined an escape route from metal for Guns n' Roses and for any other band ambitious and talented enough to follow them under the wire. At its worst, it was simply boring, and – after such a prolonged gestation – wearying. And there was simply too much of the worst material. The albums were an unquestionable commercial success – between them, at the time of writing, they have sold around an estimated 37 million copies. But for such a huge cultural moment, they created a remarkably small creative ripple. No series of bands followed in their wake; they didn't herald an ambitious new era in metal; you just don't hear either volume that much these days.

Izzy Stradlin quit Guns n' Roses on Thanksgiving of 1991 – the Wembley Stadium show would turn out to have been his last as a full-time member of the band. Forced into rehabilitation as a condition of his probation after being arrested in August 1989 for urinating on a plane, his isolation from the rest of the band had grown. He travelled separately to shows, kept to schedules when the rest of the band operated on their own clock and tried to devise ways to cover Rose's frequent onstage departures and absences, to little avail.

> The music had taken a back seat completely, there was nothing new coming from us. We didn't sit around and play acoustic guitars anymore ... We'd started out as a garage band and it became like a huge band, which was fine. But everything was so magnified ... Drug addictions, personalities, just the craziness that was already there anyway. The nuttiness. It just became ... too much. Plus, my friends, these guys ... I'm basically watching them kill themselves. Not so much Axl, but Slash and Duff – these guys were on my top ten list of guys that might die this week. And I'm thinking, 'You know what? I just don't want to be part of it.' It didn't feel like it was good.[7]

The week before *Use Your Illusion* came out on Geffen, an even more significant release for glam metal took

---

7. https://www.loudersound.com/features/izzy-stradlin-in-too-deep

place on DGC, the label's more alternative-minded subdivision that already had the likes of Sonic Youth and The Posies on its roster. A three-piece from Aberdeen, Washington, Nirvana had one previous release on the tiny independent label Sub Pop and were making their major label debut with the single 'Smells Like Teen Spirit'. The track was a hardcore mangling of Boston's 'More Than a Feeling' riff, broken up with a minimalist, watery guitar line and singer Kurt Cobain's cathartic howl of a voice. The band looked like weary, tranquilised skateboarders, a world away from the overblown pomposity of *Use Your Illusion* or the coke-bloated scene that had preceded it. A week after Guns n' Roses' midnight release party, Nirvana's own album came out. *Nevermind*.

Postscript

1992 AND BEYOND: NEVERMIND

'All of a sudden, 1980s is the kiss of death,' said Lita Ford in an interview with MTV looking back on how abruptly the guard changed in guitar music. 'If you're an artist from the 1980s now, no one wants anything to do with you.' Warrant's Jani Lane recounted a similar fall from grace to VH1. 'If you weren't wearing flannel or had a goatee you were NOT cool. You should be shot on sight ... it hurt ... it got to the point where every rock band who came out in the Eighties sucked, had no reason to live and should not be on this planet and there's no way that they can possibly do anything viable in the Nineties, so let's just burn them all at the stake.' His moment of realisation came upon visiting his label Columbia's offices in New York, and looking at the wall where a vast poster for *Cherry Pie* had once hung when it was the label's priority. Although he was there to promote the release of the band's 1992 follow-up, *Dog Eat Dog*, in its place was a poster for Alice in Chains' *Dirt*. 'I think we slipped down the priority ladder a little,' he remarked with no small amount of understatement.

For almost an entire generation of bands, this experience was replicated to varying degrees, often with little or no relation to the quality of the work that they were recording. In 1995, Skid Row released *sUB-HUMAN rACE*, their final album with Sebastian Bach on vocals. 'We could've released *Back in Black* and it wouldn't have mattered,' said guitarist Dave 'Snake' Sabo. 'It just wasn't our time anymore.'[1] In 1994, Mötley Crüe, having replaced vocalist Vince Neil with John Colrabi, released their eponymous album, showcasing a more grunge-compliant sound. For the first show of the tour, panicked by sales of only 4,000 tickets for a 15,000 seat amphitheatre in Tucson, Arizona, Nikki Sixx went on the local radio station and promised that any fans who turned up outside the station after he came off air would be put on the guest list for that night's show. Only two fans showed up. An equally brutal illustration of the band's falling stock had occurred during the recording of the album, when a night out with Dave Sabo had resulted in the group going back to their hotel with four prostitutes, who,

1. https://www.loudersound.com/features/skid-row-it-didn-t-matter-what-we-did-it-wasn-t-our-time-anymore

after their allotted hour was up, left the hotel following a raging outburst by Nikki Sixx when they informed him that any further time would require more payment. Sabo summed up the situation: 'Yeah, the bad boys of rock n' roll, Mötley Crüe and Skid Row, just had to pay girls eight hundred bucks to talk to us. We're pathetic.'[2] In another sign of the times, on September 28, 1992, host Riki Rachtman had his hair cut short live on MTV's *Headbangers Ball*.

The shorthand that grunge killed glam metal dead overnight is, of course, overly simplistic. Def Leppard's *Adrenalize* was released in March 1992 and went to number 1 in both the UK and America, while the subsequent world tour ran over 244 dates and still filled arenas and stadiums. In June of 1992, nine months after the release of *Nevermind*, Guns n' Roses still sold out Wembley Stadium for a second time. By this point in the rolling *Use Your Illusion* tour they'd acquired a new guitarist, a keyboard player, and Brian May as a special guest for the encore. But the support slots bypassed the likes of Skid Row in favour of the more voguish Faith No More and Soundgarden. In 1993, Aerosmith's *Get a Grip* would become their best-selling album worldwide. Most metal fans were comfortable listening to Nirvana and Mötley Crüe alongside one another. Nirvana appeared on *Headbangers Ball* (albeit with Kurt Cobain wearing a giant yellow prom dress to Riki

2. *The Dirt*, p. 265.

Rachtman's apparent consternation) while their first UK video play for 'Smells Like Teen Spirit' occurred on the late-night metal show *Raw Power*.

But there was a sense that the cultural energy had shifted: glam metal had reached critical mass, and the unvarnished nonchalance of grunge had suddenly made it look old, overblown, tired and ludicrous. 'You listen to Kurt Cobain and you're like "wow that's great,"' said C. C. DeVille in an MTV interview. 'You're listening to the songs and there's no bombs, no lasers ... and they're coming to the shows and he's ... breaking everyone's heart. And you're going "Ah. I have to go back to square one."'

DeVille's assessment isn't quite right though. The line that was drawn in the sand by grunge wasn't between the artificial and the real. While Nirvana's delivery may have appeared simpler and more straight-forward – and visually, it was – what it marked was the point where mainstream American rock music moved definitively from the modern to the postmodern. While glam metal had its layers of artifice and con-struction – especially in its sound and fashion – it func-tioned in a relatively one-dimensional way. Grunge looked at the world with a roll of the eyes and put things in quotation marks – glam metal was led by far simpler urges. 'Smells Like Teen Spirit' appropriated its title from a wholesome TV deodorant commercial, and interpolated the riff from 'More Than a Feeling' into live versions of the track because there's something inherently funny about independently minded punk-inspired misfits feasting on the carcass of one of the biggest mainstream rock hits of their parents' era. By contrast, Blackie Lawless shot fireworks from his cod-piece because it just looked incredibly cool and made the crowd scream. Grunge fashion recycled the quilted lumberjack shirts of manual workers as an ironic kick at macho norms. Even the title of the genre's lodestar album – *Nevermind* – came freighted with a kind of weary sigh, as though everything was just *so much effort*. Glam metal did exactly what it said on the label and traded in very obvious signs and signifiers – whereas grunge embodied a culture where everything meant something else, and everything worked on two levels. The music was heavy, but sensitive; it was pop-ular, but didn't want to be; it was noisy, but it didn't rock; it was successful, but didn't want to look like it. What glam metal was and what it stood for was glaringly obvious. Suddenly, with grunge, the whole business of what was real and what wasn't, what was permissible and what was now beyond the pale, became extremely slippery. The simple worldview espoused by glam metal was suddenly a thing of the past. When Bon Jovi returned in November 1992, it was with socially conscious lyrics, a monochrome por-trait and shorter hair – conformity was the price of sur-vival under the new regime. As Randy's love interest Cassidy asks in *The Wrestler*, after bemoaning the pernicious influence of Kurt Cobain on the music and the era that the pair both loved: 'Like there's something wrong with just wanting to have a good time?'

With hindsight, glam metal represented the final stand for white American guitar music as an evolving genre. Fifty years of styles concertinaed together from blues, folk, vaudeville, garage, glam rock, drag, punk, AOR and stadium rock. It was like the musical equivalent of a flesh golem, the mythical Dungeons and Dragons creature stitched together from other beings' body parts. It resembled the final point of progress for this kind of music before it moved into irony, repetition and a self-referential knowingness. And it's this uncomplicated nature that now dates glam metal as much as the hair or the clothes or the x-shaped guitars with upside-down pointed headstocks. It feels gauche and one-dimensional. Other older genres (post-punk, some new wave) had enough self-awareness that they still look curiously modern. But if a band arrived today dressed like Poison in 1986, one would assume it was a knowing in-joke, not a seriously intended artistic statement.

The fortunes of glam metal's standard bearers have been mixed since this musical iron curtain came down between today and the past. Aerosmith and Bon Jovi transitioned relatively easily into mainstream elder statesmen of radio-friendly rock. Heart returned to their roots with the Wilson sisters playing acoustic folk arrangements of their music. Kiss are still touring enormous venues, back in their make-up and still huge. Dokken sporadically overcame the fractious relationship between George Lynch and Don Dokken but have never fully reformed as a long-term arrangement. Poison eventually reformed their original line-up, and have overcome several health scares for Brett Michaels (in 2010 he suffered a massive subarachnoid haemorrhage). Michaels has also acted in various roles and been the subject of a reality TV show, *Brett Michaels: Life As I Know It*. Ozzy Osbourne's entire family were the subject of a similar long-running reality television show which for most of the public has now overshadowed Osbourne's musical career. LA Guns spent several years with competing versions of the band touring (one led by Tracii Guns, one by Phil Lewis). W.A.S.P. are still touring, and a superb live act, although Blackie Lawless remains the only original member. Warrant's Jani Lane married the model from the 'Cherry Pie' video, but they divorced in 1993. He appeared on the television show *Celebrity Fit Club* in 2005, where he addressed his alcohol dependency issues. On August 11, 2011, he was found dead of acute alcohol poisoning in a Comfort Inn hotel in Woodland Hills, California. He was forty-seven years old.

In December 2018, I stood in a sold-out Wembley Arena before a vast hyper-technological pyramid of luminous bars and video screens. Def Leppard were set to play *Hysteria* in its entirety, as part of an extended thirtieth anniversary tour to mark its release. Extra dates were added to their UK schedule due to public demand. This marked a significant commercial return to form from the low point of 2003 when the band had played the Brixton Academy in the same city, a venue almost a third of the size. The anniversary had also prompted a more serious reconsideration of the album – broadsheet pieces picked over its elaborate production and acknowledged the flawless songwriting which had seen other unlikely artists pick up on the band's work: Mariah Carey covered 'Bringin' On the Heartbreak', while Taylor Swift duetted with the band for a version of 'Pour Some Sugar On Me'.

The gig was an astonishingly faithful sonic recreation of an immensely complicated piece of work. As the stage set shifted through a supersize selection of neons, films and lasers, and the band strolled out on walkways that cut through the crowd, the familiarity of the material was remarkable: this is metal's equivalent of *Thriller* or *Sgt Pepper's Lonely Hearts Club Band*, one of those albums which, even if you've rarely sat down and consciously listened to it, you've absorbed by a kind of osmosis. During 'Hysteria', the band slotted neatly into the chorus of David Bowie's 'Heroes', Joe Elliott's glam rock obsessions joining up with his own glam metal achievements. The link between what came before and what these bands created was firmly underlined.

At one point the stage fell dark and a simple photo of Steve Clark appeared on the screens, with a recording of a solo guitar instrumental played by him echoing around the vast shed. Did it matter that the guitarist was no longer here? Personally, to the band and his loved ones, clearly. But musically, not really. Clark had become another component part of the Def Leppard sound, subsumed into the process. Another file stored on a hard drive to be uploaded, triggered and played back when needed. It felt like a fitting continuation of a long creative process that had always been about dissolving the boundaries between the real and the synthetic, the human and the machine.

But where does glam metal's influence live on? Beneath the level of Def Leppard, Aerosmith and Bon Jovi, a solid, moderately sized touring scene still exists for glam metal's key exponents. Hard Rock Hell's regular programme of promotions includes HRH Sleaze, whose next line-up at the time of writing promises Michael Monroe, The Quireboys, LA Guns, a version of Love/Hate, Pretty Boy Floyd and others. Other bills bring together Skid Row, the Wildhearts and Tiger-tailz. In America, the Monsters of Rock Cruise spends five days at sea between Fort Lauderdale, Cozumel and Belize, while Tesla, Krokus, Extreme, Winger, Autograph, Bang Tango, Faster Pussycat, Firehouse, Kix, Vixen and others entertain guests. But this scene exists as a period piece, with no forward momentum – it's music frozen in aspic, a ritualistic opportunity for ageing listeners to re-engage with the soundtrack of their youth's most significant moments. It doesn't impact the culture around it any more than a Sealed Knot battle re-enactment shapes contemporary politics.

What is harder to ascertain is where glam metal's influence is felt musically. Some aspects make it sound as anachronistic as skiffle to a modern audience. It hasn't been mined for samples and re-contextualisation in the way that other older genres of guitar music have. Probably the most successful modern act to consciously adapt the glam metal template was British band The Darkness, but with their handlebar moustaches and spandex jumpsuits there was always a sense that they were doing it with a nod and a wink, even if the music itself was a faithful rendering of the Eighties' sound.

Where glam metal's spirit may actually be found isn't in the world of guitar bands at all, but in the most commercial zone of dance music. Belgium's Tomorrowland festival is an industrial-sized gathering of the most mass-appeal end of EDM. To its detractors, Tomorrowland is an indictment of an entire scene: a lobotomised collective opt-out, a mass infantilisation, a cretinous procession of major-key moments of synthetic euphoria. But if you can discount the music, it all looks strangely familiar. In the round-up film of their latest festival, there's a live-for-the-weekend spirit that glam metal originally embodied. The vast crowds, private jets, supersize consumption and conversion of unattractive provincial outcasts into main-stream mini-gods seem analogous to the glam metal music festivals of thirty years ago. The clothes and haircuts have changed, but in the face glitter, body paint and shirtless muscularity there's the same desire to get under the skin of everyone who wants you to conform. In every bouncing-ball rhythm there's the same calculated offending of the sensibilities of every boring tasteful snob who thinks you should be listening to 'real' music. The walls of pyrotechnics and adventurous stage sets are the same. The build and release of every bass drop is the same as the crashing-chords that signalled the choruses of the greatest power ballads. Looked at from a distance, the spectacle and overload of something like Tomorrowland isn't so far from Nikki Sixx's vision of vast gigs that mimicked the mass sensation of a political rally. Right now, dance music is at roughly the same point in its lifespan that rock guitar music was in the mid-Eighties, and the collision of sounds and echoing snatches of the past that filter through modern EDM are as much of a cultural pile-up as glam metal represented to its own past.

Glam metal isn't going to come back, at least not in the sense that it was known and understood. But the impulse and the desire that fuelled it is a permanent feature of youth. Wherever the bored, the restless or rebellious need a release, something like it will burst into life. There's nothing wrong with being loud, nothing wrong with being brash, and, ultimately, nothing wrong with just wanting to have a good time.

Further Exploration

Honorary Glam Metal Artists Who Weren't Glam Metal

The metal press was always far more wide-ranging than people gave it credit for – Phil Collins of all people appeared on the cover of *Kerrang!* in February 1984. Fine drummer and a peerless singer of divorcee soul, but Phil was clearly not metal in any way, shape or form. A number of other artists were also welcomed into the glam metal fold for aesthetic and sentimental reasons.

Cher

As one of music's most adept reinventors, Cher has covered most stylistic bases throughout her career. After a five-year break from music (during which time she'd focused on acting) Cher returned in 1987 with her self-titled album. Her look was borderline glam metal – studded leather jacket, high heels, massive hair – while her strident, drama-laden voice naturally suited itself to crashing ballads and emotional rock. Rounding up a cast of producers, performers and co-writers including Jon Bon Jovi and Richie Sambora, Desmond Child, Bob Rock, Steve Lukather and Diane Warren, the album (and especially Michael Bolton-penned single 'I Found Someone') was a glam met-aller's guilty pleasure. Follow-up *Heart of Stone* ran with the winning formula, pulling in cowboy ballads ('Just Like Jesse James'), gospel-tinged boomer-nostalgia ('Heart of Stone') and guitar-laden epics ('If I Could Turn Back Time') to huge commercial effect. The latter track was also notable for a video shot on the deck of the USS Missouri in which Cher bared her tattooed buttocks and straddled a massive cannon while several hundred US Navy personnel bellowed their approval. The choice of the boat was especially controversial as it had previously been more famous as the site on which the Japanese government had signed the Instrument of Surrender on September 2, 1945 marking the end of hostilities in World War Two. *Love Hurts* (1991) saw Cher again working with Rock, Child and Warren, as well as Gene Simmons, Paul Stanley, Lou Reed and former Alice Cooper and Pink

Floyd producer Bob Ezrin, before sensibly bailing out of the glam metal universe before it imploded.

Sisters of Mercy

Not for their early lo-fi art-house goth productions like *The Reptile House EP*, but for the period starting with 1987's *Floodland* in which Meatloaf producer Jim Steinman helped to create an epic, chest-burstingly pompous soundtrack to support Andrew Eldritch's vocals. The end result was often like listening to an orchestra while being forced to watch a constantly changing array of satellite TV channels. From that point on you could put the key Sisters' singles – 'This Corrosion', 'Dominion', 'Doctor Jeep', 'Vision Thing', the 1992 remix of 'Temple of Love' – on at any metal night, and their ludicrous charm would win listeners over.

Meatloaf

Supersize Texan belter Meat Loaf secured honorary glam metal approval purely on the basis of 1977's deathless *Bat Out of Hell* album and the far more fun 1981 duet with Cher, 'Dead Ringer for Love'. Meat Loaf's best songs channelled the same trashy Fifties' Americana as Hanoi Rocks, but processed through a huge recording budget and a sense of drama that owed more to New York's musical theatre than LA's bars.

Still, everyone owned a copy of *Bat Out of Hell*, and 'Dead Ringer for Love' is one of metal's few great duets.

Slade

Although they enjoyed a sizeable career revival in the Eighties, and a prolific output in the Seventies, Slade's influence on glam metal effectively boils down to the component parts of 1972's *Slayed?* album, specifically Noddy Holder's paint-stripping voice, Dave Hill's preposterous, parent-baiting outfits (including a mirrored top hat, a medieval penitent's fringe and a guitar spelling out the legend SUPERYOB) and an ability to weld thumping, overdriven production together with perfect, minor key pop songs. Their influence crops up everywhere from W.A.S.P.'s circus-sized performances to Kevin DuBrow's vocals on Quiet Riot's 'Metal Health'.

Stevie Nicks

Fleetwood Mac's co-vocalist had an intermittently successful Eighties with her band – 1982's *Mirage* is a flat, overly polished album, while its 1987 follow-up *Tango in the Night* spent a long period in the critical wilderness (largely on account of its dated, glassy feel), but has latterly been reassessed and reappraised. Nicks herself was always given a free pass in glam metal circles

– while only going near the fringes of the genre sonically on solo ballads like 1989's 'Rooms on Fire', her overall appearance (clouds of backcombed hair, vast lace-dressed, lengthy scarves, gravity-defying heels) and general air of dissolute chaos secured her entry into the pages of *Kerrang!*

Rod Stewart

Only really for the later Eighties' subset of bands who reached back to booze-fuelled, blokey chaos of Stewart's band The Faces, but without Rod, no Black Crowes, Quireboys or Dogs D'Amour. His grown-out mod feathercut was also a strong sartorial influence.

Rolling Stones

Specifically for Keith Richards' herculean drug intake, raven-like hair and fondness for daft hats. Musically, the band's early Seventies' work was channelled most strongly through the material that Izzy Stradlin wrote for Guns n' Roses and his rhythm guitar style.

Books

All of these are massively entertaining books in their own right, but were also invaluable research tools while writing this book. All are well worth seeking out and reading.

Slash: The Autobiography – Slash, with Anthony Bozza

Slash's account of his musical career is entertaining enough, but several things elevate this above a regular metal memoir. Firstly, the unvarnished way that Slash recounts his own life – he treats friends, women and family appallingly and, during his prolonged heroin phase, people around him do seem to have an unfortunate tendency to overdose or otherwise come off badly. Secondly, his description of his youth in LA in the late Seventies and early Eighties is a captivatingly grim portrayal of the environment that was left behind by the burned-out heads from the Sixties who never got it together to grow up and move on. Reading this, it becomes less surprising how the Eighties turned out, given what the city's youth had grown up in.

The Dirt: Confessions of the World's Most Notorious Rock Band – Mötley Crüe, with Neil Strauss

A well-retold story that has now also been aired in the band's own individual memoirs, plus a poorly received Netflix adaptation. But Strauss' account of Mötley Crüe's squalid rise and even-more-squalid fall works not just because of the bizarre and excessive behaviour of the band, but the contrasting voices he brings in from other players in their story, including manager Doc McGhee and their A&R Tom Zutaut. The end

Films/videos

The Song Remains the Same – Peter Clifton and Joe Massot (1976)

Mainstay of every metal fan's VHS collection in the Eighties, largely on account of being one of the few feature-length metal videos you could actually buy at the time. A lengthy replaying of Led Zeppelin's 1973 Madison Square Garden gig, including narrative, mythological interludes. Far more tedious than you remember it being.

Heavy Metal Parking Lot – John Heyn and Jeff Krulik (1986)

Short documentary masterpiece capturing better than anything else just how gnarly, drunk and wild a metal show could be in the mid-Eighties.

Guns n' Roses Live at the Ritz (1988)

For a low-budget concert flick recorded in early 1988, this ragged, aggressive performance by the classic line-up of the group captures them just before real fame arrives. Before any official release, it was in surprisingly wide circulation in the UK after it was broadcast in December 1989 as part of the Heavy Metal Heaven short season on BBC2, a selection of metal concerts and documentaries 'hosted' by Cassandra Peterson's

'Elvira' character. Home video taping kept it in circulation from this point onwards.

Terminator 2: Judgment Day – James Cameron (1991)

The cinematic event of 1991: partly because it marked the high point of both Arnold Schwarzenegger's career and also James Cameron's Terminator franchise. From exploding helicopters and liquid robots to Linda Hamilton's genuinely brilliant performance, and the inclusion of Guns n' Roses' 'You Could Be Mine' in a key chase scene, this was pure metal from start to finish.

Wayne's World – Penelope Spheeris (1992)

Actually far less metal than it's remembered – released in 1992, it came after glam metal's heyday had passed, and while Alice Cooper makes an appearance, he plays 1991's 'Feed My Frankenstein' rather than his more glam-friendly hits. However, it's a genuinely funny comedy that holds up well with hindsight and marked a relatively late – and much deserved – mainstream success for director Penelope Spheeris who had previously made *The Decline of Western Civilization*.

Anvil! The Story of Anvil – Sacha Gervasi (2008)

Sacha Gervasi's wonderful telling of the story of Anvil,

the Canadian band who appeared to have the world at their feet after their 1982 album, before duly making a series of absolutely appalling decisions and judgement calls creatively and professionally that effectively reduced them to the status of a bar band. As a portrayal of life at the bottom of the heap it's an interesting counterpoint to *Decline*... and unstinting in its detail – at one point, a particularly badly attended show sees them getting paid in soup. But what absolutely shines through is the pair's unshakeable faith in the power of metal, in each other and in the need for fundamental human decency however reduced one's circumstances. An unexpectedly moving film, which has you rooting for the protagonists (if not exactly convinced by all of their music).

The Wrestler – Darren Aronofsky (2008)

Mickey Rourke's classic late period performance as a washed-up novelty wrestler, brutalised by life in and out of the ring and trying to scrape together a living from what remains of the wrestling circuit while his personal life collapses around him. Strong parallels with the glam metal story, and great use of the music of the time throughout.

Not Dead Yet – Jesse Vile (2012)

Jesse Vile's brilliant documentary from 2012 tells the

story of the rise of guitarist Jason Becker and his subsequent battle with Lou Gehrig's Disease. Even if you've got no interest in what Becker did musically – and if you like metal, you really should have – the story of the young man and his family and how they dealt with an unimaginably cruel series of events makes this story a must-see. Becker is one of the absolute good guys of metal and his talent shines through every frame of this sensitively told story.

Acknowledgements

Special thanks to everyone who pledged on the original crowdfunder and without whom this book would never have been published.

I would like to thank everyone at Unbound involved in the development of this project: Mark Brend for originally working on the proposal; Anna Simpson, Becca Allen and their team for overseeing publication; and Mark Eglinton and Sharon Ayre for their work editing the original manuscript.

Thank you to Darren Aronofsky for permission to quote the dialogue from *The Wrestler* that appears at the start of this book. And to John Heyn and Jeff Krulik who allowed me to use footage from their film *Heavy Metal Parking Lot* in the original trailer for the book's crowdfunding campaign.

Numerous people helped shape the original idea for the book, encouraged me to pursue it and read various sections at different points, but special thanks have to go to: Andrew Emery, Andrew Mueller, Jonathan Spence, Josh Woodfin and Paul Woodgate.

I've been enormously fortunate to have spent my professional life working for and with people who have encouraged me, indulged my obsessions, supported my writing and developed ideas along the way which all ended up somewhere in this book. I wouldn't have had the career that I've enjoyed without the support and encouragement of Steve Beale, Dan Flower, Anthony Noguera, Mat Smith, Kathy Sweeney and Ben Wilson.

My friends have been a constant source of encouragement, support and advice throughout the writing of this book and in many cases for several decades beforehand. A special mention to: Dan Anderson-Ford, Chris Bostock, Matthew Green, Katie Green and the entire extended Green family, Lulu Levay, Beth McLoughlin, Julia Montero, John Power, Alex Rayner, Céline Stella (plus Lily and Gizmo), Aubrey St Louis, Luke Sweeney and the wider Sweeney family. I would also like to specially thank Helen and Hughie Furlong and the entire Furlong, Foale and Edgar families for the lifetime of love, support and encouragement that I've had – and continue to have – from them all. And to Martin Boston, who would have hated nearly all the music in this book, but whose encouragement (and liberal attitude to home taping) did a huge amount to spark my original love of music as a small child.

Finally, and most importantly, this is for my parents Nuala and Joe, and my sister Hannah. For the love, support and encouragement that you've given me and the way that you've constantly encouraged me to try new projects irrespective of whether they were going to work out or not. I couldn't – and wouldn't – have done any of it without you.

Unbound is the world's first crowdfunding publisher, established in 2011.

We believe that wonderful things can happen when you clear a path for people who share a passion. That's why we've built a platform that brings together readers and authors to crowdfund books they believe in – and give fresh ideas that don't fit the traditional mould the chance they deserve.

This book is in your hands because readers made it possible. Everyone who pledged their support is listed at the front of the book and below. Join them by visiting unbound.com and supporting a book today.

Sarah Bee
Matthew Blakout
Leonie Blatchford McDonald
David Booton
Chris Bostock
Kevin Braddock
Kimberly Bright
Johnno Burgess
Jim Butler
Alex Callaghan
Steve Carr
David Cashmore
Adam Chisholm
Léo Chupin
Ed Clews
Lauren Cochrane
Ellen Cole
Nicolas Constantino-Russell
Benjamin Cooke
Martyn Daniel
Mark Day
Anna Delaney
Neil Denny
Anna Devlin
James Donaghy
Jamie Donnelly
Adrian Dunne
Alison Dyton
James Edgar
Carly Eiseman
Manu Ekanayake
Andrew Emery
Matthew Fearn
Robert Fitzpatrick
Ben Foad
P. Fontayne
Ken Ford
Tim Foster
Clare Fowler
Shuna Frood
Vim Fuego
Richard Galpin

Mischa Gilbert
Ian Gittins
Travis Glover
Alvaro Gonzalez
Sean Goodall
Katie Green
Robert Green
Mike Griffiths
Darren Dean Vincent Groves
Alan Hake
David Hannah
Pete Harris
Andrew Harrison
Adam Harvey
John Henderson
Peter J Hobbs
John Hobson
Markus Hofpointner
James Holden
Mark Hooper
Holly Howe
Paul Hunt
Kate Hutchinson
Anton Ingham
Andrew Jacobs
Ian Jago
Timothy Jan Adams
Derek Jeffrey
Dafydd Jenkins
Rob Jenkins
Michael A Jones
Dan Kieran
George J Kokonas
Jimmy Lacey
Simon Landmine
Michael Leader
Craig Leckie
Andrew Leitch
Nick Letchford
Ted Linehan
London College of
Fashion Library

Greg Martin
Chris Matthews
Claire Maugham
Niall McCaffrey
Kirsty McFadden
Mhairi McFarlane
John McHugh
Tracy McKenzie
Clare McKinney
Beth McLoughlin
Lucy McLynn
James Medd
Joe Minihane
John Mitchinson
Julia Montero
Jonathan Moore
Rik Moran
Liam Murphy
Carlo Navato
James Nicholson
Mikkel Nørgaard
Paul O'Connell
Sinead O'
Bryan Paisley
Michael Paley
E. Pardee
Stuart Parkins
Alexis Petridis
Ashley Pfeil
Simon Philby
Scott Phillips
Justin Pollard
Doug Pollock
Benjamin Powell
John Power
Pauline J Power
Melissa Ramos
Alex Rayner
Stuart Reed
Darryl Reeves
Pam Ribbeck
Wyn Roberts

Jude Rogers
Michael Rola
Victoria Rowland
Kate Ruth
Dan Saitta
Richard Sheehan
Ramon Silva
Lee Simmons
Jonathan Spence
Jim Stafford
Jørgen Stamhus
Celine Stella
Alan Stephen
Suzanne Stephenson
Ian Stewart
Zane Stillings
Will Storr
Richard Sutcliffe
John 'Johnny Waaczz' Swartz
Luke Sweeney
Ed Taylor
Anthony Teasdale
Damon Tennant
Gaz Tidey
Arto Tuomola
Stuart Turnbull
David Uranga
Cara Usher
Sonja van Amelsfort
Tony Vanderheyden
Lulu Vay
Samantha Veal
Colin Vipurs
Marge von
Munchingindahausen
Annica Wainwright
Melissa Wallis
Nathan Walters
David Ware
Lisa Watt
John Whitfield
Claire Williamson

Mark Wood
Paul Woodgate
Ian Wright

Monica Yam
Ahmed Zambarakji